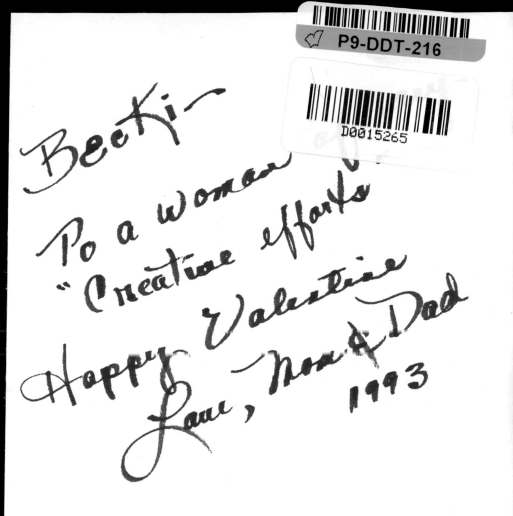

Becki —

To a woman —
"Creative efforts

Happy Valentine
Love, Mom & Dad
1993

HEARTS ON FIRE

Books authored or coauthored by Muriel James:

Born to Win: Transactional Analysis with Gestalt Experiments
Born to Love
Winning with People
Transactional Analysis for Moms and Dads
The Power at the Bottom of the Well
The OK Boss
The People Book: Transactional Analysis for Students
The Heart of Friendship
Techniques in TA for Psychotherapists and Counselors
A New Self: Self-Therapy with Transactional Analysis
Marriage Is for Loving
Breaking Free: Self-Reparenting for a New Self
Winning Ways in Health Care
It's Never Too Late to Be Happy:
The Psychology of Self-Reparenting
The Better Boss in Multicultural Organizations
Passion for Life: Psychology and the Human Spirit

HEARTS ON FIRE

Romance and Achievement
in the Lives of Great Women

MURIEL JAMES

JEREMY P. TARCHER, INC.
Los Angeles

Photographs of Abigail Adams, Sarah Bernhardt, Charlotte Brontë, Elizabeth Browning, Catherine the Great, Emilie du Châtelet, Marie Curie, Aurore Dupin, Mary Ann Evans, Helen Hayes, Katharine Hepburn, Elsa Lanchester, Margaret Mead, Anne Morrow Lindbergh, Georgia O'Keeffe, Eleanor Roosevelt, Margaret Sanger, Gertrude Stein, Harriet Tubman, Queen Alexandrina Victoria, and Mary Wollstonecraft courtesy the Library of Congress.
Photograph of Akiko Yosano courtesy of Yomiuri Daily.
Photograph of Simone de Beauvoir courtesy of UPI Bettman.
Photograph of Josephine Bonaparte loaned by the French Cultural Services.
Photograph of Suzanne Carvallo Schulein's oil on canvas portrait of Karen Horney courtesy The National Portrait Gallery, Smithsonian Institution.
Photograph of Alexandra Kollantai courtesy Virago Press.
Photographs of Käthe Kollwitz and Clara Schumann courtesy German Information Center.
Photograph of Mary Leakey courtesy of UPI/Bettman Newsphotos.
Photograph of Beryl Markham courtesy North Point Press.
Photograph of Golda Meir courtesy the Sophia Smith Collection.
Photograph of Beatrix Potter courtesy The Free Library of Philadelphia, Rare Book Collection.

Library of Congress Cataloging-in-Publication Data

James, Muriel.
    Hearts on fire ; romance in the lives of great women / Muriel James.
        p.   cm.
    ISBN 0-87477-592-2
    1. Women—Biography.   2. Love.   3. Interpersonal relations.
I. Title.
CT3203.J36   1991
306.7'092'2—dc20
[B]   90-10984
                                                              CIP

Copyright © 1991 by Muriel James

Jeremy P. Tarcher, Inc.
5858 Wilshire Blvd., Suite 200
Los Angeles, CA 90036

Distributed by St. Martin's Press, New York
Design by Tanya Maiboroda
Manufactured in the United States of America
10 9 8 7 6 5 4 3 2 1
First Edition

To Ernie, with love

CONTENTS

CHAPTER FOUR
LOVE AND TRADITION 120

ACKNOWLEDGMENTS

This is to express my deep gratitude to many who were part of my life while I was in the process of researching, constructing, and writing this book.

Originally I was going to write it with Camille Minichino, a friend and a physicist, because we are both interested in women's biographies. However, our professional commitments interfered with our having sufficient time to work together, and early in the process she dropped out of the project. Nevertheless, I want to give Camille special recognition and thanks. I might not have written this book without her initial involvement and enthusiasm.

Betty Fielding is another friend whose help has been invaluable. She read and reread much of the manuscript and made numerous important suggestions. Furthermore, she was always willing to listen when I talked on and on while developing my ideas.

The research of this book was enormously aided by Sue Hughes, who helped me many times by hauling books back and forth from Stanford and San Mateo libraries and by commenting on parts of the manuscript.

I am also grateful to Michiko Fukizawa of Tokyo, who has translated some of my other works, and who introduced me to Akiko Yosano's life and poetry. Gloria Noriega of Mexico City escorted me through Frida Kahlo's home, which is now a museum, and translated some material on Frida Kahlo that was not available in English. Kathy Seacrest's feedback toward the end of the project was most helpful. Others who helped in the process because they were willing to engage in conversations about women's biography include: Joan Marshall, Shirley Madsen, John James, Mary Goulding, Barbara and John O'Hearne, Linda Albert, Margaretta Jeffery, and Yolando Santiago. Their interest was most encouraging.

I thank my agent John Brockman and his associate Katinka Matson for their honesty and commitment. I also thank my publisher, Jeremy P. Tarcher, for his interest. Connie Zweig, my editor at Tarcher's, was a joy to work with. She responded to every inquiry and offered ideas in ways that invited cooperation.

Last, and definitely not least, I am indebted to my husband, Ernest Brawley. Frankly, he has not read all of my other fourteen books and my many articles—and I can understand that! Now in our seventies, in the mellow twilight of our lives together, he continues to show by words and actions that our romantic love is still alive and well.

INTRODUCTION

Romance is important to anyone who delights in the warmth and tenderness, excitement and passion that usually accompany this powerful event. Even a person who has never known romance often dreams that such an experience is possible and longs to find the right person who will be sympathetic and understanding, ardent and inspiring.

At the same time, many women struggle to integrate romance with busy lives—or busy lives with romance. Men seem to have been able to do this for hundreds of years, but their beloveds have not so easily dovetailed their creative, innovative, professional capacities with a soul-shaking love that endures. Certainly, there are limited numbers of women who have accomplished both, and they are scattered haphazardly throughout history.

This book has been created to bring such women together, so that they may serve in one way or another as models of creative, accomplished, *and* romantic people. These thirty-three women achieved something important to them because they felt they had no choice; their mission drove them toward specific goals. And at the same time, each one also had a rich romantic life.

Of course, romance is an important part of many people's lives, whether they are famous or not. For many, it has alternating extremes of ecstasy and agony. But in spite of actual, possible, or imagined misery, people seek romance, fight for romance, languish—even die—for romance. And though some have considered great love to be a "disease" of youth, this book will attest to the fact that people of all ages, from thirteen to eighty-three, survive and thrive with hearts on fire for their lovers and for their work. Each woman you are about to become acquainted with is special, and each romance is different. Some women were romantic and sexually active until death; others were not. All of them knew the power of romance.

This book is built around portraits or sketches of thirty-three great women. Whereas a sketch does not reveal the deepest details of color or form, it can indicate action and mood. And the actions of these women reveal not only their moods but also their values, commitments, and depth of character. Although these brief biographies can be read as single units, the sequence in which they are arranged is intended to add meaning to the whole, as are the six chapters they are grouped into: "Romance at Any Age," "Women with Many Lovers," "Love and Social Action," "Love and Tradition," "Variety in Sexual Choices," and "Love without End."

The lives of some of these women illustrate several of these themes. Astounding women, these stories will tell us, led astounding lives; we cannot help but want to know more. What is romance like, for example, between two brilliant people who love each other and work together for fifteen years, until she dies giving birth to another man's child while working on her translation of Newton's works? This is revealed in the life of Emilie du Châtelet.

Or how can a woman be a lover, mother, feminist, author, politician, revolutionary, Bolshevik commissar, Communist ambassador, and also be nominated for the Nobel Peace Prize? The life and romances of Alexandra Kollontai tell us how.

Or how does a famous psychoanalyst with many lovers liberate people from the Freudian belief that women have penis envy? Karen Horney's life responds to this question.

Brief details of each woman's background show how later choices sometimes refer directly to childhood experiences and decisions, and indicate how emotional strength and personal commitment to work, to romance, or to both often develop in the face of overwhelming adversity. They all indicate the power to break out of contemporary myths about what women should and shouldn't do.

Every life and love story has its own special flavor. Some lives, more than others, appeal to the desire to ignore statistics, overcome obstacles, and laugh in the face of common sense.

A popular belief today, for example, is that educated, intelligent women in their thirties have a very slim chance of finding a mate. But history offers novelist George Eliot, whose real name was Mary Ann Evans. A physically unattractive woman, Mary Ann lived in an open romance, without marriage, for twenty-four years until the death of the man she loved. She then married, for the first time, at age sixty-one.

It is also believed by many people today that people who are sexually intimate with one another have difficulties if they also work together. But just such an arrangement was ideal for Simone de Beauvoir and Jean-Paul Sartre. They met as students and won for themselves not only love but worldwide acclaim as writers and existential philosophers.

And what are the chances for a thirteen-year-old girl who becomes seriously crippled to meet and marry a famous artist whose paintings she admires—and also become a famous painter in her own right? Frida Kahlo discovered that anything was possible during her romance with well-known Mexican artist Diego Rivera.

Even in government, romance can flourish. Abigail Adams, wife of the second president of the United States,

John Adams, made her own mark on history while remaining deeply in love with her husband. After eighteen years of marriage, she wrote to him when he was overseas that the breadth of the ocean could not quench their love.

The greatness of all these women can be found in their dedication to love, to their career, to a cause, or to a combination of these. They have either left a legacy of beauty or bettered the world politically or socially, but in all cases they have brought forth ideas of independence and embodied what it means to be fully a woman. Each had a strong commitment to her beliefs and the courage to live by them. When courage was necessary for physical or emotional survival, they found it within themselves. They fought for their values, for their romances, and for their work. They fought for their children. They fought for understanding, and they challenge us to do the same. We may not agree with some of their choices and might make different ones in similar situations, but we can surely honor their dedication and integrity.

Selecting which women to write about was difficult; there are so many astonishing ones. I wanted some who are widely known and some who are relatively unknown, but all whom I would want to know personally. Because our world is rapidly developing a global culture, I included women from various cultures and family backgrounds to demonstrate the universal desires of women to experience romance as well as to develop their own potentials. All of them lived within the past 250 years, a period during which a worldwide awareness of women's remarkable abilities and accomplishments developed.

My considerations in the selection processes were that these women exemplify competence in their field and that their romances reflect intensity and variety. Some lived in what could be called traditional ways; others chose unusual lifestyles. Yet all are intriguing and exciting, and their lives appertain to what transpires in the world today.

I explored biographies and autobiographies, diaries and

letters—each source seemed to focus on certain aspects of these women's lives, while overlooking others. I wanted to analyze different points of view to see how romance and work affected each woman and how knowing this might expand our awareness of women's choices. In the process of reading five or more books related to each woman, I grew to more deeply understand how their thoughts and feelings motivated their career choices and lifetime actions. I learned about their private lives as well as their more public lives, and I got to know them as romantic women as well as achieving women.

Although none of us have identical experiences, we can learn from each other. I became more aware of the potential greatness of any woman who sets personal goals and is willing to do what is necessary to achieve them. These women stretched my mind and enlarged my vision, and I hope they do the same for you.

Only you, the reader, will be able to tell me if this is true. I hope you let me know.

Muriel James
Lafayette, California

CHAPTER ONE

❦

ROMANCE AT ANY AGE

FROM ROMANCE TO LOVE

Romantic dreams and the longing for romance begin early in life and for some women continue into old age. Romance may begin in childhood, with someone who lives around the corner or sits on the other side of the schoolroom. It may come during early adolescence, when hormones change and "falling in love" is experienced as nothing less than cataclysmic.

Romance can swoop down suddenly, at any time, and lift one to the heights of ecstasy, erasing hopelessness or skepticism; or it can develop slowly, culminating in a long-term romantic commitment or marriage. It can die as suddenly as it was born, or stay with you until death, remaining a warm and tender, sometimes painful, memory.

Romance is not the same as love. It is more exciting, more dramatic; it feeds on dreams of love and glory. Romeo and Juliet, Antony and Cleopatra, Heloise and Abelard are but a few who represent a tragic form of romantic love throughout the centuries.

In romance, each person sees the other through rose-colored glasses that magnify only the positive qualities of the beloved. Beauty and strength, intellect and skills receive ex-

7

aggerated attention. To lovers, such attention feels wonderful, and it is not unusual for them to spend hours talking to each other, gazing into each other's eyes, or melting into each other's arms.

If, by any chance, a woman thinks that she is unable to fall in love, or to attract someone she desires, or that she is too old or lacks sex appeal, or that potential partners are simply not available, then the women in this chapter will illustrate how wrong she may be. Romance is not limited by time, place, or situation. It can come at any age.

The women featured in this chapter are testaments to passionate romance that came in unexpected ways and developed into lifelong love. Hundreds of letters between Elizabeth Barrett and Robert Browning, for example and hundreds of photographs of Georgia O'Keeffe by Alfred Stieglitz bespeak a romantic intensity that endured until death.

In order for some romances to flourish, great obstacles must be overcome—geographical separation or societal, religious, or family objections among them. But these kinds of obstacles didn't stop such women as George Eliot from living out of wedlock with her lover in the days when that was most rare. Nor did other people's opinions stop actress Katharine Hepburn, who did not live with the man she loved, from being loyal to him until his death, in spite of his alcoholism.

Both poet Elizabeth Barrett Browning and concert pianist Clara Schumann came from families in which their fathers directed their lives, and they were obligated to rebel in order to get married.

In contrast, Georgia O'Keeffe was much more independent. She originally had no interest in the man who became her life-long love, so angry was she at him for displaying her art in his studio without her permission. But then she fell in love.

Anthropologist and author Margaret Mead was also romantic and independent and, like the others in this chapter, was not interested in social approval. Work and romance were far more important. An observer of life and of herself, Margaret Mead constantly recorded bits and pieces of one culture and compared them with bits and pieces of another. She trusted her powers of observation and intuition, of "recognizing that the other person is different from oneself, and of paying enough attention to find out just what the differences are."

Women, regardless of age, seek romance for many reasons. Some yearn to find again the excitement of a previous heady romance that may have faded or even ended in disaster. Others may never have experienced the intensity of something like it and may fear they are missing something. If they don't find romance soon, they reason, perhaps they never will.

The dream of romance as a prelude to marriage and having children is a motivation for many middle-aged women who realize that the years they have left to bear children may be running out.

After a time, single women may find themselves motivated, too, by a kind of social pressure reflected in the fact that most of their friends have become couples, and that many social events revolve around couples. Others recognize that as they grow older the pool of potential partners gets smaller.

The biographies in this chapter reveal the intense appeal of romance and the different ways it has entered the lives of great women. In some cases romance is based solely on sexual fulfillment; in others, it comes into its own as a "marriage of the minds." Certain women as they get older might appear unlikely romantic mates because of their circumstances or their personalities. Yet their lives reflect the power of possibilities in romance and love. Whatever the reasons, romance often comes unexpectedly. The greatness of these women lies not in their genius but in their being themselves, developing their potentials, and having the courage to believe in the importance of love and to follow where it takes them.

HOW DO I LOVE THEE?

Elizabeth Barrett Browning (1806–1861)

Elizabeth Barrett was a semi-invalid for twenty-five years before she met and fell in love with poet Robert Browning. In spite of her considerable health problems, she married, raised a son, wrote about pressing issues concerning Italian politics and U.S. slavery, and enjoyed fifteen years of romance before her death at age fifty-five. She is best remembered for her novel in verse form, *Aurora Leigh*, and for her love poems *Sonnets from the Portuguese*, which were published when she was forty-four. Her best-known sonnet begins

> *How do I love Thee? Let me count the ways.*
> *I love thee to the depth and breadth and height*
> *My soul can reach . . .*

It has been spoken and written thousands of times in the repertoire of romantic lovers. Robert Browning said they were the finest lines since Shakespeare.

Poetry is often the language of love. It evokes emotion. In good poetry one can hear a person speaking through the voice of a romantic lover. This "voice" conveys the heart of the poem. In the case of Elizabeth's sonnets, it conveys the heart on fire of a woman who was willing to risk losing her father's precious love for romance.

Elizabeth, the oldest of eleven children, was a brilliant

student who was reading Greek by the time she was eight. Her father, always authoritarian, became even more so after her mother died when Elizabeth was twenty. A major obstacle to her independence, he did everything possible to prevent any romance from flourishing. And what he could not accomplish through his dictatorship, Elizabeth's own body abetted with its infirmity. In compensation, her dog Flush became the young woman's chief companion and "loving friend," about whom she even wrote a poem.

Then Robert Browning entered a not-so-young Elizabeth's life: She was thirty-eight years old, and he was thirty-two. He became smitten even before meeting her. He had only read her poems when he wrote his first letter to her and said, "I love your verses with all my heart, dear Miss Barrett . . . and I love you too."

By this time Elizabeth had a fine reputation for her articles and poetry. Naturally, the thin and frail shut-in, an invalid since the age of fifteen, worried greatly about having him see her. "It would be unbecoming," she wrote, "to lie here on the sofa and make a company-show of an infirmity." But Robert was persistent and later claimed that Elizabeth's four walls were the dearest that had ever enclosed him, despite the fact that the room was deprived of sunlight and fresh air in order to control the temperature.

The nature of Elizabeth's illness is still not certain. Various hypotheses include a spinal injury, tuberculosis, and psychosomatic reaction to stress. Whatever the diagnosis, her biographers continue to differ as to the cause. Elizabeth had grown up in the country, then moved to London, then returned to the country. When her brother died by drowning, she became a recluse and semi-invalid.

After a year of courtship, Robert Browning proposed to Elizabeth Barrett, declaring that his uttermost pride and privilege would be to live in her sickroom and serve her forever. Each of his visits required elaborate plans to accommodate both Elizabeth's physical well-being and her father's strict rules about how often and how long they could be together.

During the romance, more than 600 letters were exchanged between the lovers. One, from Elizabeth to Robert, dated July 13, 1846, reads, "I loved you yesterday. I love you today . . . I shall love you tomorrow. Every day I am yours." This same sentiment was echoed in letter after letter.

At times their letters seem a competition of superlatives, with each declaring more debt to the other and more happiness derived from the union. Each also begged to be led by the other's requests and rejoiced that the other was more intelligent and more full of goodness. "Consider," Browning wrote, "how much of my happiness would be disturbed by allying myself to a woman to whose intellect, as well as goodness, I could not look up." The lovers also claimed in their letters to each other and to friends that neither had a thought that the other did not finish.

They worried that if her father became aware of how close they had become he would keep them from meeting or writing further. Elizabeth wrote to Robert that she so feared her father's raised voice that she would shut her eyes to keep out the sight of his displeasure and to try to avoid having "fainting fits."

Three months after they finally met, Elizabeth and Robert were married secretly, against her father's wishes. For the first week she lived with her father and sisters, afraid to share her secret with any of them. Her greatest pain, she said, was having to remove her wedding ring in order to maintain the fiction. The situation became so intolerable that the lovers finally fled to Italy to begin married life. Her father never communicated with her again. Ironically, that seemed to have been just what she needed. Elizabeth's health improved enough for her to travel often and even give birth to a son.

In spite of her towering romance, life was not easy for Elizabeth, either as a woman or as an author. She challenged certain traditional values, confronting, as she did in *Aurora Leigh* ten years after her marriage, the problems of male domination and love between equals. Because of this, the *Edinburgh Review* accused her of being "more coarsely masculine than any other woman writer." She resented this comment nearly as much as she did the condescending approval of other male reviewers; she said that their comparative respect for her as a woman actually meant absolute scorn.

Elizabeth also struggled with criticism from women writers who often treated other women writers more harshly than they did men. She wanted to be judged only by the value of her work and said that any inequality of intellect could be proved by the way the works of gifted women were received by other women.

Robert and Elizabeth lived in Pisa and in Florence, where their only son was born. Although they visited London twice after being married, Elizabeth's father died without forgiving her and returned her letters unopened. Nevertheless, she dedicated her collected works to him.

Elizabeth, never completely healthy, died, after fifteen years with Robert, peacefully in his arms. Asked how she was feeling at the time of her death, she responded simply, "Beautiful." Equally romantic, Robert defined his years with Elizabeth as his "real life," as if everything before and after meant nothing to him.

TWO GEORGES IN LOVE

Mary Ann Evans, a.k.a. George Eliot (1819–1880)

She was described as an unattractive literary scholar, brokenhearted over being rejected by her first love. Yet Mary Ann Evans fell in love again and lived happily for twenty-four years outside the bounds of matrimony. And then, at the age of sixty-one, she married for the first time as a culmination of yet another romance.

Better known as George Eliot, the novelist and literary critic, our protagonist lived out a happy romance in an unconventional yet highly stable relationship with George Henry Lewes, who never divorced his unfaithful, legal wife. Their romance, which began when Mary Ann was thirty-four, resulted in her often being socially ostracized. And while the world may have changed sufficiently in the last hundred years to make living together outside of marriage fairly common, a first marriage when one is over sixty is as uncommon now as it was then.

Mary Ann grew up in the country in the Midlands of England. Her father was a builder and land agent. Life was pleasant there, but she and her siblings were sent to boarding school because of her mother's ill health. In a letter to her favorite teacher she described herself as never satisfied and constantly living in an imaginary self-created world. Mary Ann read extensively and did well academically, but she was socially awkward and self-doubting. She changed her name to Marian when in school, as she thought it fit her better, but shortly before her death she took back her childhood name.

Her first grief came at sixteen when her mother died. She took over the care of the house and continued studying on her own, but she also began to develop phobias due to perfectionism and fear of change. In spite of those fears, Mary Ann became a prominent figure in London as a successful magazine editor, writer, and scholar. Hoping for romance as well, she became interested in several men and finally fell for Herbert Spencer, the well-known writer and popularizer of scientific and social issues. Mary Ann wrote him many letters in which she declared her love and asked for his. But Spencer did not return the feeling. He claimed that he was unable to fall in love with anyone, and while he greatly valued Mary Ann's companionship and the intellectual stimulation of evenings with her at concerts, lectures, and plays, he warned her that their status as friends would never change. Despite this, Mary Ann's love persisted. Unhappily, her stature in literary circles and the respect and affection of many interesting and loving friends were not nearly as important to her then as her unrequited passion. Those were lonely and unfulfilling years.

And then, one night at the theater with Spencer and friends, Mary Ann met George Henry Lewes. He did not, however, appear in her life to become her second great love without his own set of unusual circumstances. George not only lived with his wife and several other couples in a large house that was similar to a commune (a situation as unusual then as it would be now) but also had discovered that his wife, the mother of his children, was sexually involved with his friend and partner, Thornton Hunt, who also lived in the house. In fact, when George met Mary Ann, his wife was pregnant by Hunt, and would have two sons by him while still living with her husband.

Ironically, it was George's tolerance of this occurrence that prevented him from obtaining a divorce. Under English law at that time, a man could divorce his wife if she bore one illegitimate child, but if he waited for a second, it was too late! In the eyes of the law, he was then condoning her adultery and thus forfeited his right to dissolution. In addition, the cost of divorce was enormous. Lewes was a most generous man and, as Thorton Hunt was often short on funds, would help support Hunt's children as well as his own. Years later, even after her lover's death, Mary Ann continued to send money to Hunt's children.

At first George did not impress Mary Ann very favorably. He was physically unattractive, and though he was generally considered a brilliant author and editor, his literary efforts did not meet her high standards. She doubted that he was serious enough to be a scholar. But despite this, George Lewes began to replace Herbert Spencer as Mary Ann's es-

cort. After a few months of evenings together at the theater
and concerts, her opinion of him changed. She confided to
her diary that he was a man of heart and conscience who only
wore a mask of flippancy. About her he wrote, "To know
her was to love her."

Gradually the two grew closer both professionally and
emotionally, and finally, at age thirty-four, Mary Ann moved
into lodgings of her own and received George as a frequent
visitor. Then George's ill health prompted still another step
considered to be quite bold for those times: They traveled
together to Germany for his recovery, and from then on lived
together as man and wife.

One of the great heartbreaks of Mary Ann's life was
when her adored brother, Isaac, refused to see her because
she lived with a married man. But George was the man who
had brought her the happiness and passion in middle age that
she had longed for so deeply in her youth. To a friend she
wrote, "Few women, I fear, have had such reason as I have
to think the long, sad years of youth were worth living for
the sake of middle age."

Because in those days the works of women novelists
were not taken seriously, Mary Ann chose the pen name
George Eliot—George because it was her lover's name and
Eliot because, she said, it was "a good, mouth-filling, easily
pronounced word."

Originally, George Lewes had been as prejudiced against
professional women as were others of his time. Before meeting and being influenced by Mary Ann, he granted that
women could write fiction only because they were more
emotional than men. However, he said, as men were "more
intellectual," they should be the writers of philosophy, history, and poetry. He also believed that women writers should
know their limitations and stay out of work best accomplished by men. But during their romance he realized that
his thinking was faulty, and that women could write well in
any field.

All their problems—his initial prejudice, the troubled past of each of the lovers, their inability to marry, and their social ostracism—did not mar the couple's happiness. Through his inspiration and encouragement Mary Ann, under her pen name, gained even greater fame as a novelist than as a literary scholar, and many of her novels, such as *Silas Marner, Adam Bede,* and *The Mill on the Floss,* rank among the classics of literature.

George Eliot's identity was discovered when a friend recognized that Mary Ann was the author of *Adam Bede.* Her anonymity was further at risk when her novels won acclaim and a man named Joseph Liggins, who lived in the town where Mary Ann had been born, began calling himself George Eliot and encouraging people to think of him as such. This proved too much for George Lewes, who wanted to disclose her identity. Her publisher foresaw an avalanche of social disapproval at the revelation of Eliot's identity—and in particular at her domestic arrangements. But Lewes insisted that anonymity had been necessary only so that the book could be judged on its own merits. Now that this had been accomplished, that no longer mattered. The public now knew that George Eliot was a woman as well as a great writer.

Gradually the stress of writing and defending her writing took its toll, and both became ill. Yet the writing continued, and the relationship between the two Georges prevailed, as close and fulfilling as either could have desired. At the start of their romance, Mary Ann had written, "The blessedness of a perfect love and union grows daily." And, despite not actually marrying, they often referred to themselves in this way. One of her dedications read, "From George Eliot to her dear husband." They were together for twenty-four years, separated only by his death.

After two years of grieving, Mary Ann became more aware that she was happiest when she had a man to share her life. She married John Cross, a longtime friend twenty years her junior, who was also in publishing. At sixty-one, it was her first legal marriage.

Ironically, Mary Ann had lived with George Henry Lewes for so long outside of marriage that she received strong disapproval from others when she bound herself legally with Cross. Her brother, however, was an exception. After twenty-five years of silence, he wrote to congratulate her! And when she answered him, she signed her new name, Mary Ann Cross. Eight months into this short, happy union, Mary Ann died of a cold that she caught when attending the theatre.

PASSION AT THE PIANO

Clara Schumann (1819–1896)

At the same time Elizabeth Barrett Browning and George Eliot were writing poetry, essays, and novels in England, a brilliant pianist was seeking independence and romance in Germany. Clara Schumann was a child prodigy whose father was devoted to her success. Yet when she wanted to get married, that same father did everything possible to stand in the way; he even collected the money due her from her concerts and kept it for himself.

Clara, an accomplished composer and concert pianist, became intensely associated in the course of her lifetime with two other great musicians, Robert Schumann and Johannes Brahms. Yet the greatness of all three did not prevent their unhappiness. When still relatively young, the genius Robert Schumann, then Clara's husband, became mentally ill and committed suicide. With their seven children to support, Clara faced the struggle of single parenthood with little money. In spite of that, she found love and creativity one more time, against all those odds.

Born Clara Wieck, she began to study the piano when

she was very young, made her debut at age nine in Leipzig, and went on her first concert tour at eleven. By the time she was twelve, Clara had composed and published four polonaises. At age thirteen she gave her first concert in Paris and was widely acclaimed for her brilliance, and by sixteen she was famous and received honors from the Austrian court. Goethe, Mendelssohn, and Chopin admired her, as she played the music of great composers in many of the major cities of Europe.

Clara's mother was a soprano soloist and pianist; her father was a demanding, conceited piano teacher who sought credit for everything Clara accomplished. Her parents divorced early in Clara's life, but because German law of that time decreed children to be their father's property, she was permanently separated from her mother

Herr Wieck's domination of his daughter was relentless, down to reading the diaries Clara started to keep at age seven and writing comments in the margins. Later, he dictated business letters to those who hired her, and in these letters she was forced to complain about fees and reviews.

Yet Clara always loved her father. She was miserably unhappy when they were alienated, and in romance she chose two men, Schumann and Brahms, who would advise her much as her father had. But Clara's father did not want romance to interfere with her financial support of him. He believed that her success would reflect positively on his teaching ability as well as provide him with a substantial income.

Robert Schumann, an author and a prolific composer who published thirty works in one year, was a family friend who became involved with Clara against her father's wishes. Entranced with Clara, he wrote that he felt like a willing slave to her: "I should often like to follow you from afar at a distance, and await your slightest bidding."

Herr Wieck's wrath drove them to meet in secret and shoulder the burden of being torn between Clara's love for her father and their love for each other. Robert also suffered from chronic depression, which was exacerbated by this situation: "I beg you to whisper my name to the Almighty now and then that he protect me, because I can tell you that I am so depressed and worn out with pain that I can hardly pray. I am carrying a great burden of guilt—I separated you from your father—and this often torments me."

Although her father's opposition grew, he could not destroy their romance. Anger mounted, and the two men began to vilify each other in public. In Germany at this time, parental permission was a prerequisite to marriage, so the couple filed a legal suit and went to court to prove that Schumann would in fact be a suitable husband and that Clara's father was not justified in withholding permission.

They won the case, but it was a painful victory. Clara's father turned his back on them. She became disconsolate over both the alienation from her father and her husband's increasing depression, which also led to a marital alienation. One of her diary entries reads:

> My state of mind is indescribable. I cannot forget the words in Robert's last letter—they torture me. I have endured everything. I have lost my father, I have stood up to him in a court of law, what battles have I fought with myself, but Robert's love made up for all this. I believed his faith was immovable, and now he hurts me so much. I can barely calm myself.

Beyond wanting parental approval to marry, Clara wanted also to follow the custom of giving her bridegroom a dowry when they were married. Clara's father, who had been serving as her manager, refused to part with any of what she had earned from her concerts. In desperation, Clara gave additional concerts without using him as manager so that she could earn a dowry that her father could not touch.

Perhaps her father was professionally interested in Schumann's musical abilities, or perhaps he just didn't want to lose the income he derived from Clara—whatever the reason, three years after the marriage he wrote them an unexpected letter asking to be invited to hear Robert's music. And he pressured the couple to agree by reminding them that he had once been Robert's teacher as well as Clara's. All of them were glad for the opportunity to heal the wound. The pain of the past was put aside, not to be discussed again.

But an even more serious problem arose. Robert became increasingly depressed and so emotionally disturbed that the last two years of his life were spent in a private mental institution. He died there at thirty-seven by suicide, without ever seeing his youngest child. Their seven children, all between the ages of two and fifteen, suffered greatly from the loss. They remembered him because of his playfulness, whereas Clara was obligated to be their disciplinarian. Clara tried to protect Robert's image after his suicide by pointing out his good points: "Ah! if only you were a little older and more capable of understanding, that you might know how to appreciate him, for he was a man of godlike qualities, one who had few equals."

After her husband's death, Clara felt unable to be both mother and father to her children and also maintain herself as an artist. Forced to work hard to support her family, her piano understandably became her priority.

It was during the time when Robert was institutionalized that Clara first met Johannes Brahms, another composer. He visited Robert in the hospital to thank him for writing complimentary reviews of Brahms's music, which had done much to advance his reputation. He was also grateful to Clara for her superb playing of his compositions.

In the beginning, their relationship centered on Johannes Brahms providing Clara emotional support during the confinement of her husband. He was twenty-two years old at the time; she was thirty-four. They gradually became close friends. In time he also became a father surrogate for her children, and she increasingly turned to him for guidance. As their love grew, so did her defense of it in her diaries and in letters to her children.

Johannes and Clara also wrote often to each other. A typical letter of his would begin:

> My beloved Clara, I wish I could write to you as tenderly as I love you and tell you all the good things that I wish you. You are so infinitely dear to me, dearer than I can say. I should like to spend the whole day calling you endearing names and paying you compliments without ever being satisfied. If things go on much longer as they are at present I shall have, some time, to put you under glass or to have you set in gold.

After this, Johannes asked her for more letters; they would, he said, be "like kisses." Her letters usually detailed her recitals, complimented his compositions, complained of various things, and sometimes admonished her beloved about how to spend money and advised him as to where he ought to live.

Clara Schumann had two great needs: music and money. Regarding music she said, "I feel called to reproduce great works. . . . The practice of art is, after all, a great part of my inner self. To me, it is the very air I breathe." But her greatness as an artist could not earn her enough to support her family, and she was short of money throughout her life. Still, when Brahms offered it to her, she refused. Financial independence was as important to her as it is to many women today.

Her last public performance was in Frankfurt in 1891, at the age of seventy. After this, arthritis in her hands and an increasing hearing loss made it necessary for her to leave the concert stage. From then on she shared her love of music only through teaching others.

All her life Clara worked hard to support herself and her children with her passion for the piano; she also worked hard for the three men in her life whom she loved so deeply. Each of the men had a passion for music, for Clara, and for her great ability to interpret love through the piano.

Her relationship to Brahms, which began when she was thirty-seven, lasted until her death at seventy-five. We do not know whether he ever proposed marriage to her. Perhaps he did not, because of her children or because of their prominent positions in the musical world. On the other hand, perhaps he did propose, only to be rejected. What is known for certain is that Brahms never married, and that he and Clara Schumann remained close until death.

AN ALMOST PRIVATE LOVE

Katharine Hepburn (1907–)

Although their hearts and acting careers were linked for twenty-seven years, he remained married because divorce was against his religious beliefs. In addition, he was an alcoholic. Yet neither circumstance interfered with Katharine Hepburn's lifetime loyalty to Spencer Tracy. Outspoken, self-determined, from a prestigious and well-educated family, Katharine—or Kate, as she was known to most people—had a strong sense of personal identity and gave her parents full credit for her success: "The single most important thing anyone needs to know about me is that I am totally, completely, the product of two damn fascinating people who happened to be my parents. What they did for me is me. I could never repay them."

Kate's mother was a feminist and suffragist who campaigned for birth control with Margaret Sanger and for a woman's right to vote. She was an unusually independent woman who was awarded a master's degree from Radcliffe in 1900 and then decided her career was to be a wife and mother. Her father, also very independent, was a urologist who spoke out publicly about venereal disease in the days when this was considered most indecent. He was so concerned over the high death rate due to syphilis that he could not be stopped. Nor could her mother, who publicly spoke about syphilis, gonorrhea, prostitution, and birth control at a time when such outspokenness was deemed shockingly unladylike.

Their five children were encouraged to be similarly forthcoming and independent. Kate's strong spirit displayed itself at an early age. By three she was climbing tall trees; by four, she was hanging by her toes from a trapeze. The entire family exercised daily and took cold baths. In her preadolescence she called herself Jimmy and became a tomboy. In the summer she would shave her head so that when she wrestled with boys they would not be able to pull her hair.

Kate was a redhead with many freckles, which she thought were very unattractive until her father, who called her Redtop, proclaimed: "I want to tell you something, Kathy, and you must never forget it. Jesus Christ, Alexander the Great, and Leonardo da Vinci all had red hair and freckles, and they did all right."

One of the tragedies of Kate's life occurred when, at age thirteen, she discovered the body of her beloved fifteen-year-old brother hanging from a rafter. An athlete with honors in school, there was no final explanation for his death, which could have been due to suicide or an accident during a hanging stunt, which he sometimes engaged in for the purpose of shocking people.

After her brother's demise, Kate struggled with her emotions. She began to fail in school, so she was removed and tutored until she went to college. Although she was not brilliant, she made honors because of her determined studying. It was at this time that she became seriously interested in acting, much against her father's wishes; he thought it a poor way for Kate to spend her time. (Spencer Tracy's father said the same to him.) Many years later, after Spencer died, Kate hypothesized, "I think Spencer always thought acting was a rather silly way for a man to make a living. But he was of such an emotional balance, you know, that he had to be an artist. Of course he never realized this. . . ."

Married at twenty-one to a wealthy broker, Ludlow Ogden Smith, Kate decided Smith was too common a name for her, so she dropped it and called herself Mrs. Ludlow Ogden. Her marriage, however, was more of a convenience than a romance. Her husband, entertaining and a good escort, was so fascinated by the high goals she set for herself as an actress, he agreed to whatever she wanted to do. After four years they dissolved their marriage, remaining friends for many years. Kate believed that women were coming into their own, that men were blocking them, and that it was too difficult to have both a husband and a career. She claimed that she wasn't fit to be married, that she always had her mind on herself and couldn't pass a mirror without looking into it. Furthermore, she said, "Keeping a husband on the string is almost a full-time job." In an interview she philosophized:

> For the independent woman the marriage problem is very great. If she falls in love with a strong man she loses him because she has to concentrate too much on her job. If she falls in love with a weakling, who[m] she can push around, she always falls out of love with him.

Kate's greatness in her profession has been in the dedication she has given to acting and to developing her roles. Whenever she failed or was fired, as occurred several times, she did not let it deter her from trying again. Kate, always a perfectionist, whether playing comedy or drama, has enjoyed more than fifty years on stage or in films. Her colleagues claim she was absolutely honest in her dealings with people.

Kate also had many long and sustaining friendships. A

number of men were deeply interested in her—some romantically, others as friends. One of her friends was Howard
Hughes, who liked her independence and wit. He taught her
to fly, and she liked his golf playing. A fine golfer herself,
she appreciated the fact that he could out-putt her.

Often cast as a free, independent woman, Kate displayed
her own brand of feisty individualism even as she performed.
Once, when playing Portia in Shakespeare's *Merchant of Ven-
ice*, someone in the audience rose and took a flash photo. Kate
stopped, faced the audience directly, and boomed, "There
will be no more of that or we won't go on." She then continued in her role.

Kate was thirty-five years old when she first met actor
Spencer Tracy, usually called Spence. At the time both were
big box-office names. Kate had made many films, had won
her first Academy Award, and had successfully played on
Broadway. Both of them had had affairs with other people.
Although he admired her work, he did not like it that she
was so independent and wore slacks. She had long admired
him for the naturalness, warmth, and ruggedness he displayed
in his films—the same qualities that she had admired in her
father.

Kate, often thought to be eccentric in her dress, was
well-known for wearing both high black turtleneck sweaters
to hide her long neck and black pants to get around having
to wear the garter belts required in that pre–panty hose era.
In her home stands a statue, a Lifetime Achievement Award
presented to her by the Council of Fashion Designers of
America for "not giving a damn about clothes." Standing
five feet, eight inches tall, Kate, when meeting directors or
producers for the first time, would also often wear custom-
built platform shoes that increased her height another four
inches.

This last predilection had a particular bearing on the first
meeting Kate and Spencer Tracy had, at the initiative of
film director Joe Mankiewicz. Spencer was five-foot-nine,

and at first glance Kate looked him up and down as though buying him and then commented, "You're rather *short*, aren't you?" The director, trying to extinguish Spencer's glare, intervened with, "Don't worry, honey, he'll cut you down to size."

Although he was married, the two stars developed a mutual attraction and twenty-seven-year-long romance that lasted until his death. It was as private a romance as can be possible in publicity-hungry Hollywood. Although there was some gossip, their privacy was generally respected by friends and the press. In one story, Spencer was discovered looking repeatedly over the back edge of a hotel roof in Paris while waiting for Kate. Asked why he was looking over the back instead of the front, he replied, "Kate always comes in the back way. Gotta be discreet, ya know."

They enjoyed many of the same things—walking on the beach, listening to music, and painting together. They both shared a passion for their work and appreciated each other's dedication to excellence. There is no doubt about their greatness.

Yet all was not well between them. Spence was an argumentative alcoholic who would not take advice from his friends or loved ones and was often depressed. It was not unusual for him to go on week-long drinking binges and to be found by friends or colleagues in the worst possible condition. Although he damaged his liver, he was unable to stop drinking for long. As a father, he was very impatient with his son, John, who was diagnosed as deaf when he was ten months old. A staunch Irish Catholic, Tracy would not consider divorce, but he did move out of the family home and continued to drink. His wife, Louise, committed herself to teaching their son how to communicate. Spencer led an independent life and visited them from time to time. Yet he and Louise remained friends until his death.

Once when Kate and Spencer were on their way to a private picnic at Malibu, he collapsed with severe chest pains. A rescue squad rushed him to the hospital, from where Kate immediately called Louise. The two women kept alternate vigils by Spencer's bedside until his sickness was diagnosed as a temporary congestion of the respiratory tract. He was then released, with Louise Tracy's approval, to Kate's care.

Always in the Hollywood spotlight, Kate and Spencer preferred privacy and seldom discussed their relationship with others. In an interview given when she was almost eighty years old, Kate expressed herself: "I don't understand why people care about things like that. I'm sure you've slept with one or two people, too, if that's your sport, and I certainly don't want to hear about it. So why would anyone be interested in whom I've gone to bed with?"

For the last ten years of Spencer's life, Kate went with him whenever he traveled. Although he eventually stopped drinking, it was too late; his liver deteriorated further and his heart weakened. He became even more withdrawn. Spencer Tracy died alone in his small house in 1965 while drinking a glass of milk. Louise and Kate were notified, and the curtain came down on a sad romance between two great stars.

Throughout the pain and the joy, Kate always adored Spencer, much as her mother had adored her father. Whether out of adoration or, as some people thought, to de-emphasize her height, she often sat at his feet, looking up into his face. To her, "He was like water, air, earth. He wasn't easily fooled. . . . Yet he was enormously complicated and tortured."

Through the years of loving and caring for him, Kate remained a disciplined artist. Once she was playing the role of Clara Schumann in love with composers Robert Schumann and Johannes Brahms in the film *Song of Love*. Arthur Rubinstein was to perform the actual music for it, and Kate was expected to mime the moves on a nonworking piano. She refused, insisting that she learn the instrument well enough to play the opening bars. And after studying hard with a fine

professional, she was indeed prepared to do this. In the film-
ing, she played the opening, then Rubinstein took over and
commented, "That woman is incredible! She actually does
play as well as I do! And when she ends and I begin, only I
in the whole world could tell the difference."

Fiercely autonomous, Kate was also a dreamer who, as
a child, had studied the inscription on the marble fireplace in
her father's study: LISTEN TO THE SONG OF LIFE. She often asked
her parents what this meant and was amazed by the depth of
its meaning. Although often indifferent to society's expectations, she lived by listening to the song.

WITH PAINTBRUSH AND LENS

Georgia O'Keeffe (1887–1986)

Couples frequently claim that incompatible temperaments
can undermine romance. But this was not true for Georgia
O'Keeffe and Alfred Stieglitz. She became one of the great
American artists of the twentieth century; he is remembered
as the father of modern photography. And their romance
endured until his death, despite their very different temperaments. Stieglitz for example, loved to be surrounded by
people, whereas she preferred solitude. Georgia loved to paint
the flowers and dry bones of desert landscapes; he photographed people and big-city buildings.

Although Georgia painted the buildings of New York
City when she lived there with Stieglitz (which is how she
always referred to him), her heart perennially longed for the
solitude of the American Southwest, with its rugged hills,
snowy peaks, and blistering hot desert sand. She returned
there often, moved by what she saw. She often carried a
heavy stick when walking in the desert to fend off a rattle-
snake if one came too close!

The second of five children, Georgia was born to happy

parents on a very large ranch in Wisconsin. Her mother, who was greatly concerned about her children's education, spent many hours reading to them. Georgia especially liked stories about Texas and New Mexico. Later these became her favorite places to live in and to paint.

Painting was always a great interest. Georgia had lessons even as a child, and by the time she was twelve was developing her own style. Once when asked about her unique approach she replied, "It's as if my mind creates shapes that I don't know about. I get this shape in my head, and sometimes I know what it comes from and sometimes I don't."

By the time she was sixteen, the young artist's ability was sufficiently developed to be more fully tested at the Art Institute of Chicago, where her talent deepened, her spark intensified. From there, Georgia proceeded to the Art Students League of New York, where a friendship with Anita Pollitzer began. Both were outstanding students, and when each left to work at teaching assignments, Anita initiated a correspondence with Georgia. In her memoirs, Anita takes credit for stimulating Georgia's career in 1915 when she took some of her friend's sketches to Alfred Stieglitz. Greatly impressed, he hung O'Keeffe's drawings in his New York City gallery—but without her permission. O'Keeffe, very much put out, marched over to the gallery to protest it. Stieglitz, however, prevailed, and Georgia, ever the independent, strong-minded artist, was somehow persuaded to leave her drawings—and come back again and again.

Georgia, however, never quite forgave Anita for her presumption. Many years later, when Anita asked for Georgia's approval of the book she had written about O'Keeffe, it was refused on the basis that the book was not accurate. Anita then dedicated her unauthorized biography to Stieglitz.

Stieglitz's gallery was a lively center for artists of the day, both photographers and painters. It was the only place to see contemporary art like Picasso's and Rodin's, and Georgia began to drop in more often, between trips to Amarillo,

Texas, where she taught drawing and penmanship. She had the opportunity to teach in New York, but she preferred her beloved Texas. One time, after returning to Texas, Georgia wrote, "Anita, he is great." After another trip to New York, she wrote even more directly to Anita in a letter, "Stieglitz —well, it was him I went up to see. I just had to go, Anita, and I'm so glad I went. I believe I would rather have Stieglitz like something—anything I had done—than anyone else I know of. . . ."

As their romance became more compelling, Stieglitz persuaded Georgia to stay in New York and to spend time painting the city. Although he was married, they lived together for six years. Eventually Stieglitz's wife agreed to a divorce and they were married. Georgia was then thirty-seven years old, and her art career well established. Yet he sometimes directed her like a child. Later in their marriage, he was attracted to younger women.

Although Georgia never liked the city, she painted the skyscrapers in a special way, based on her vision of them as tall, thin bottles going ever upward. One painting of New York at night, *The Radiator Building*, reveals some of her feelings for Stieglitz. What at first glance looks like a solid blur of red from a neon sign really encloses the name Alfred Stieglitz in a lighter hue. Once asked if her thirty years off and on in New York were a sacrifice, she replied romantically, "I never thought of sacrifice. Stieglitz was there. It was where I belonged."

Romance united O'Keeffe and Stieglitz, but when she went into her room and closed the door, he knew that it meant "keep out," and he respected that message. Their life was one of alternating intimacy and separateness that allowed their differences to thrive. O'Keeffe sought privacy, while Stieglitz preferred society; she opted to spend her summers alone painting in the desert, while he hung her paintings in his New York gallery and took his camera into the rainy city streets. And although she chose this lifestyle, it was not always without its complications. Once Georgia brought a barrel of bones all the way from Texas to New York so that she could paint the bleakness that she loved while being with the man she loved.

Alfred Stieglitz photographed Georgia more than five hundred times, although she claims not to have enjoyed it and was ninety years old before she decided to publish some of the photographs. The collection includes a whole range of poses. Some are erotic, with Georgia lying among crumpled bed sheets. Others are creative compositions, with Georgia standing beside her paintings. All of them portray her as strong and ageless.

When Stieglitz died in 1946, Georgia, then fifty-nine, moved permanently to the land that became her home, the American Southwest, and continued to paint into her nineties.

Her long life presents countless instances of her ability to get what she wanted. Once, when she was in art school, she persisted in getting a space in the school where she could paint—even after she was told repeatedly that the spaces were filled. Later in life, she rented a house for three years near Ghost Ranch in New Mexico before she could persuade the owner to sell it to her. Here she was happiest and did some of her greatest painting. Of this site she joked, "It's my private mountain. It belongs to me. God told me if I painted it enough, I could have it."

When interviewed about her marriage to Stieglitz and why it had worked so well, Georgia replied, "I was interested in what he did, and he was interested in what I did. We were interested in each other's work—very interested." And he had described Georgia as "absolute Truth—Clarity of Vision to the Highest Degree."

In 1973, when Georgia was sixty-six years old, a young man named Juan Hamilton came knocking on her door, asking for work. His father was a Presbyterian missionary, and his early years had been spent in South America. At fifteen

Juan had returned to New York, graduated from college, studied sculpture, had been married and divorced, and was in debt. He had been recommended to Georgia by one of her friends. She hired him to help her with chores partly because she was beginning to lose her eyesight. With time, Juan became her eyes, her student, her friend to joke with. He helped her manage her affairs, encouraged her to learn pottery, and then to paint, even with her shadowed vision. In spite of objections by her agent, friends, and family, he also became her heir—and, according to several of her biographers, her lover.

At her death at ninety-eight, Georgia's will was challenged by her family. If she had been alive she might have been embarrassed for them and herself, for she did not feel comfortable being a celebrity and preferred to live without the rumors and intrigues that often go with fame. On the other hand, perhaps she would not have cared. Georgia claimed, "When I think of death, I only regret that I will not be able to see this beautiful country anymore, unless the Indians are right and my spirit will walk here after I'm gone."

COMING OF AGE

Margaret Mead (1901–1978)

Anthropologists seek to understand cultures by studying native peoples. To cultural anthropologist Margaret Mead, love was something that has been created and may or may not last. She did not believe love was necessary for a long marriage. Most remarkable was not necessarily what she said, or how "right" she might have been, but how willing she was to express her feelings openly. In one interview she commented: "Love is the invention of a few high cultures . . . it is cultural artifact. To make love the requirement of a lifelong marriage is exceedingly difficult, and only a few people can achieve it. I don't believe in setting universal standards that a large proportion of people can't reach."

During Margaret's long career she wrote forty books, eighteen of them with coauthors, and over one thousand monographs and articles. From 1961 to 1976 she authored a monthly column for *Redbook* magazine. In addition, she developed and gathered an extensive collection of tapes, films, and artifacts. She wrote myriad letters and kept carbon copies of them. When engaged in her fieldwork, she sent boxes of letters back home, letters that have provided rich insight into her life and loves. She often apologized for her letter writing as if it were a supplement to her real work, but also said it was a form of self-indulgence to which she felt entitled.

Instant fame came with the publication of her first work, *Coming of Age in Samoa*, a study of adolescent girls in an island culture. When Margaret first went to Samoa in 1925, little was known of its culture. The island was idyllic, unspoiled by tourists, still largely primitive and sexually permissive, yet with a very low rate of premarital pregnancy. Her popular book began to open the eyes of fellow researchers and the public as well to other cultural styles and choices. It was written in a way to help an average reader understand the implications of behavior being culturally rather than biologically determined. In addition, it made the point that teenage romance and sexuality did not have to result in pregnancy.

Romance can come at any age, and Margaret found herself at high romantic peaks when she fell in love during high school and became engaged for three years, and then married—not once, but three times, in the space of thirteen years. She loved her three husbands, her only child, and innumerable other children and friends, especially anthropologist Ruth Benedict. She was also one of the hardest-working anthropologists of all time, committing herself to promoting a cross-cultural understanding of childbearing, sex roles, and personality.

Born in Philadelphia, the daughter of a professor of economics and sociology, Margaret was the oldest of five children. She always felt wanted, was glad to be a girl, and adored children. She was especially close to her brother, Richard, who was overprotected because of poor health. Margaret claimed to have grown up two generations before her time, referring to her own independent thinking about how to raise children who appreciated other cultures and were also independent in their own thinking.

In her autobiography, Margaret lovingly describes her parents as highly educated social scientists who brought her up in an academic world. Her father believed that adding to the planet's store of knowledge was the most important thing anyone could do. Completely insistent on facts, he was also firm and opinionated, occasionally sarcastic, and most affectionate with his family. He expected and encouraged women to succeed.

Her mother, an independent thinker, was committed to being a responsible citizen and to inculcating this in her children. Always a serious student and researcher, she was highly concerned with social issues and would argue that extra money should not be spent on presents for herself but on worthy social projects. Studying for her doctorate when pregnant with Margaret, she was particularly interested in immigrant Italians, and the family often moved so that she could further her research on them. With each move she always sought out a variety of friends for her children.

Margaret's paternal grandmother, greatly respected by her family, shared their household and often conducted family meetings in her room. She had been a teacher, highly advanced in her thinking, and taught Margaret and her siblings the foundations of fieldwork. From both her mother and grandmother, Margaret learned that all races are equal and all cultures are of comparable worth.

Both mother and grandmother were avid observers and recorders of words and behavior. When Margaret was a child, her mother took frequent and copious notes on her development, and Margaret was trained to do the same with her younger siblings. The family also believed in schools that encouraged creativity rather than conformity. Because they moved so often, some years Margaret and her siblings would go to school, and sometimes they wouldn't. They were encouraged to learn from anyone who had useful skills, and each day Margaret studied in her grandmother's friendly room, always the largest and sunniest, no matter where they lived.

Margaret was in high school when she fell in love with Luther Crissman, a college senior. Then war came, and during the years he was away, the two of them wrote poetry and letters to each other daily. Although she considered herself to be engaged before Luther left for the service, when he returned and they told her father of their plans, he strongly objected and offered his daughter a trip around the world instead. Margaret chose to be married, however—and also to keep her own name, which was unusual then.

By this time Luther was a graduate student and part-time pastor in East New York. To both of them it was, in some ways, an ideal marriage: They were working toward goals they shared. He looked forward to being a minister full time. She liked attending an Episcopal church and hoped to become a pastor's wife someday, with six children. But Luther's interests slowly turned from religion to sociology. Margaret, meanwhile, became more interested in anthropology. As their mutual concerns drifted, their romance died, but they remained friends.

In her early years Margaret was quite uncertain as to what career to follow. Her interest in painting and creative writing segued into psychotherapy, and then to politics and world change. But it wasn't until she took a course in anthropology with Franz Boas that she made her career decision. Long conversations and a close association with anthropologist Ruth Benedict, fifteen years Margaret's senior and Boas's teaching assistant, cemented a commitment to what beckoned as fascinating life work. The two women shared a professional respect and deep friendship that endured throughout their lives. Each read everything the other wrote—a major commitment, considering how prolific they both were. Eventually, Margaret would write a biography of Ruth Benedict, as well as edit some of her papers.

The particular focus of Margaret's work developed after she attended a small conference of leaders in cultural anthropology and decided to select a specific culture in which to do fieldwork. She chose Polynesia to study the ways in which culture changed or remained the same—as in, for instance, child-rearing practices.

While Margaret was still married to Luther but no longer romantically involved with him, she met New Zealand anthropologist Reo Fortune on the boat back from her first trip to Samoa. A romance developed. Margaret, who had been told she was unlikely to bear the children she wanted, overlooked Reo's general unsuitability as father material and plunged into the union. After her divorce from Luther, they were married in a flush of passion and mutual interest in their work. Their first collaboration was to study the Manus people. Then, at Margaret's insistence, they returned to New York to write up their findings before embarking on another project.

While there, they each wrote three major books, after which they returned to New Guinea to study the Arapesh, a very nurturing and placid people. Not finding the situation sufficiently stimulating, they next went to study the head-hunting Mundugumors, also in New Guinea. In contrast to the Arapesh, with their overlapping male and female nurturing of children and one another, the Mundugumors were taught to be fierce, possessive, and sexually aggressive. Infanticide was common among them. Mothers would throw girl babies into the river to drown, and fathers their boy babies. Margaret was so appalled that she determined then to have a baby of her own, no matter how many miscarriages she might suffer, until she could successfully carry one to term.

Difficulties were arising between her and Reo. His idea of shared fieldwork was to pursue whatever was most interesting to him, and to leave what was left over to Margaret. By now in a state of deep fatigue, Margaret sought an end to the alliance. On one of their trips upriver through New Guinea they met Gregory Bateson, whose reports on the Iatmul people were beginning to get some professional attention. This meeting led to a new romance. Reo in his self-absorption had not recognized Margaret's severe fatigue, but Gregory did. "You're tired," were his first words to Margaret, as he pulled out a chair. These were the first cherishing words she had heard in months. His kindness overwhelmed her, as did the joy she felt in talking about their work. Gregory, a biologist first, with a secondary knowledge of physics and genealogy, added a new dimension to Margaret and Reo's approach as social scientists. As the three shared their insights from different perspectives, the relationship between Margaret and Gregory deepened.

Divorce from Reo and marriage to Gregory Bateson followed. The relationship lasted fifteen years and yielded the daughter Margaret so deeply desired. The couple's love for each other and interest in Mary Catherine were evident from the beginning. When, for example, the baby was born while Gregory was away in England, Margaret insisted on waiting to name her newborn until Gregory returned, so intent was she on including him in their infant's life.

Margaret was an innovative, greatly observant, self-confident, and loving mother. After all, she had herself been loved in this way as a child, so it was only natural that she treat her daughter similarly.

Mary Catherine also became an anthropologist and wrote in her memoirs what it was like to have two such famous parents. They were all on a first-name basis, and her mother, a compact five feet tall, had a great lap to cuddle in. Her father, she said, was six-foot-five and "more like a jungle gym rather than a nest." When World War II came, the family moved into a large house with the family of Lawrence Frank, also a social scientist, and there were always lots of people around. It was an ideal childhood; her parents played with her, read aloud to her, and talked to her about their work. Her father taught her the rudiments of biology, and her mother, cultural anthropology.

Unhappiness came to this ideal family when Gregory became interested in another woman and moved out. Margaret tried to hide her grief, but finally they were divorced so that Gregory could remarry. Cathy, eleven at the time, was encouraged to be independent. Throughout her growing up years she was always surrounded by Margaret's close friends and relatives, who would take loving care of her when her parents were away.

More years passed, and Gregory divorced and remarried again. Margaret never said anything unkind about him, because she wanted the love, respect, and good times between father and daughter to persist. Although exceptionally busy, Margaret strived for her own concentrated times of joy and intimacy with her daughter. As the director of the Museum of Natural History, for example, she delighted in giving Mary Catherine full rein to wander through those halls and exhibits for hours.

Because of her fear of being an overprotective mother, she encouraged Cathy to be autonomous, and she was successful. Cathy lived independently her senior year in high school when she went to stay in Israel with friends, and continued living on her own from then on.

Margaret always spoke of her three husbands with affection, and of Gregory with continuing love. Friendships with women and men were of great importance to her; some

were sexual, others were not. Her longest intimate relationship, with anthropologist Ruth Benedict, started long before
marriage to Gregory and continued after that time.

Psychiatrist Rollo May, who knew her for many years,
said that there was no doubt that Margaret was androgynous.
One of her other friends said: "She fell in love with women's
souls and men's bodies. She was spiritually homosexual, psychologically bisexual, and physically heterosexual. She had
affairs—with both men and women—though never with two
men or two women at the same time.

Margaret Mead was always in the process of coming of
age. She resisted the aging process by her adaptability to
changing ideas and situations. Her living will, in which she
specified her wishes as she approached death with cancer,
reflects her poise and flexibility. Margaret said she was willing
to continue living if she became blind or deaf, but not if she
lost both of those faculties. She was also willing to lose the
power of writing or the power of speech—but, again, not
the power of both. Perhaps the love and life of this busy
woman is best summarized in one of her favorite poems,
"First Fig," by Edna St. Vincent Millay:

> My candle burns at both ends;
> It will not last the night;
> But ah my foes, and oh, my friends—
> It gives a lovely light!

LOVE CONQUERS ALL

In today's world, many educated, intelligent women of all
ages want love and question their ability to find romantic
partners and to be self-actualizing at the same time. But there
is no end to the list of competent women who have been
able to do so regardless of age, physical handicaps, difficult
situations, objections from family, and social disapproval.

They have not been controlled by myths about women's roles and destinies.

One of the most pervasive myths is that romance is only for the young and that career success, if achieved at all, comes later. Yet many great women develop the most important love of their lives after they are already involved in a significant vocation. Their romantic relationships are not destroyed by their competence, because dedication to their chosen work provides a sound foundation for self-esteem.

Women with self-esteem do not focus their energies on bemoaning possible barriers to romance. To them, most barriers are myths or figments of the imagination. One common myth involves either-or thinking—that you can't have romance and be whole-heartedly involved in a career at the same time. Yet the lives of all the women in this book reflect the fallacy of this belief.

Whereas every culture has ideas about the "shoulds," the life stories of these women are so diverse that it is foolish to conclude that this is the way women are. Studies by anthropologists such as Margaret Mead show that in some cultures women are passive and peaceful, while in others they are aggressive and warlike; in some they are the dominant sex, in others the subordinate one.

Styles of courting differ as much as beliefs about how women should treat their friends, children, and other family members. In some cultures monogamy is important and premarital and extramarital sexual liaisons are kept secret. In other cultures such secrecy is unimportant. This was true in Margaret Mead's life.

The need to conform to some arbitrary cultural definition of beauty to be able to attract romance is another myth. Yet the women in this chapter demonstrate the truth of the phrase "Beauty is in the eye of the beholder." Margaret Mead, for example, was short and overweight by Western standards; Georgia O'Keeffe and Katharine Hepburn were tall and thin. In these cases height and shape did not interfere with romance. Each woman had a distinct presence that reflected self-esteem.

Yet another myth is that only the healthy are fit to be loved. Whereas radiant health is beautiful, many women who do not have health do have romance as well as successful careers. Semi-invalid Elizabeth Barrett proves this. In the passionate love she shared with Robert Browning, health was not the issue; the meeting of their minds and interests was more important.

In a similar vein it has been said that a woman who is intelligent and esteems herself could not possibly be romantically involved with an emotionally unstable man. Yet two of the great women in this chapter loved men with severe psychological problems. Clara Schumann's husband, Robert, was probably manic-depressive; Katharine Hepburn's lover, Spencer Tracy, had a severe case of alcoholism. The loyalty of these two women was not destroyed by the problems of the men in their lives.

Another common belief is that happiness in the face of family disapproval is impossible. Yet four out of six of the women in this chapter had just that experience. Elizabeth and Robert Browning, even after marriage, had to flee in secret from her father's wrath. Clara Schumann was forced to fight her father in court in order to release herself from his parental authority and get legal permission to marry. Mary Ann Evans, also known as George Eliot, lived for many years in a romantic relationship with one man in the face of severe criticism from her brother and the wider culture. Katharine Hepburn, in spite of her high admiration for her mother, ignored her advice not to become involved with Spencer. It seems clear that disapproval from others does not necessarily deter women who think for themselves, make their own decisions, and are willing to pay the price when going against family or cultural values.

Of course, as any single parent who loves children and is also commited to a vocation can tell you, the allocation of time and energy is often difficult. But the myth that it can't be done successfully is contradicted by Clara Schumann, who was often impoverished and had to support herself and her seven children after the suicide of her husband.

Alternative lifestyles are not unusual for great women, and love can come more than once, even in later years. It did for Mary Ann Evans and Georgia O'Keeffe. Taking their destinies into their own hands, they acted according to their own values.

An even more pervasive myth is that a man will not give emotional support to a competent woman. Instead he will be controlling or competitive. That may be true with the man who has some uncertainty about his own worth. But it is not true for the romantic partners of these great women, who were encouraged or directly assisted by those they loved.

Perhaps it is true there are no insurmountable barriers and that love conquers all for those who affirm, "How shall I love you? Let me count the ways!"

CHAPTER TWO

WOMEN WITH MANY LOVERS

WITH HIGH DESIRE

Some women love one man for a lifetime and are fully satisfied with a monogamous sexual relationship. They pledge themselves to this style of romance, and they keep the pledge. To other women, fidelity to one partner is not ideal. Whether due to excessive sexual energy, changing emotional needs, or boredom and a resulting desire for variety, some women have many romances and many lovers.

In the past, women in a very few cultures have claimed the same sexual freedoms that men commonly have had. But in most other cultures, women have been expected to fully restrain themselves before—and, to a certain extent, even during—marriage. While men through the ages have openly discussed their sexual escapades, using slang and pejorative language, found even in Shakespeare, to describe them, women seldom have done so, even with their lovers or husbands. During the nineteenth century and what became called the Victorian era, many people believed discussing sexual needs was not "ladylike." In fact, women were not even expected to have sexual needs, only to be available to meet men's needs. Open discussion of sexual matters was frequently censored by law or custom, and euphemisms were used for sexual parts of the body. This led to widespread ignorance about many sexual matters. Only since the advent of psychology, sociology, anthropology, and the women's movement has the study of sexual conduct received a certain acceptance in Western culture.

Today, many professionals and lay people agree that there is no way of determining what is "normal" sexual behavior. What is normal to one person may not be so to another. For example, abstinence from sexual intercourse while a partner is gone for months or years may fit one cultural value of what is normal but not another.

The enjoyment of sex is considered immoral to some people, even after marriage. These kinds of moralists say the only justification for sex is procreation; pleasure plays no part. Women have been expected to remain virgins until marriage, and to remain faithful afterward regardless of circumstances.

Strangely enough, the idea of having many "romances" is sometimes interpreted as more acceptable than having many lovers. The word *romance* implies an emotionally overpowering attraction that one is not able to control. Whereas "taking a lover" may mean creating a romantic relationship, it also refers to a sexual relationship, with or without a romantic component. And it can by extension imply casual sex.

In contrast to the tradition of women being virgins and always sexually faithful, for men to "play the field" has been considered normal, even admirable. If a man is called a Don Juan or a womanizer, it is often with indulgence rather than condemnation. The argument has been that "that's the way men are; they can't help themselves." A woman behaving similarly is said to be a home wrecker—either of her own or of someone else. She is labeled "promiscuous," a "nymphomaniac" or said to be "acting like a prostitute."

In spite of cultural expectations and labels, some women enjoy many lovers, whether the relationships are romantic or not, whether secret or well known. In this chapter we will meet five women, from different cultures and times, whose sexual desire was high and who expressed it with more than a few men.

Catherine the Great, empress of Russia, was never faithful to a man for more than a year or two. Although she did not flaunt her torrid affairs, they were widely acknowledged. Most of them could be called romances, because each time she fancied herself to be in love and trapped by her passion.

The famous aviator Beryl Markham, an extremely competent professional woman, also had many lovers. Her greatness lay in her courage and adventuresome spirit, which were well demonstrated in her professional skills in training racehorses, as well as in her incredible record-setting flight across the Atlantic.

Sometimes partners in a long-standing relationship choose to have additional lovers by mutual consent. Bisexual Mexican artist Frida Kahlo had an open relationship with fellow artist Diego Rivera. Her seriously crippled body did not keep her from marrying him twice while having other sexual partners, including various women and Leon Trotsky, the Russian revolutionary.

The great French philosophers Simone de Beauvoir and Jean-Paul Sartre, lovers for fifty years, also had numerous sexual partners. Their value systems contraindicated marriage or monogamous commitment. Yet they were utterly dependent on each other, and her writing shows how agonizing it can be for a woman to take charge of her own sexuality.

The great actress Sarah Bernhardt, also independent, was often in the spotlight. She had many romances with younger men and continued her acting career even after the loss of a leg.

All of these women, with the exception of Sarah Bernhardt, found their life work—as ruler, artist, and philosopher—in occupations traditionally dominated by men. Yet all of these women had hearts on fire as well. Each succeeded in her chosen field because of her energies and interests, her learned skills and the commitment to use them. Although they came from different cultures (Russia, Kenya, Germany, Mexico, and France), each lived a life of courage and confidence. We may not agree with some of their choices in expressing the fire of their sexual desires, but it is impossible not to admire their work and courage.

TOO MANY TO COUNT

Catherine the Great (1729–1796)

Catherine II had too many lovers to count and was also one of Russia's great rulers. She was charming and had high energy, intelligence, and great ambition. She became empress of Russia via a coup, organized with one of her lovers, to overthrow her husband, Peter III, who was then ruling the country and threatening to dispose of her.

Catherine's achievements had a major impact on Russian life. She personally rewrote the laws of her country, effectively limiting the rights of government and church officials. Her thinking was ahead of her time in many ways. She believed, for example, in the decentralization of industry to reduce the constant threats of plague and fire that often demolished large urban populations, made vulnerable by overcrowding and wooden construction.

She also reorganized the administration and rewrote the laws so that they would be more compatible with those of other European countries. During her rule she expanded Russian territory by over 200,000 square miles by taking over the Crimea, gaining access to the Black Sea, and adding much of Poland to the empire.

She also founded the first Russian school for girls and the first medical college. She regularly corresponded with many of the intellectuals of Europe, and her ambition was boundless, for both herself and her adopted people. According to one biographer: "Everything that she desired she obtained by patience, intelligence, toughness, courage, taking incredible risks when necessary, suddenly changing course in order to reach the goal more surely."

Catherine was born in Germany as Sophie Friederike Auguste and came from modest nobility. Her mother was cold and ambitious; her father, a minor German prince, was loving yet distant. At the age of fourteen she was called to the Russian court to be evaluated as a potential wife for the man who was to become Peter III, then a grand duke and the grandson of Peter the Great.

Unfortunately, Peter did not inherit his grandfather's greatness. He was immature, unattractive, and poorly educated. These liabilities did not, however, deter the ambitious Catherine. When called to the court, she converted from Lutheranism to Russian Orthodoxy and changed her name from Sophia to Catherine to please Peter's aunt, who was then the Empress Elizabeth.

To advance her political interests further, Catherine studied the Russian language—so long and hard and feverishly that she became ill, a development that did not go unnoticed or unappreciated by either the people or the ruling empress. Catherine was hence chosen from the pool of candidates; her engagement to Peter was announced, and they were married when she was fifteen.

Peter was seventeen at the time, yet he remained a virgin for the first eight years of their marriage. He pretended to be a womanizer but actually preferred to play with toy soldiers in bed. In contrast, Catherine enjoyed dancing, fun, and laughter, as well as spending huge sums of money.

Peter was voyeuristic and especially interested in watching the sexual exploits of his promiscuous aunt, the empress. At one time, he bored holes in the wall of her bedroom and invited his friends and his young wife to join him in watching his aunt with her lover. The empress was enraged. Catherine wrote in her memoirs:

I might have been fond of my husband had he only wanted
or known how to be pleasant. But I came to a terrible con-
clusion about him within the first days of my marriage. I said
to myself, If you love this man, you will be the most miserable
creature on this earth.

Then, to make things worse, Peter fell prey to a bad case
of smallpox, which left its mark on both his brain and his
face. Recognizing her inability to love this man, Catherine
tried many outlets for her sexual frustration, including stren-
uous horseback riding. She also embarked on a series of love
affairs. Serge Saltzkov, a minor official, was the first; she
became pregnant by him three times. The first two pregnancies resulted in miscarriages, the third in a male child.
Peter was seemingly unable to father a child; so to protect
himself when Catherine first became pregnant, Serge Saltz-
hov suggested to the empress that Peter have a simple operation that would "allow him to be fertile." This done, Peter
and Catherine were then commanded to have sex to please
the empress, Peter's aunt. When a boy was born, it was
announced as Peter's to ensure an heir to the crown. Catherine
rarely saw her son, so completely did the empress insist on
directing the child's life. Nor was Catherine particularly interested in rectifying this situation; the child was as mentally
disturbed as her husband.

Life was not easy for Catherine in the court. When her
beloved father died, for example, she was told she could have
one—and only one—week in which to grieve. Because he
was not a ruler, anything of longer duration would be inappropriate. She was only twenty-two when this occurred,
and after her week she was obliged to resume her court duties.

To keep herself intellectually occupied and insulated
from the boredom of court, Catherine, who had a brilliant
mind, read widely, especially the historical works of Voltaire,
with whom she conducted an active correspondence. Reading
was one of her favorite occupations, and she spent three years

plowing through the enormous five volumes of Bayle's *Dictionary, Historical and Critical*. In her memoirs she rejoiced at how a fire in the palace in Moscow had, despite destroying many things, spared her precious books. Her love of reading was unusual at a time when at least half of the court was illiterate.

Of the many affairs Catherine entertained herself with, most were terminated by lovers who were politically ambitious and ultimately bored by her commitment to Russia, her addiction to romance, and her sexual insatiability. Even Catherine admitted this. When writing about a young Polish aristocrat, Count Stanislas August Poniatowski, one of the many men she seduced, Catherine remarked that he "was loving and beloved from 1755 to 1758, and the liaison would have lasted forever if he himself had not got bored by it."

A frail daughter was born to Catherine, fathered perhaps by Poniatowski. This child, like her son, was also controlled by the aging empress. Catherine was permitted to see her children exactly once a month.

When the empress died and Peter was crowned emperor his behavior became even more bizarre. Often drunk and irrational, he constantly ridiculed Catherine in public. He despised Russia, and his cruelty was so well known that he enraged both the military and the clergy. This created a climate ripe for a coup, and exactly such a thing occurred in 1762, when Gregory Orlov, Catherine's lover by whom she was pregnant at the time, led, along with his brothers, a successful revolt that lasted for two days. Catherine, at age thirty-three, was declared empress; Peter was forced to abdicate, and a week later he was killed.

But Catherine would not marry Orlov. He was from an insignificant family and politically naive. Her advisors also objected on the grounds that such a union would have confused the issue of who would inherit the throne, already in dispute because of her son Paul's continuing poor health. So Orlov was given jewels, palaces, and thousands of peasants.

He was made a prince. And then he was also given some responsibilities. One was to oversee the relocation both of Russians who had earlier fled the country and some 30,000 immigrants, mostly Germans, to whom she had promised religious freedom and land on which to settle. Another of his tasks was to govern Moscow when the great plague broke out. But their torrid romance did not last. As Orlov gained power and wealth he developed a preference for his fifteen-year-old cousin.

Catherine's primary interest was to be a good ruler, and her first achievement after being crowned was to reform Russia. To do so she decided to be an absolute ruler and become fully involved in straightening out the corruption in many parts of the government. She began by calling the senate to accountability: "Messieurs Senators are to be in the Senate from half-past eight until twelve-thirty, and in nowise pronounce irrelevant speeches." One of her next reforms was focused on the Orthodox Church. She ordered the divestiture of many of its lands and the transfer of two million peasants from church control to government control.

Not content to rule from the palace, she visited many parts of Russia and tried to improve the conditions of those who lived there. The cost of food was checked regularly, and bread prices were strictly controlled for the benefit of the poor. Catherine also reorganized the army and navy, denounced torture, and forbade capital punishment except in extraordinary situations. From her personal funds she established the first free public hospital in Moscow for the poor and an orphanage to reduce infanticide. As a result of a small-pox epidemic, she initiated inoculation at a time when it was unknown in Russia. Later, the bubonic plague hit, and three to seven hundred people died daily in Moscow. To try to control it, she reorganized the health department, instituted quarantine, closed factories that were at risk, and relocated others outside the city limits.

Along with these activities she took another lover, Gri-

gory Potemkin, a distinguished military man whose abilities
and ambition were as high as Catherine's. Although most of
her lovers were in the military, she did not involve them in
significant political decisions. Potemkin was the exception.
She was forty-five; he was thirty-five, blind in one eye, intelligent, and evidently most virile.

Catherine wrote him impassioned love letters proclaim-
ing that he was much superior to Gregory Orlov in bed.
They had many nicknames for each other: "my darling pet,"
"my twin soul," "my dearest doll," "dear plaything," "tiger," "little parrot," "infidel," "my little Geisha," "my
golden pheasant," "golden cock," "lion of the jungle,"
"wolfbird." Like other men, Potemkin often played hard-
to-get. Their quarrels were frequent. Though often humiliated, Catherine would bribe him with gifts, titles, and passionate letters: "I am burning with impatience to see you
again. It seems I have not seen you for a year. I kiss you and
so much wish to see you because I love you with all my heart.
My beloved falcon, you are staying away far too long."

Some historians claim the two were secretly married.
The truth of this is unknown. Each also had other lovers.
After two years, their infatuation decreased, although their
admiration did not. Until death they maintained their close
association while continuing to plan for Russia's development.

As their passion faded, Potemkin began to act as a procurer to help Catherine find men to sexually satisfy her, while
three of his young nieces became his mistresses. Catherine's
new lovers each paid Potemkin large sums of money for her
favors. Then, when the affairs broke up, as they always did,
she would reward them financially and politically with land
and titles. To assist in the selection of men, Catherine had a
confidante whose task was to try out men sexually before
their skills could be approved for the empress's bedchamber.

Throughout life, young men continued to attract Catherine. In her fifties, she was still sexually aggressive and had

many lovers—for their convenience as well as hers. But her liaisons were not all sexual; some of the most brilliant minds of Europe were her lifelong friends. Generous and loyal, Catherine was nonetheless sometimes domineering and egotistical. She developed extraordinary administrative capabilities, partly due to her careful study of Montesquieu's great work *Spirit of the Law* and his concept that a good ruler should be concerned about the enlightenment of the people and gradual social change. She also called on other European legal sources for reference and, by writing it herself, codified Russian law from its disorganized state into an astute and scholarly document. During her reign, more than one hundred towns were built, and many others were expanded and improved.

Platon Zubov, the last of her lovers was, like his predecessors, financially greedy and politically ambitious. He was twenty-two, less than half her age, when she bribed him into her bed. He exploited her to the end, however, and continually tried to undermine Potemkin's high goals for Russia.

Catherine never lost her love of life. At age sixty-five, when she had become so obese she could hardly walk, she claimed that she was like a child of five who enjoyed playing childish games because she still loved to laugh. At sixty-seven she died of a stroke, falling off a commode, while her young lover Zubov awaited her in his adjoining suite.

On hearing of her death, Prince de Ligne of Vienna, who had first called her Catherine the Great, proclaimed, "Catherine le Grand is no more. These words are frightful to pronounce! . . . The most brilliant star that illumined our hemisphere has just been extinguished."

The drama of her many romances was not finished. Three of her lovers became part of a new scenario. Her son Paul, supposedly by Peter III, decided to take revenge. He forced her early lover Gregory Orlov, who had overthrown his father so that Catherine could become empress, to lead a procession to dig up Paul III's coffin. Paul then decorated it with honors and put it beside the coffin of Catherine under the words "Divided in life, united in death." Next, the bones of her lover and procurer, Potemkin, were exhumed and thrown away. Then Paul, becoming more and more insane, began to systematically terrorize Russia. Finally he was assassinated by a group led by Zubov.

To Catherine, men were necessary as friends and advisors, beyond their capacity as sexual and romantic partners. Most of them could be attracted by favors and paid off with more favors, and because she did not hold grudges when one of them moved on to someone else, they usually remained friends afterwards. To men, Catherine the Great was the key to titles, serfs, and unlimited funds. This astute and generous ruler, with great political and sexual appetites, showed throughout her life that sexual passion in women and avarice in men can be two strong motivating factors in romances.

ADVENTURE IN FLIGHT

Beryl Markham (1902–1986)

Racehorse trainer and licensed pilot Beryl Markham was a bewitching and glamorous woman. She had numerous adventurous, passing liaisons, but none could match the excitment of her chosen work.

Beryl Markham met professional challenges from which many brave men would shrink. A bush pilot in Kenya, she flew a light two-seater plane, often in darkness, without earphones for ground contact or lighted airports to guide her. She said she liked this lonely job because it freed her from "the curse of boredom."

Beryl was also the first person to fly solo from England to North America, the first woman to be a licensed racehorse trainer in Africa, and the first licensed female bush pilot who delivered goods, passengers, and mail. Before her record-setting aviation triumphs, she developed six Kenya Derby winners. As a writer, she became best known for her memoirs, *West with the Night*, first published in 1942 and reissued forty years later.

Born Beryl Clutterbuck in England, she grew up among the children of British East Africa; when her mother left the family, her father, a trainer of racehorses in Nairobi, brought Beryl to Africa when she was four. To her, Africa was the "breath and life of childhood." Eventually both parents remarried, but Beryl disliked her new stepmother as well as her teachers and was allowed by her permissive father to do without both. Beryl was emotionally close to her father, who first worked to create a farm out of a wilderness and then built a mill using power from old railway engines. Beryl found a mother substitute, Lady Delemere, on a nearby ranch, and was always willing to listen to her.

Feeling self-confident and full of energy after dropping out of school, Beryl found her own way, mostly among the young boys of the nearby Muran tribe, and learned to ride and to hunt barefoot with a spear as they did, as well as to speak Swahili and several African dialects. Her fearlessness served to put her on equal footing with them. All her life she retained the teeth and claw marks of a lion who attacked her when she was a child.

At sixteen, Beryl was already a tall, strong-willed beauty, with fair skin and light brown hair, successful at any physical task she undertook. But she had no real friends or close relationships and was unable to deal with her emotional life. She could ride and tame the wildest horse and hunt feral animals, but she was unable to get along with any of the tutors or governesses who tried to "tame" her.

During her unusual life, Beryl had three husbands and many lovers. But it was at sixteen that she married her first, Alexander "Jock" Purves, a successful sportsman and farmer in his early thirties—twice Beryl's age. Although Beryl enjoyed the first year, successfully racing horses and becoming

the toast of upper society of the Europeans in Kenya, she and
Jock soon began to argue, sometimes violently, often in public. She often left Jock for weeks to stay either with friends;
with her mother, who had returned to the area; or with a
lover.

When a severe drought came, her father's farm could no
longer function, and the mill that ground grain into flour was
closed. Her father, leaving to work with racehorses in Peru,
invited Beryl to come along, but she loved Africa too much
to leave. Besides, the family's bankruptcy and the sudden
death of her twenty-one-year-old brother had left her shaken
and vulnerable.

Beryl was divorced from Jock when she was in her early
twenties, but not before she had earned a reputation for infidelity and promiscuity. After their separation, she was alternately poor and well-to-do, living for short periods with
friends and lovers. Among the well-known people who supported her in various ways were Denys Finch Hatton, a man
of many interests, and Karen Blixen, who, writing under the
name of Isak Dinesen, produced such works as the well-
known *Out of Africa*.

Beryl worked hard to establish herself as a successful
trainer of winning horses and to earn a respected place in the
male-dominated racing profession. She also earned a place in
the social gossip columns, especially in 1927, when her en-
gagements to two different men were announced within a
few months of each other. Beryl followed through on the
second announcement and married Mansfield Markham, one
of the richest young aristocrats of their society.

Under Markham's tutelage, she became even more of
an admired socialite, complete with a wardrobe that contributed to her fame as an international beauty. Her tall, slender
frame perfectly suited the fashions of the 1920s. She continued
to have affairs and openly declared that she was not "in love"
with Mansfield but only "liked" him. One of her romances
was with Prince Henry of the British royal family, to whom

she had been presented in court. In fact, when Beryl became pregnant, she did not know which man was the father.

Soon after the birth of her baby the marriage broke up, and her son was then raised by Markham's mother. This allowed Beryl and Prince Henry more freedom to continue their liaison. Their affair, which attracted worldwide attention, ended quietly. Beryl claimed that he was kind and rather firm, but that she had not yet found the ideal man, one who could earn her complete love and respect, as her father had done.

It seems, however, that Denys Finch Hatton quite nearly measured up. Polished, intelligent, and extraordinarily charming, this man whom Beryl had first met at eighteen captured her heart as well as her admiration. Brilliant and adventuresome, he became her lover, brother, mentor, and friend. He tutored her in literature, introduced her to music, and took her on flying adventures.

Beryl and Denys were at the peak of their romance in 1931 when Denys died in a plane crash while he was scouting for elephants. Before his death, Beryl and others had had uncomfortable premonitions. One friend, when asked to accompany him on the flight, responded, "Good God, Denys! Do you want me to commit suicide?" The daughter of another friend saved her mother's life by pleading, "Mummy, please don't go, you'll crash, you'll die." Beryl had also been invited, but she was late, so Denys took off without her. In her memoirs she wrote: "Someone will say that he was a great man who never achieved greatness, and this would not only be trite, but wrong; he was a great man who never achieved arrogance."

Denys's funeral was the only one Beryl ever attended. She described him as "a keystone in an arch whose other stones were other lives. If a keystone trembles, the arch will carry the warning along its entire curve."

Beryl now poured more of her energy into flying, passing her tests, and entering into a long-term affair with her instructor, Tom Black, who was also a skilled horseman. She became not only the first woman pilot in Kenya, but also, in 1933, the first Kenya-trained pilot to be granted a commercial flying license—this at a time when only a few women from anywhere in the world flew planes at all. "My girl," she said to herself at this accomplishment, "you are getting somewhere at last." As a commercial pilot, Beryl took clients on safaris and delivered mail and supplies to outposts of the African bush. She was the first pilot to offer aerial elephant scouting trips.

As lovers and coworkers, Beryl and Tom made elaborate and adventurous plans to be together. But Tom flew to England alone to prepare for a race, and neither realized it would change their relationship forever. Beryl read in the newspaper that a few days after the race Tom had married English actress Florence Desmond.

Once again abandoned by a man she loved and admired, Beryl worked even harder for achievement as an aviator. Two years after Tom's marriage, in 1936, she had her greatest triumph, her transatlantic flight.

As much as Beryl had struggled to be considered a pilot and not a "woman who flew planes," the press persisted in using their own terms. "Atlantic Has No Terrors for Flying Woman," newspaper headlines read. One critically referred to a "young mother" who would attempt a transatlantic flight. Other headlines shouted, "Daredevil Society Woman Leaves Today" and "Beauty to Fly Today." Beryl's response was to entreat the papers not to use such phrases which reflected on her appearance but instead to give her credit for being a competent professional pilot undertaking a job.

And Beryl did the job well. After a flight of twenty-one hours, in a small aircraft not much bigger than her tanks of fuel, Beryl executed a forced landing on fumes. She landed not at her ultimate destination of New York but on a bog of mud in Nova Scotia. Yet her record flight was accomplished, and when she finally reached New York, crowds congratulated her for conquering the Atlantic.

But Beryl still had not conquered the events of her private life. Soon after her internationally hailed crossing, Tom was killed in an aircraft accident. Although they were no longer lovers by then, he had nonetheless remained a friend and tutor and was still the most important man in her life. At thirty-eight, Beryl found herself lonely once more, and again without money.

Encouraged by friends, among them writer and fellow aviator Antoine de Saint-Exupéry, Beryl began to prepare parts of her personal journal for publication. Her autobiography, *West with the Night*, which she dedicated to her father, was released in 1942.

By this time Beryl had married again. Her third husband, Raoul Schumacher, was a handsome, entertaining, well-read Hollywood producer, five years Beryl's junior. For a short time both of them wrote to earn a living, though it was not a very substantial one. The marriage turned sour, complicated by—or perhaps because of—a combination of Raoul's drinking, their joint financial problems, and Beryl's own pattern of preferring affairs to monogamy. For Beryl it meant another divorce, another period of depression and loneliness.

Finally, in her mid fifties, Beryl decided to reclaim the name of her second husband, Markham, and turned once again to horses. Her body remained fit (she rode well into her seventies), but her life remained fragmented. She was never able to keep herself out of financial disaster. At the end she won acclaim when *West with the Night* was reissued and documentaries of her flying career were made. Shortly before the fiftieth anniversary of her famous flight she died, still alone and seeking her place in the world. When people asked why she undertook the dangerous task of flying across the Atlantic against the headwinds, her response was both revealing and practical: "I believe in the future of an Atlantic air service. I planned this flight because I wanted to be in that air service at the beginning. If I get across I think I shall have earned my place. Don't you?"

A BROKEN WOMAN

Frida Kahlo (1907–1954)

Mexico's most famous woman painter, Frida Kahlo, was an ardent revolutionary. Severely crippled in an accident, she nonetheless had many lovers. Her greatness lay in an ability to focus and communicate on canvas her personal values and her pain.

Diego Rivera, who married her twice, was also a famous painter and once described the paintings of his wife as "acid and tender, hard as steel, and delicate and fine as a butterfly's wing, lovable as a beautiful smile, and profound and cruel as the bitterness of life."

Frida's paintings are famous for reflecting her Mexican tradition and her personal pain in realistic and unconventional ways. Although others considered her art surrealist, she said she painted only what she saw and was not influenced by the Surrealism movement. Frida described the beauty and bitterness in her life in terms of accidents: "I suffered two grave accidents in my life. One in which a streetcar knocked me down . . . the other accident is Diego Rivera." Unlike most artists, both of them were best known by their first names.

Both artists viewed death as part of life and saw everything as interconnected. Especially in Frida's work one can find skulls, skeletons, and rotted flesh. This is not surprising, considering the thirty-two operations she had on her spinal column after it was broken.

Frida was born in Mexico City, one of six children. The home in which she grew up, now a museum, is painted royal blue and set in lush gardens surrounded by a high stucco wall. Her Mexican mother, intelligent, diligent, and pious, managed the family and their finances. Frida regarded her with a mixture of love and disdain. Her relationship with her father, however, was quite different. To begin with, Frida was her father's favorite. Of Hungarian and German descent, he worked as a professional photographer of Mexican archeological findings and was also an amateur painter, a lover of books, and a pianist. Frida greatly looked up to him for his courage and ability to "see" with his camera. Although he had epilepsy for sixty years, he never stopped working; her portrait of him is signed "With adoration."

At age six, Frida was stricken with polio, which left her with a withered leg for which she was ridiculed, even when she tried to hide it by wearing several pairs of socks. To further disguise her infirmity, she developed a unique style of walking, as if she were lightly flying.

When she was a seventeen-year-old high school student, Frida's already compromised body was further seriously injured when she was riding on a bus that was rammed by a streetcar. An iron bar from the streetcar was driven through Frida's back, impaling her. Three lumbar vertebrae were broken. Further, there were three injuries to her pelvis, eleven breaks in one foot, a broken elbow, and a deep cut in her stomach.

These injuries, numerous operations, and a series of steel and plaster corsets caused her great pain for the rest of her life. One plaster corset that she wore became so tight as it hardened that it pressed against Frida's lungs, nearly suffocating her.

While Frida recuperated from the accident, her mother had a mirror installed in the canopy ceiling of her bed. Lying there, she could stare up at herself for hours. While it was meant to be comforting, it served only to be confronting, offering as it did no place for her to hide from what she saw. In this position, lying on her back, Frida began to paint her many self-portraits, often with the great detail that her photographer father always encouraged her to observe. She once said her paintings were like photographs because of the detail that is most noticeable in the clothes she painted, such as the lace ruffle completely surrounding her face in one of her self-portraits. She also painted pictures of herself in emotional and physical pain.

Frida's physical presence was as dramatic as the events that marked her life. The strong features of her face bore witness to her independent character. Dark, heavy eyebrows crossed her forehead, dipping slightly in the center to give the appearance of a perpetual frown. Although she lived in pain, she participated fully in the world around her, a vibrant, sensuous, successful woman. She dressed always in the colorful costumes of her native Mexico, even when traveling, and had many lovers before and during her two marriages to the famous Diego.

Frida's sexual energy fanned out in many directions. As a teenager she was seduced by a female teacher, and throughout her life she continued to take women lovers. One of her first male lovers, Fernando Fernandez, was her tutor in drawing. Another, Alejandro Gomez Arias, was a student leader in their high school, who in a recent taped interview called her "a daughter of the revolution."

As a teenager she was also infatuated with Diego Rivera, who was commissioned to work in her school. In fact, Frida once told her classmates that she planned to have a child by Diego. She might well have at a later date, had the bus accident not doomed her attempts at childbirth to a series of miscarriages.

Her first self-portrait was painted as a gift to win back her estranged lover Alejandro. In this, Frida depicted herself as calmly reserved but very feminine, with her breasts showing prominently through the fabric of a low-cut dress.

In letters to him, Frida tried to dispel gossip that branded her as "loose" and told him that he was her only love. For months she wrote him long, sentimental letters, but they were seldom answered. He could not endure her possessiveness or her emotional neediness. The romance faded, yet Alejandro remained a lifelong friend.

Frida was eighteen when she took her first canvases to Diego Rivera, already Mexico's most famous painter, to evaluate. It had been five years since she had first met and been attracted to him. Diego was encouraging and asked if she had other paintings he could see. Despite his obesity, Diego had a reputation for being a womanizer, and Frida, acutely aware of this, minced no words: "Look, I have not come to flirt or anything, even if you are a woman-chaser. I have come to show you my painting. If you are interested in it, tell me so; if not, likewise, so that I will go to work at something else to help my parents."

Diego began to come to Frida's home to see her, and after several visits her father asked if he was serious about her. When Diego said yes, Frida's father warned him against her cleverness; there was in her, he said, a "concealed devil."

Meanwhile, Frida joined the Communist Party. She had the spirit of a revolutionist, which she said started when she was four years old and witnessed the revolutionary armies fighting outside the window of her home. In fact, she changed her birth date from 1907 to 1910 to match the year of the Mexican Revolution. Well-known Marxists became her heroes, and her many paintings of them hang on the walls where she once lived.

Frida was twenty-two and Diego forty-three when they first married in 1929. It was said to be a marriage between two monsters, a dove and an elephant. During this marriage, Diego and Frida continued to take other lovers. Diego's affairs included one with Frida's sister, Cristina. Although he did not mind Frida's lesbian affairs, he was terribly jealous of those that were heterosexual. Among Frida's lovers was the famous Russian revolutionary hero Leon Trotsky, who was also a close friend of Diego's.

Frida and Trotsky desisted when his wife became disconsolate over them. They feared that if their relationship became public it could be detrimental to the Russian revolutionary movement. As a farewell statement, Frida, as she had done with Alejandro, painted a self-portrait. In it she stands as an aristocrat, dressed in striking colors, looking beautiful and regal.

Frida and Diego, both strong-willed and independent artists, both sensuous and openly seductive, found monogamy impossible. Diego's account of the reasons for their divorce sheds some light on how each of them felt about marital infidelity:

> I simply wanted to be free to carry on with any woman who caught my fancy. Yet Frida did not object to my infidelity as such. What she could not understand was my choosing women who were either unworthy of me or inferior to her. She took it as a personal humiliation to be abandoned for sluts.

Their marriage had lasted ten years. The divorce lasted one year. During this time, Frida worked hard so that she would not have to accept money from Diego. She also painted to express her passion. Once she cut off the long hair that Diego loved and painted a self-portrait. In this painting Frida sits with pieces of her hair all around her, while holding a pair of scissors at her crotch in a symbolic portrayal of how she cut herself off from Diego.

A year after her divorce, one of Frida's American doctors wrote to recommend that she come to the United States for medical treatment. He also recommended that she remarry Diego in spite of the fact that he would never be monogamous. Frida followed the doctor's advice. When she remarried Diego she was thirty-three and he was fifty-four. She insisted that it become a celibate marriage. She turned more and more to women for comfort, often to the very women with whom Diego himself was having affairs.

After their remarriage, Frida and Diego became closer friends while maintaining sexual autonomy. They nurtured each other intermittently, as a loving parent will a child. She enjoyed bathing him as though he were her fat little boy. Sadly however, after so many operations her leg became gangrenous, requiring much medical care. During the year she was hospitalized, he took a room next to hers so he could sleep there and rock her to sleep.

Through it all, they both continued to have affairs, to fight with each other, to separate and reunite. But Diego was the undeniable center of her life. Her journals are full of references to him as her "universe," and her paintings of herself, reflecting her suffering from Diego's infidelities, belie her casual public attitude toward his philandering.

A final operation in 1953 resulted in the amputation of Frida's leg. She never completely recovered, yet she never lost hope. One of her last diary entries reads:

> *I have achieved a lot*
> *I will be able to walk*
> *I will be able to paint*
> *I love Diego more than I love myself.*
> *My will is great*
> *My will remains.*

Frida's will may well have remained, but her health became worse, and during her last months she faced death as she had faced life, with utmost honesty. When her death seemed imminent she freely discussed it and pleaded that she not be buried lying down, as she had had too much pain in that position. Her wishes were granted, and she was cremated. She left a great legacy to Diego when she told him that all her tragedies served only to remind her that she loved him more than her own skin.

ALWAYS FAITHFUL, NEVER FAITHFUL
Simone de Beauvoir (1908–1986)

Feminist writer, teacher, and leftist politician Simone de
Beauvoir maintained a lifelong committed relationship with
a lover who was equally talented. Simone first met Jean-Paul
Sartre in 1929, when they were taking tests at the Sorbonne
for teaching diplomas in philosophy. He placed first; she
placed second. He nicknamed her *le castor*, "the Beaver," so
hard and energetically did she work.

The two of them wrote novels, plays, and philosophical
essays and became known as important French existentialists.
(Existentialism is a post-war philosophy concerned with freedom of choice, personal responsibility, and the need to find
one's own reasons for living.)

During their fifty-year romance their sexual and intellectual relationship remained constant. As Simone wrote, "I
followed him joyfully because he led me along the paths I
wanted to take." Yet she rejected marriage on the basis of
principle. In her famous book *The Second Sex*, she raised
questions that were new for many women: How can a
woman find fulfillment? Which roads are open to her and
which are blocked? How can independence be recovered
when a woman is in a state of dependency? What circumstances limit women's freedom, and how can they be overcome?

Simone's childhood was spent in Paris with her parents
and younger sister. A rebel from the beginning, she often
felt like an outcast as a young child and had raging temper
tantrums with her parents and their friends because they alternately ignored and spoiled her. She decided she "would
never forget that a five-year-old is a complete individual."

Her mother, a devout Catholic, was affectionate with
her children, but also distant and capricious. Moreover, she

was so puritanical that when Simone was reading George Eliot's *Adam Bede*, which she labeled slow and dull in spite of its popularity, she hid the book lest her mother discover it and declare it scandalous, because the heroine was pregnant and such words were never used in their home. But Mme. de Beauvoir was also a crossword puzzle enthusiast, and just before she died she bought herself a large dictionary, of which no doubt Simone frequently availed herself. Simone's adored father was an atheist, a wealthy, politically conservative man of the world. Although he encouraged her to read extensively, he also censored what she read. Simone managed to get hold of forbidden books anyway. And she read continually. Although deathly afraid of sex and profoundly ignorant about it, Simone nonetheless longed for her life to have an all-consuming passion, and she managed to become independent of many of her parent's middle-class values.

Jean-Paul Sartre was, from his early adolescent years until his death, sexually involved with many women. He said that he wanted to conquer a woman, almost as if conquering a wild animal. Then, he added, she would be equal to a man. Simone, one can confidently assume, was equal to him. Throughout their fifty-year union, they continually encouraged each other's love of freedom, dedication to writing, and commitment to each other. This commitment always took first priority, despite the fact that each had other lovers. Simone described their early love: "We were two of a kind, and our harmony would last as long as we ourselves . . . and nothing could take precedence over this alliance. . . . For me, his existence justified the world."

Simone and Jean-Paul spent endless hours playing together. Sometimes they would dress up and go out on the town, assuming fictitious names and characters for the evening. Often they joked and played with ideas, making up comedies, nursery rhymes, and fables.

But they also spent hours discussing every aspect of their

writing. They showed each other everything they wrote and looked to each other for honest criticism. When parted from each other, they usually kept up a daily correspondence.

World War II and the German occupation of France brought important changes to their relationship and their work. Until this time Simone had been carefree and optimistic. During the war, however, she became deeply involved with politics. To her, ethics and politics were one and the same. She was critical of Western capitalism and also of Marxism, because to her neither recognized the importance of individuals. Individual freedom and commitment to others became the basis of her philosophy. Some of her friends became wartime collaborators; others became active in the French Resistance. Jean-Paul was called into the army. "If you were sleeping on the little bunk next to me," his first letter to her read, "I would be completely at ease and my heart would be light. Oh, my love, how I love you and need you."

Although Sartre needed her sexually as well as intellectually, often during their years together, Simone found herself unfulfilled sexually and began to repress that part of herself. Then, in 1947, she met Nelson Algren while traveling in the United States, and with him she rediscovered her sexuality. Nelson, a journalist and short-story writer who came from a poor family and often associated with tramps and criminals, was fascinating to Simone. During the next four years she visited him annually in Chicago for several weeks, though she refused to remain there, despite his pleading. And although he enjoyed Paris, Algren himself refused to live there. The affair finally ended in 1951, when it became clear that Simone would not allow Nelson to be her first priority. It would always be Sartre.

The Second Sex was published in 1949 and sold 22,000 copies the first week. Carefully written with passion and historical documentation, the book considered women from biological, psychological, and historical points of view. It created a storm because of the ideas expressed concerning the oppression of women. Simone insisted that the object was not to help women demand rights, but to help them clarify and understand how the fact of being a woman affects their lives.

One of her main theses was that much of the difference between men and women came from the different ways in which they were educated. In schools, "domestic science" was deemed a necessary subject for young women. This kind of educational discrimination, de Beauvoir insisted, led women to take secondary roles, being trained as they were to support men's endeavors rather than to live up to their own free and independent values. The book had a revolutionary effect on women throughout the world, but it did not bring about the freedoms she and Jean-Paul hoped for. "We had the same attitudes then, we believed socialist revolution would necessarily bring about the emancipation of women. We've sure had to change our tune."

Although they were not members of the Communist Party, Simone and Jean-Paul supported its principles and visited Russia frequently, along with Cuba and other countries that put the welfare of the state over that of the individual. To her, "The only public good is that which assures the private good of all its citizens."

Simone sometimes wrote documented reports using the pseudonym Daniel Secretan. In that way she could speak of serious social problems without implicating some of her friends who were involved in activities that were considered subversive. She also wrote strongly against cultures that treated women as inferior and allowed children to starve. An ardent feminist, she became president of the League for the Rights of Women, a group organized to help working women who were also single parents and battered wives.

It was their passion for individualism as much as anything else that prompted Simone and Jean-Paul to have other affairs. Simone, occasionally jealous or hurt by Jean-Paul's liaisons, said that by confessing his infidelities, he inflicted a "double violence" upon her. For his part, Jean-Paul claimed that he did not feel at all jealous, that both hers and his were merely "contingent" affairs. Nor, he boasted, were these affairs even discussed. Their letters, however, reveal that the couple spent many hours in just such discussion.

These "contingent" loves were often part of a trio arrangement. Sometimes the third person was a close friend to one, sometimes to the other, often to both. Jean-Paul freely wrote about these other women to Simone; she freely wrote of her loves to him. Occasionally, her passion almost consumed her and her jealousy threw her into despair. She did not like this conflicting feeling: "There was something innately shameful about this obscure resentment on my part, and I consequently found it harder to endure than I was prepared to admit."

Simone and Jean-Paul did not live together and sometimes were many cities apart. When Jean-Paul was in Le Havre, for example, Simone commuted between Marseilles and Rouen. When they were both in Paris, he had a room at the end of the hall in the hotel where she lived.

Each year they usually managed several weeks together hiking or bicycling throughout Europe. She enjoyed these trips more than he did and sometimes took similar jaunts with other lovers. Once Jean-Paul complained of her hiking enthusiasm, it all made him feel like a boy scout.

They differed on many issues. As a child she loved nature and continued to do so; he disdained it. She liked Bach, he liked Beethoven. Yet despite their frequent disagreements, they respected each other so much that they felt incomplete when alone. Although they acted with great independence, to Sartre the relationship was that of a "we" instead of two "me"s.

Fearful all her life of old age and death, Simone started writing about it when only twenty-six. She recognized this fear as one of her own mortality, of her own body gradually, inexorably deteriorating to the point when a sense of powerlessness would be pervasive. She particularly dreaded what would happen to her at the death of Jean-Paul and expressed this in her book *The Prime of Life*. "I know that no harm could ever come to me from him—unless he were to die before I died."

Jean-Paul died first, in 1980, after four years of blindness during which he stayed with Simone. She died six years later, to the day, and was buried in the same grave. The words she wrote for his funeral were also read at hers: "His death separates us. My death will not unite us."

Simone's most recent biographers, who interviewed her over a period of years and also had access to her unpublished letters, describe her as an "extremely self-controlled, aggressive, self-demanding person; on the other hand, she overflowed with vitality, sensuality, and a tremendous capacity to enjoy life."

Simone agreed. Writing about herself, she claimed, "I have never met anyone, in the whole of my life, who was so well equipped for happiness as I was, or who labored so stubbornly to achieve it."

IN SPITE OF EVERYTHING

Sarah Bernhardt (1844–1923)

There is no end to the list of women who have been in the spotlight and have had many lovers. Of legendary fame is Sarah Bernhardt, who won the hearts of entire nations and was called "Divine Sarah" because of her golden voice and the depth of emotion she brought to the stage.

In addition to being a great actress, she enjoyed embroidery and tapestry making, painting and sculpting, had several of her plays published, and kept a private zoo of exotic animals that often roamed in her home.

She was able to play the roles of both young men and adolescent girls until she was in her late fifties. At age sixty-five, she was able to bring down the house with her portrayal of the fourteen-year-old Joan of Arc. She was also one of the first great stage actresses to play in silent films when she appeared as Queen Elizabeth in 1912.

Sarah was the illegitimate daughter of a sixteen-year-old Dutch mother of Jewish descent who moved to Paris to become a courtesan. Sarah saw her father only a few times. When he died, he left his very young daughter a small dowry.

With little attention from anyone, Sarah had a difficult childhood. In infancy she rolled near a fireplace, and a spark ignited her clothes. Only the fast action of her nurse, who plunged her into a bucket of milk, saved her from bad scarring or death. From then on, Sarah was phobic about fire.

In her memoirs Sarah tells of this nurse, who called her "Milk Blossom" because she had to be plastered every two hours with milk and butter while her skin was healing. When her nurse moved to an ugly basement room, Sarah was banished by her mother to go live with her. There, Sarah felt as if she were in prison; she could not even see the sky.

One day she noticed one of her aunts passing along the street, an aunt who was not the slightest bit interested in this ugly, dirty child. Running to escape the dreariness of her surroundings and reach her, Sarah fell and broke her arm, also injuring her kneecap. Her mother visited the aunt's home only long enough to arrange for Sarah to be sent to boarding school. She visited her twice in the two years Sarah was there.

Some of Sarah's earliest memories are of herself as a precocious redhead acting in school plays. At the time, however, she was told that she was much too skinny and her hair much too curly for her to ever become a successful actress. "You'll never do anything on the stage, so you'd better get married," advised one of her teachers.

At the age of eight, Sarah was often teased for not yet knowing how to read. Her temper outbursts became more common and violent. She wrote that they were like "attacks of madness," during which she would yell, hit, and kick at anything and anybody. Because of these tantrums, Sarah was transferred from this school to a convent.

Fortunately the mother superior there took pity on her, and she slowly began to make friends. At age ten, Sarah rescued a four-year-old who was sinking into a deep pool of mud. But it was the private garden she planted and the animals of all kinds that she befriended that touched her heart most deeply. She felt animals were more trustworthy than people.

Sarah applied for admittance to the Paris Conservatoire at the suggestion of her mother's friend the great Alexandre Dumas, who had complimented her for being able to express emotion so easily. The day she passed the entrance examinations was the day she decided to create a stage personality by dint of sheer will and find a career in the theatre, in spite of the fact that her godfather had advised her against it.

But her explosive temper continued to give her problems; she was fired from the Comédie Française after only three performances because of it. Shortly after this she left the house of her aunts and mother to take an apartment of her own. One day a fire broke out and destroyed everything she owned, including her two pet tortoises. Although Sarah had arranged for fire insurance the day before, she had neglected to sign the papers on schedule, so was unable to collect on her loss. In fact, she was sued for the damage to other apartments in the building.

At about age eighteen, Sarah became very sexually active. Her affairs were all very passionate, but none lasted. Her mother and aunt encouraged her to consider the role of a courtesan, as they had. But Sarah wanted to choose her own lovers, and not for their wealth but because she cared for them.

At twenty, she gave birth to Maurice, who, like Sarah, was illegitimate. She kept the father's identity a secret, although at the time she was without a job or money and could have used support from him. Twenty-three years later, the father, Prince Henri de Ligne, unexpectedly visited them, offering to make the boy legitimate. Maurice, who was devoted to his mother all her life, politely refused.

The Franco-Prussian war erupted. It was 1870, and Sarah, at twenty-six, established a war hospital with seventy beds for injured soldiers and begged and borrowed food from many sources. She also begged overcoats from her friends, because in winter it was impossible to keep the hospital heated. Actively caring for those who were injured, she slept in the hospital herself. Food was scarce, bread was rationed, and furniture was burned for fuel. Before the city finally fell, it was bombarded daily, yet Sarah went out into the battlefield to help bring in the wounded. Years later, when World War I arrived, Sarah's name was on the list of hostages sought by the Kaiser.

Meanwhile, Sarah had sent her beloved son to live in the country with her mother and aunt. But they, in turn, had taken him to Western Germany where he might be safe. It took her seven days, traveling through the horrors of the battlefields, to reach him. Unlike her own mother, Sarah was anything but indifferent to her child. She never turned away from him, even when he didn't measure up to her expectations. And she grew to be an adoring grandmother.

For years, Sarah stayed in control of her romances and remained uninterested in marriage. But then she met Jacques Damala. This handsome Greek diplomat, a combination of Casanova and the Marquis de Sade and a frequent user of morphine and brandy, changed everything. While he pretended to be disinterested, she became so hopelessly infatuated that she proposed marriage. He accepted.

She was thirty-eight and he was twenty-seven. Sarah was by this time a famous actress—which was convenient for Jacques, since he wanted to switch careers from politics to acting. But despite Sarah's insistence that he be given good roles, he had little talent. Moreover, he often ridiculed Sarah publicly, even when she was performing. She was gullible; he was a failure. At thirty-four, he died of an overdose of cocaine mixed with morphine.

Sarah often took her leading man as her lover. These men were always much younger and usually not very good actors, but her infatuation and optimism made her blind to these deficiencies.

Noted for her rich voice, which could mesmerize thousands of listeners Sarah was idolized by her coworkers and appreciated by royalty. The call-boy in the Paris theater would notify her of the first-act curtain with the words, "Madame, it will be eight o'clock when it suits you." When onstage, she sometimes put so much into her acting that she fainted, vomited blood, or forgot her lines. She played in every conceivable kind of theater, even beneath a folding canvas roof under which four thousand spectators could sit. Because of her success, some of her jealous colleagues spread malicious rumors that became incorporated in some of the books written about her.

Sarah's legendary preoccupation with her own mortality may be related to her frailty and childhood illnesses. While still in her teens, Sarah visited the local morgue often and talked her family into buying her a lovely coffin to assure herself that she would not be "laid away in an ugly bier." She kept the coffin in her bedroom and often lay in it while studying her parts. After frightening a maid who came in inadvertently while she was asleep, Sarah frequently had herself photographed in the beautiful cherrywood coffin, sometimes surrounded by candles and flowers.

Perhaps some of Sarah's eccentricities were brought about by her general boredom with social situations and the constant social pursuit brought on by her notoriety. She found animals often more interesting than people. At different times in her life she had a kind of private zoo inside her house. Another great actress, Cornelia Otis Skinner, tells of the time Sarah had three dogs, a parrot, and a monkey and also wanted to buy a set of lion cubs, but resisted when she saw their size. As substitutes she bought a cheetah, a wolfhound, and six chameleons, as well as a miniature prehistoric "monster" with protruding eyes that often crossed. She had a jeweler fashion a tiny chain around its neck and pinned it to her jacket when she felt herself in a "reptilian mood."

The more exotic these creatures the better, it seemed. On one of her tours she purchased two large black snakes that so frightened her hairdressers the creatures had to be thrown off the train. She also had a small alligator, Ali-Gaga. Quite tame, it followed her around, lay at her feet, and even joined her in bed. Ali-Gaga died of too much champagne. Sarah arranged for a successor that happened to be hibernating at the time and shipped it to France. Unfortunately, when it wakened it swallowed her small dog and had to be killed. Then there was the boa that wakened and swallowed a sofa pillow, so it, too, had to be put down. At yet another time she had a lynx and baby tiger, which were occasionally allowed in the house on leashes, to the discomfort of her guests. For her death scene in Cleopatra, she used one of her live garter snakes.

And through it all, Sarah had lovers. One of her last was Lou Tellegren—handsome, not very bright, and a poor actor to whom she gave many parts. A young Don Juan, he was her constant companion from the age of sixty-five to sixty-nine.

Eight years before her death it was necessary for her to have her leg amputated because of an injury she had received while acting in Rio de Janeiro ten years earlier. She refused to wear a prosthesis, hopped on one leg when at home, and was carried when away from home. She chose never to walk again on stage rather than be seen limping and some of her greatest acting was performed when she was either sitting or lying down.

Sarah's sense of humor remained one of her most endearing qualities. At one time, she lived in a Parisian apartment many floors up, and an old admirer toiled up the stairs to see her. When he had recovered his strength a little, he inquired, "Madame, why do you live so high up?" "My dear friend," replied the actress, "it is the only way I can still make the hearts of men beat faster."

An actress to the end, Sarah Bernhardt designed a life with many spotlights and more romances and lived by her motto, "In spite of everything."

SEXUALLY INDEPENDENT

Although there have always been women who have made independent choices about how to express their sexuality, only recently has this sexuality become the subject of research. In the process many myths have been exploded, and women have gained new understanding and confidence in themselves as sexual beings.

One long-standing myth is that women lack the intensity of sexual desire that is attributed to men. Yet the lives of the women in this book show this is not universally true. Some women who have hearts on fire in their work also have passionate sexual desires.

Another myth is that women who willingly express their sexual desires are evil. This myth was acted out in its highest intensity during the Middle Ages when thousands of women were slaughtered daily, accused of unabashed sexuality due to "cohabiting with the devil." By the early eighteenth century witch hunting had been abolished, but women continued to be persecuted for expressing their sexuality, especially outside of marriage. Throughout the world, including the United States, it was acceptable for a husband to kill his wife if she was adulterous. The same standard did not apply to men who took lovers.

It was believed that a "good" woman is one who remains a virgin until marriage. After marriage, she must submit to her husband's sexual whims and proclivities. The women in this chapter did not live by these kinds of myths. Frida Kahlo, for example, was sexually active in her early teens. And the universal myth that women's enjoyment of sexuality and romance inevitably stops at the age of menopause is not true: Catherine the Great and Sarah Bernhardt remained sexually active well into their sixties.

Taking a lover is not always related primarily to sexual passion. Sometimes the need for companionship or for intellectual stimulation is a motivating factor, as in the case of Simone de Beauvoir. Although Beryl Markham's classic beauty captivated many men, the myth that physically handicapped are not sexually attractive is invalidated by Sarah Bernhardt and Frida Kahlo. In spite of their physical challenges, each attracted many lovers.

When a woman chooses sexual independence, the assumption of responsibility that comes with it can be agonizing. Yet some women believe they have no choice. They live by the spirit of Frida Kahlo's last painting, completed just a few days before her death. Hanging in a museum which was once her home, the painting shows a ripe watermelon cut into pieces, accompanied by the words "Viva la Vida"—live life.

However, independence does not always bring happiness or self-confidence. Simone de Beauvoir, who wrote so strongly in favor of sexual freedom, lived fully but did not always enjoy her own independence. She felt miserable when her lover, Jean-Paul Sartre, boasted about his sexual experiences. Beryl Markham's lifestyle of moving from one man to another left her with feelings of emptiness and loneliness. And Frida Kahlo's lovers, women as well as men, ultimately did not bring her happiness. Therefore, the myth that sexual independence leads to happiness is untrue, but on the other hand, so is the belief that sexual fidelity to one man is the road to happiness.

Regardless of how they freely expressed their sexuality, and whether or not we agree with their choices, each of these women accomplished important goals. They were dedicated to governing wisely, perfecting their art, or pioneering in a typically male-dominated field. Their lifestyles and intellectual commitments reflect their independent thinking and unwillingness to be treated as just a member of "the second sex." This attitude had a tremendous impact on the world, and many men are recognizing the unique contributions women have made and are rejoicing in them.

CHAPTER THREE

LOVE AND SOCIAL ACTION

THE PURSUIT OF RIGHTS

The human rights movement is concerned with everyone's happiness and legal and ethical rights, including those of women. In more countries than ever before, women today are increasingly recognized as full citizens who are concerned with other people's rights as well as their own.

The struggle for human rights has existed in many forms throughout history. Sometimes the focus has been on physical freedom, sometimes on the freedom to think for oneself and make autonomous decisions or to speak up against authority. Other times the emphasis has been on the freedom to have a homeland or to be free of the terror of war.

The concept of human rights for all people first gained importance at an international level in 1948 when the General Assembly of the United Nations adopted the Universal Declaration of Human Rights as a standard. It took almost twenty more years for the General Assembly to approve the two detailed covenants concerning the rights of individuals and the duties of governments. Finally, in 1976, this was ratified by enough nations to become a force in defining international values and relationships. The declaration affirms that equal and inalienable rights for all people are essential to freedom, justice, and peace, and that international order is necessary for these rights and freedoms to be realized.

In part, the United Nations declaration reflects the earlier United States Declaration of Independence and Bill of Rights, which proclaimed certain inalienable rights, among them "life, liberty, and the pursuit of happiness."

Women, the largest minority group in the world, are claiming their rights with more determination than in the past. They want to make their own decisions about their own lives. They are not willing to stay locked inside their homes, as was common in ancient cultures. They are not willing to be excluded from political organizations and institutions of higher education, as was common until the middle of the nineteenth century.

Women are claiming rights to worship as they please, to freely assemble, to have equal protection before the law, and to be free from slavery, forced servitude, and other forms of brutal or degrading treatment. They are claiming other rights also specified by the United Nations declaration, including the right to own property, to take part in the government of their country, to receive an education, and to be able to work gainfully, as well as to have leisure to rest from work.

Whereas some women feel happy only if they are involved in an exciting romance, others are willing to give up romance if they perceive their work to be necessary for important social change. These women feel unable to pursue personal happiness if they ignore the plight of others.

Although many women seek both romance and improved social conditions, few are courageous enough to seek the latter if sacrifice is required. Some women who have hearts on fire put their passions to work in the cause of human rights and also are committed to romance. Others feel forced to choose between them.

This chapter is about six women who fought for human rights: Mary Wollstonecraft, Harriet Tubman, Alexandra

Kollantai, Käthe Kollwitz, Golda Meir, and Eleanor Roosevelt. Each fought in her own way—for herself and for other people. Each experienced successes and failures, joys and heartaches, especially if she had to sacrifice romance and marriage, or safety and social approval, for social action.

Mary Wollstonecraft, an early feminist, was writing in eighteenth-century England when men still sold their wives as though they were pieces of furniture. There was no effective birth control, and death by childbirth was common. Women who held jobs outside the home had only a few occupations open to them: companion, teacher, governess, and a few trades that were controlled by men. Poorly treated and poorly paid, very few women lived a pleasant life, nor did they dare complain about its dreariness. Yet at the same time in France, just across the English Channel, women were organizing themselves into groups, marching in the Revolution, and demanding bread from an overly affluent court. In England they were not yet that bold, and Mary Wollstonecraft's writing became a mobilizing force.

But women's rights were not the only human rights attracting attention at that time. Courageous women, desperate women, great women were fighting against slavery in the United States. Women were generally uneducated and not allowed to vote, own property, or control their own money. Furthermore, they were not expected to speak out in public and were ridiculed if they did so. For slaves, of course, the situation was even worse, and the women's movement was closely aligned to the abolishment of slavery.

Physical freedom is the most basic human right anywhere, and Harriet Tubman, a black American slave, lived in this dangerous period when death or chain gangs were the punishment for any slave seeking freedom. Brutalized as a child by three white masters, she risked further mistreatment to help her people escape from slavery and also gave up marriage to a freed man to do so. This was a time when almost one third of the population of the southern states consisted of slaves, mostly field-workers. Cotton, rice, sugar, and tobacco were cultivated by slaves who had no rights. Harriet was determined that they would obtain some, and she risked her life for her vision.

When women feel obligated to choose between a lifelong commitment to romance or to their fight for human rights, the choice is sometimes difficult. Work can be so important and stimulating that they may prefer romantic liaisons outside the responsibilities of marriage. To Alexandra (sometimes spelled Alekandra) Kollontai, Russian revolutionary and nominee for a Nobel Peace Prize, her commitment to her country was primary. This was a woman behind not a husband but two political leaders, Stalin and Lenin. Although politically admired, she was also kept out of the central decision-making group in Moscow by being sent to Norway and then Sweden as an ambassador.

Women have also been deeply concerned with the right to live without the overpowering fear that comes with war. Many women have put their lives on the line by confronting their governments, opposing war in favor of peace. In Germany, Käthe Kollwitz was a threat to the Nazis with her antiwar posters and sculptures. In creating this kind of political art, she did not lose the love of her physician husband, although both were put on the Nazi "wanted" list because of her work.

Some women prefer, rather than work alone for human rights, to channel their passions into political organizations. This political involvement may precede romance, as it did with Golda Meir, whose belief in the right for a homeland began when she was nine years old. Or it may be accelerated after a broken romance, as in the case of Eleanor Roosevelt, who chaired the United Nations commission to develop the Universal Declaration of Human Rights.

In whatever way women express themselves in favor of change, they may be perceived as threats to the status quo and suffer for their actions. Yet the willingness to live and die for human rights continues to grow throughout the world. Great women recognize this danger but do what they believe is right. They feel as if they have no choice.

LIBERATED IN WORDS ONLY

Mary Wollstonecraft (1759–1797)

In England in 1792, serious and widespread discussion of women's status was launched when Mary Wollstonecraft published *A Vindication of the Rights of Woman*. This became a basic text in women's long struggle for legal rights. A woman capable of intense jealousy and prone to emotional excesses, Mary's romantic ties to three men created great inner conflict with her intellectual beliefs about women and independence.

In her private life, Mary was a self-proclaimed romantic who insisted on being first with any friend or lover. As a fourteen-year-old schoolgirl, she wrote to friend Jane Arden, after they quarreled about Mary's jealousy, that she had romantic notions of friendship and must have the first place. At age eighteen, she repeated this pattern with another young woman. Her overwhelming possessiveness and her demand to be first priority created many lifelong problems for her, especially with the men she cared for.

Her earliest bouts of jealousy came from envy of her brother, who was her mother's favorite. First born and two years older than Mary, he was a spoiled child who inherited a large fortune from his grandfather when he was seven years old and Mary five. Mary, who got nothing, thought this unfair. But there was not much solace to be had from her unstable family, fraught with its own problems. Her father drank heavily and initiated many moves back and forth from business in London to farms in different parts of the country.

Educated in a village school, Mary learned only to read and write—skills that nevertheless served her well in later life when, in an effort to support herself, she became a companion in an educated family where reading was encouraged. Later she taught school, and when the school failed, she wrote her first book, *Thoughts on the Education of Daughters*. This manuscript opened the doors of the editor and publisher, Joseph Johnson. As his protegé, not a romantic partner, she moved into his house and was thereby introduced to literary circles and radical thinkers.

Tall, fair, and very attractive, Mary received considerable attention from men, acting dependent and adoring toward them. In return she demanded they give her exclusive attention and also be dependent on her. Three men were placed in this position: Henri Fuseli, an artist and scholar; Gilbert Imlay, an American army captain and businessman; and William Godwin, a radical intellectual like Mary herself. She made desperate attempts to be "the one and only" to each of the three and succeeded, finally, with one.

Henri Fuseli, a friend of her publisher and a professor of painting at the Royal Academy in London, was characterized by his contemporaries as vain, sardonic, eccentric, and lecherous. He was known for his erotic nude figures in positions reflecting strong emotions and was criticized for drawing pornographic sketches for his own amusement and that of his clients. He was also delighted by Mary's passionate attachment to him. She was twenty-nine at the time, and he was forty-seven. But Henri did not want to be limited to one woman and, perhaps to protect himself, quickly married an uneducated artists' model when Mary became too possessive. This inflamed Mary all the more; she wrote him long letters of love, while Henri retreated harder and faster.

It was typical of her to try to develop symbiotic relationships. Yet this deep emotional need was in direct conflict with her intellectual championship of autonomy for women.

When Mary began to think about human rights seriously, the first "vindication" she wrote was about the rights of men. She also argued for social justice, suggesting that the lands of the rich be divided into properties for the poor.

Another social issue that interested her was the institution of marriage. Her disdain for the state of matrimony was based on her belief that women who settled for domesticity actually opposed equal rights. After being with a happily married couple, she wrote, "I cannot help viewing them as if they were my inferiors—inferior because they could find happiness in a world like this."

Mary's major work, *A Vindication of the Rights of Woman*, was written in six weeks, and its somewhat poor organization testifies to how important its speedy publication must have been to her. The book, however, was ground-breaking in its philosophy and is still read by women studying feminism.

Mary's theme is the humanity of women. She proclaims that they are the intellectual equals of men, that they have been regarded as sexual objects and denied economic independence and freedom. She was not against men but against the society that put women in such a degrading situation.

Mary wrote with the passion of her convictions and was the first to use the term *legal prostitution* for some kinds of marriages that are based on sex for the man and financial convenience for the woman. Mary also wrote that it would be better if passionate love were excluded from marriage; women would then be freer to think for themselves, instead of focusing all their attention on trying to please men.

She claimed that the subjugation of women by men was not good for either sex, because it not only deterred women from developing their potential but deprived men of the possibility of companionship with an equal. This was a very new idea at that time.

In a chapter on the undesirable effects of unnatural social distinctions between men and women, Mary pleaded that men remove the chains placed on women and be content with rational fellowship instead of slavish obedience:

> [Then] they would find us more observant daughters, more affectionate sisters, more faithful wives, more reasonable mothers—in a word, better citizens. We should then love them with true affection, because we should learn to respect ourselves.

After the publication and success of *A Vindication*, Mary became one of the best-known feminists in Europe. But despite the popularity and economic rewards, Mary was still tormented by her passion for Henri Fuseli, who continued to treat her casually as it suited his own purposes. In desperation, then, she went to his wife, Sophia.

Mary told her that she could not bear to be separated from Henri for even a day and begged to be allowed to join their household as his spiritual partner. Sophia furiously and indignantly refused. As for Henri, he did nothing, and Mary had to be persuaded by friends to accept the humiliation and quietly leave town.

The next man to capture Mary's emotions so intensely was Gilbert Imlay, an American she met in Paris at a time of great political upheaval. Once again, Mary's heart burned with fire, and she flung herself at him. She was gullible, he was manipulative, and her passion was not reciprocated. Although they lived together for a while and she became pregnant, Gilbert left her for other women.

Once again, Mary turned to writing, this time about the necessity of carrying on the fight for equality and also about the political revolution surrounding her in Paris, where she was then living. It was a dangerous situation. The French Revolution was coming to an end; soldiers roamed the streets, and food was hard to find.

In addition to her political writing, Mary sent desperate

letters to Imlay, begging him to return. He did so, but stayed
only for the first three months of their daughter's life. He
then left them both without means of support for a series of
affairs with younger women in England.

As Mary had once pleaded with Henri, she now begged
Imlay to allow her and their daughter to join him and his
current lover. Refused, she followed him to England. Twice
Mary attempted suicide when her desperate letters proved
ineffective:

> I would encounter a thousand deaths, rather than a night like
> this. . . . Should your sensibility ever awake, remorse will
> find its way to your heart; and, in the midst of business and
> sensual pleasure, I shall appear to you, the victim of your
> deviation from rectitude.

Even when she wrote to tell him where and when she
would try to take her life, he did not rise to the occasion.
Next, Mary spied on his affairs by questioning servants and
friends. They reminded her that his desertion was perfectly
in accord with her theories of freedom in marriage and the
undesirability of maintaining formal ties when feelings had
changed.

Deeply humiliated, Mary finally accepted what was inevitable, broke her emotional ties, and became involved with
the third important man in her life, William Godwin. Mary
and William were in the same literary circles, and both were
well known for their opposition to marriage and for upholding women's need for independence. They began to share
their work, commenting on each other's essays. He was in-
finitely kinder to Mary than the previous men in her life had
been, yet initially she showered him with similar doses of
dependency, jealousy, and possessiveness.

Once again Mary struggled with an emotional involvement not under her control, and she initiated a series of letters
attempting to sound out the degree of William's romantic

attraction to her. This time she was rewarded; William's passion matched hers: "You set my imagination on fire on Saturday. For six and thirty hours I could think of nothing else. I longed inexpressibly to have you in my arms."

Mary and William's relationship grew in ways dissimiliar to either of her previous romances. He was able to convince her that jealousy did not enhance what they had together. He told her that he wanted to be her friend first and also be free to see what else might evolve. They quarreled and wrote frequently to each other, and even managed to keep their sense of humor. Mary even asked him for a "bill of rights" with which she would tease him sometimes. When she became pregnant, they both abandoned their philosophical position against marriage, albeit with some embarrassment. But Mary died ten days after delivering their child. She was thirty eight years old.

William Godwin's great grief at his wife's death could not be expressed in words. In his diary entry for that day there were only three strokes from his pen. At first he was unable even to look at her letters and writings. Within two weeks, however he began his own book, *Memoirs of the Author of a Vindication of the Rights of Women*. In so doing, he displayed the qualities of a great man who could recognize that women should have the same rights as men. This was a tribute to Mary's beliefs and to their full but short-lived romance.

LIBERTY OR DEATH

Harriet Tubman (1828–1913)

Brutalized by many masters, Harriet Tubman, an illiterate slave, spent almost twenty years secretly leading other slaves to freedom. To do this she had to leave her husband, who was a free man. But so strongly did she believe in the human right of freedom that there was no question for her that liberty—or even death—should take precedence over love.

Born Araminta Ross, the granddaughter of African slaves, she chose to be known by her mother's name, Harriet, and by Tubman, her married name. Less than five feet tall, her greatness of spirit and work in freeing others from slavery led her to be known as "the Moses of her people."

In the United States at this time, the southern states believed in slavery while the northern states experienced a growing awareness that it was wrong. In the south, one third of the population were slaves and their education was highly restricted. Marriage between blacks was ignored by white owners, who sold them for the best price they could get. Consequently, couples were often separated from each other and children from their families. This was so painful for some parents that they killed their children rather than let them be sold.

In the North, many women who saw the tragedy of this formed female antislavery societies—a new development in America, where women were not involved in politics and had no voice in the government. The first such group originated in Salem, Massachusetts, in 1832 by black women. In Boston and Philadelphia, more groups formed with both black and white women. Still other groups were white only and often consisted of well-educated women from prestigious families.

By the end of the 1830s, more than one hundred such groups had adopted constitutions, based on the one designed by the Philadelphia society. The group's purpose, it declared, was to collect and disseminate correct information on the character of slavery and to dispel prejudice against people of color, to assist slaves because they had the right to immediate emancipation. The society would be open to all women who agreed with this view and would also "be willing to entirely abstain from purchasing the products of slave labor."

For a slave to seek freedom was to court death, so Harriet had to do her work with the utmost care. One of her strategies was to sing spirituals that conveyed a hidden message. "Go

Down Moses" was her battle song; "Steal Away" was her call to other slaves to come to a secret meeting. Blacks singing spirituals was so common an occurrence that the hidden messages went unnoticed by the whites. Harriet became increasingly skilled in planning her escape strategies and helped more than two hundred slaves to escape. None of them were recaptured or lost.

When only five years old, Harriet was sent out on her first job. It was to work for a poor white family as housekeeper and child's nurse. Poor whites as well as wealthy plantation owners had slaves. In this family she was ill-fed and soundly whipped by the children's mother if she fell asleep while her charge slept. At the age of nine she was given such tasks as setting traps for muskrats and carrying wood for fires. Without enough sleep or food, and with the constant beatings, Harriet's health failed; she was returned to her original master.

Next, she worked for a man who was even more cruel and demanding. Again her health collapsed, and she was returned to her master as worthless. At the age of thirteen, she was hit on the head by a two-pound weight flung at her by a white overseer when she tried to protect another slave from his wrath. For weeks her survival was in question, since the blow had pushed part of her brain against her skull. For the rest of her life she wore a turban to hide the injury. Another permanent effect of this blow was that for years Harriet would pass out briefly several times a day, and then return to consciousness as though nothing had happened.

After two of her sisters were put into chain gangs, it seemed clear to Harriet that she was scheduled for the same fate. Desperately she began to spend many hours in prayer. She finally decided her only choice was to escape because she believed she had the right to choose between liberty or death.

Most of the information we have about Harriet comes from one source, Sarah Bradford, a white friend who published a biography of her in 1886. At this time Harriet was still very active, and Mrs. Bradford wanted to raise money for her support. Unable to read or write, Harriet explained to her friend how she made her liberty-or-death decision:

> I had reasoned dis out in my mind; there was one of two things I had a *right* to, liberty, or death; if I could not have one, I would have de oder; for no man should take me alive; I should fight for my liberty as long as my strength lasted, and when de time came for me to go, de Lord would let dem take me.

In 1849 Harriet begged her husband, John Tubman, who was a free black, to leave with her and go north to freedom. He refused. He did not have to fear the chain gang, because he had been granted his freedom through his master's will, and he was not sufficiently concerned for her safety to change his own life. Harriet had to escape alone. This was an extremely risky venture for those times. The first women's rights convention, in Seneca Falls the year before, had forged new awareness and heightened concern with issues of slavery. Whereas white women who led this movement were merely ridiculed, black women were still at great risk for their own involvement. But Harriet was not deterred.

In the North, working as a maid, cook, or laborer, she carefully saved small amounts of money both to help others escape and to arrange to be reunited with her own beloved family. It took two years to save enough to lead her sister and two nieces to safety. She also tried, for the second time, to persuade her husband to join her. But marriages between blacks were not considered legal, and he had in the meantime married someone else.

Once again her husband's rejection of both herself as a woman and her fervent belief in freedom did not diminish her commitment to the rights of slaves to choose either liberty or death. She continued her careful strategy to stay safe while helping others to safety through the "underground railroad"—an escape route neither underground nor focused on railroads, but consisting rather of a network of people, mostly white and often Quakers, who provided food and ingenious hiding places to slaves.

Harriet demanded that those who were escaping also believe, as she did, that life without freedom was worse than death. When, out of fear or fatigue, some slaves changed their minds en route, she gave them a choice with her revolver: "You go on, or die. Dead niger tell no tales." She would not risk having the precious escape route discovered. Nineteen times "little Moses" went south, and nineteen times she led her people into freedom. Like her biblical namesake, she led her people through marshes, mountains, and wilderness out of slavery.

At first, slaves were safe in the northern states. But when the Fugitive Slave Law was reinstated in 1851, they were again at risk, so Harriet led them on the longer trip to Canada.

Deeply religious, Harriet always attributed her success to God, whom she consulted constantly in her prayers. She also believed God talked to her on a daily basis, directing her activities and providing for her safety.

As the antislavery movement grew slowly, resistance to it also grew. A reward of $40,000—an astoundingly large sum for those days—was put on Harriet's head. But the challenge went largely ignored, due to the great respect Harriet commanded. In 1868 Frederick Douglas, a black leader who ran against Lincoln for president after defeating him in the race for senator of Illinois, wrote to her: "I know of no one who has willingly encountered more perils and hardships to serve our enslaved people than you have."

In addition to her underground work, Harriet later nursed soldiers in army hospitals, was a scout and spy for the Union Army, and even led military raids. She was called "General Tubman" because of her bravery, wisdom, and integrity. As if this weren't enough, she became involved in women's rights, concentrating especially on the right to vote, and she was often sought out as a convention speaker.

Later, Harriet again found romance and marriage, this time with Nelson Davis, a Union enlisted man from Philadelphia. Their happiness, however, was short-lived; he was in such poor health that he died shortly thereafter.

Harriet, always very poor, spent her last years nearly penniless, with a pension from the government that amounted to only eight dollars a month. After a long struggle with Congress, her pension was raised to twenty dollars when she was eighty years old. This was surely deficient for a woman who had given so many years to her people and had loved freedom so passionately.

Harriet's first husband may have twice rejected her, but it seemed most of the rest of humanity embraced her. At Harriet's funeral the great Booker T. Washington offered the eulogy for this woman whose life itself was a lesson in courage, and who gave everything she had to the cause of freedom. In Washington's words, she had "brought the two races together and made it possible for the white race to place a higher estimate on the black race." This was a remarkable achievement in the long struggle for human rights.

COMMITTED REVOLUTIONARY

Alexandra Kollontai (1873–1952)

There is a great difference between a slave, such as Harriet Tubman, a working-class woman, and a woman of a higher class who chooses to work. Alexandra Kollontai was from a wealthy background, but she was passionately concerned about the working class and devoted her life to the working-woman's movement in Russia. She was also a wife, lover, and mother; a feminist and author; a politician and revolutionary; a Bolshevik commissar; a Communist ambassador; and she was nominated for the Nobel Peace Prize. She is another model of what a woman can accomplish whose heart is on fire for her people.

Alexandra's greatness lay in her utter commitment to equal rights for women and in her idealistic belief in the potential of socialism to solve problems of poverty. This commitment was so great that she was imprisoned for her ideas on one occasion and went into semiexile two other times. The first exile Alexandra herself chose for five years to escape police, returning to Russia only to assist Lenin when he came into power. Later, under Stalin, she was sent into semiexile when he assigned her to political tours and made her an ambassador. Clearly, she was too powerful and outspoken in favor of women's rights and free love to be allowed to stay in Moscow, the center of decision making.

Alexandra was a prolific writer of fiction, essays, and political works. In 1918, for example, she had twelve of her articles published on a number of diverse subjects: "Why the Bolsheviks Must Win"; "Old Age Is Not a Cross but a Deserved Rest"; "The First All-Russian Conference on Working Women"; and "The Priests Are Still at Work." Her writing, which was ignored for many years, is resurfacing today largely because of the women's movement.

Alexandra, nicknamed Shura, had free-thinking and well-educated, aristocratic parents who usually distrusted hierarchies. Her mother, the daughter of a wealthy timber merchant, had been forced to marry against her wishes, yet continued her romantic attachment to her first love, who later became Alexandra's father. When the two met after a ten-year separation, their passion flamed anew and Alexandra was conceived. Her father, a czarist general, was, because of his aristocratic background, able to influence church officials to allow Alexandra's mother to get a divorce, but only after they admitted to their adulterous relationship. The two remained in love until death. Although sharing traditional values, they were also progressive—but not radical, as their daughter was to become.

Alexandra's mother was a self-educated woman who read the works of John Stuart Mill, Herbert Spencer, George Sand, and Louis Pasteur, and her father was also an avid reader. Alexandra thus had the benefit of a large library at home, as well as liberal-thinking parents. She became fluent in four languages. Winters were spent in St. Petersburg, summers on her mother's inherited estate in Finland. A restrictive English nanny was followed by tutors, who opened up to her the world of literature and ideas.

At the age of nine, Alexandra became aware of the widespread serious illness and poverty of peasants and factory workers in Russia. She dreamed of becoming involved in political action against poverty, and this remained one of her life-long goals. One of her tutors, Maria Strakhova, a political activist, was not allowed to teach political theory; it was against the law and could lead to imprisonment. With police spies and political hangings as part of everyday life, Alexandra turned to books to learn what she wanted to know. At the same time, she decided to write.

Romance first entered her life when, at the age of fifteen, she was kissed by a depressed, confused young man who suffered such guilt at this loss of self-control that he shot himself. At eighteen, Alexandra fell in love with Vladimir Kollontai, her Polish second cousin. Her parents disapproved of him and, to interrupt the romance, took her on an extended trip to Berlin and Paris. There, Alexandra started reading some of the French socialists as well as the *Communist Manifesto* and Friedrich Engels's *Origin of the Family*. Her parents became so worried about her political activities that they reluctantly gave her permission to marry.

Although at first Alexandra was romantically in love with her husband, an engineer, being a housewife and mother had little appeal; marriage to her was like being in a cage, with time and energy wasted in endless love tragedies and their complications. One day a visit to a factory and the sight of the conditions of the workers prompted her to study Marxism. Her husband, it soon became clear, did not share her intellectual interests. In fact, he and Alexandra soon began to disagree on many political issues, including a woman's place in the home. She argued that work, not love, is the most important thing in a woman's life: "If she must choose between love and work, she should never hesitate: It is work, a woman's own creative work, that gives her the only real satisfaction and makes her life worth living."

Because of her dissatisfaction with marriage and her commitment to human rights through social change, Alexandra left him and left their five-year-old son with her parents to go to Zurich to study, as many upper-class Russian women were doing. At this time, the early 1890s, the universities were open, and she could study political economy. After a year in Zurich, however, she became lonesome for her son and returned to Russia, where she became deeply involved in the underground political movement of Russia's Social Democratic Party. She began teaching classes to workers, writing pamphlets against the Czar, and instigating ways to free women from stereotyped roles.

At the same time that Alexandra was developing her views on socialism and feminism, a strong countermovement was burgeoning in Germany, led by Rosa Luxemburg, who believed a Marxist revolution must precede the liberation of women. But for Alexandra, women's liberation needed to come first, so that women could then assist in wider reforms.

With the first revolution in 1905, when women workers began to become aware of their civil rights, Alexandra became a controversial, outspoken figure. She organized working women and wrote the "Social Basis of the Women's Question." Each night she was compelled to hide from the police. Finally, in 1908, Alexandra fled to Berlin, where she joined the German Socialist Party and continued to speak out publicly. While touring other countries, she spoke out on such issues as voting rights and maternity insurance, as well as the housewife strikes in France.

When Germany declared war on Russia in 1914, Alexandra organized women's meetings in Berlin against war and joined the Bolshevik Party. Then forty-two years old, she wrote political tracts on class struggle, sexual equality, society, and motherhood. She also started an active correspondence with Lenin, then living in Switzerland, who had sought her out to collaborate with him on an article. Lenin not only was in favor of women's equality as part of his socialist program, but had several women, including his wife, with whom he worked closely. This greatly appealed to Alexandra. On the strength of her dedication to the cause and her prolific writing, she was then sent to various countries, including the United States, to pique interest in and raise money for Bolshevik causes.

With the coming of the great Revolution, which overthrew the czar and gave power to the Bolsheviks, feminist organizations became increasingly powerful. By 1917 women had won professional equality, the right to vote, and the right to receive equal pay, along with protective legislation for mothers and children.

Alexandra persuaded Lenin to establish a women's department. She also expressed concern that if women were involved in monogamous sexual relationships, they would be in danger of losing their own personalities. She believed that male and female relationships should be open and based on equality and friendship, that possessiveness and jealousy were inappropriate. In her autobiography she claims her vision was "the abolition of the slavery of working women" and that "all women would be free of any economic need to bargain with their sex." Lenin, however, claimed there needed to be more discipline and less freedom, and recommended monogamy for both sexes, no homosexuality, and no sex outside of marriage.

Alexandra's views on such social issues as the humane treatment of prostitutes conflicted with his views, and her writings on sexuality were so frank that they raised considerable controversy. Yet her travels to raise funds in other countries to support the movement continued, and in time she became commissar of social welfare. In that capacity, she believed her most important achievement was the founding of the Department for the Protection of Motherhood and Childhood.

In 1917, when she was forty-five, Alexandra met and fell in love with a man seventeen years younger, who became her second husband. Pavel Dybenko, from a peasant family, had become a Bolshevik and a sailor. He was not an intellectual but was "passionate, steadfast, and totally decisive," according to Alexandra. Alternately referred to as the "most famous lovers of the revolution," and ridiculed for the disparity in their ages, they were not approved of by Lenin. "I will not vouch," he said, "for the reliability or endurance of women whose love affairs are intertwined with politics." Their relationship lasted five years, until she realized she could not play the accepted traditional role. She was more committed to her work, speaking in many congresses and negotiating trade agreements between Russia and other countries. Finally, "I am not the wife you need," she wrote to him. "I am a person before I am a woman."

When Stalin was appointed general secretary of the party in 1922, he began investigating workers' opposition, including the influence of the women's movement. He soon found it convenient to appoint Alexandra ambassador to Norway to get her out of Moscow. According to Germaine Greer's foreword to Alexandra's *The Autobiography of a Sexually Emancipated Communist Woman*, the appointment signified "nothing but prestigious banishment and defeat." From then until her death twenty-eight years later, she wrote very little at all, and even less about controversial issues.

In 1930 Stalin closed the women's department. Divorce and legal abortion were no longer allowed. The government claimed they were not necessary, because no woman had to marry out of economic need, now that socialism was a reality: "The Soviet woman has the same rights as the man, but that does not free her from a great and honorable duty which nature has given her: She is a mother, she gives life. And this is certainly not a private affair but one of great social importance."

Under Stalin, Pavel became commander of the Leningrad Military District, but he was demoted, tried for treason, and later shot as part of the massive purges in 1938. Although her passion had waned, Alexandra's love for him remained, and her grief at his death was profound.

Meanwhile, Alexandra became skilled at trade agreements and negotiated peace between Finland and Russia, the two countries of her childhood. In 1935 she became part of the Russian delegation to the League of Nations, working on women's rights. At the age of seventy-three, she was nominated for the Nobel Peace Prize.

This great woman, dedicated to the have-nots, considered herself sexually emancipated; she did not endorse promiscuity or double standards but rather the right of a woman to live by her own values in intimate relationships. There were several short romances in her life, but her work always came first. The only time she experienced an inner conflict of choice was when she was separated from her beloved son, who through the years remained, with his wife, a lifelong revolutionary colleague.

Alexandra died at eighty of a heart attack, still believing fervently that "woman will be judged by the same moral standards applied to man. For it is not her specific feminine virtue that gives her a place of honor in human society, but the worth of the useful mission accomplished by her."

A ONE-WOMAN PEACE MOVEMENT

Käthe Kollwitz (1867–1945)

Käthe Kollwitz, one of Germany's greatest artists, confronted the Nazis publicly with her art, and for this she was put on their list of those to be imprisoned. Although she lost both a son and a grandson to war, she did not lose her own humanity or her commitment to her country. Nor did she lose the love and emotional support of her husband.

Although the pinnacle of her work was a condemnation of war, all of her art confronted viewers with the need for social action to overcome major social issues. Käthe's work first received major attention when she portrayed a group of weaver peasants who revolted in 1844 because of low factory wages and inhumane living conditions. This revolt, which occurred before her birth, became the theme of a play, which, despite its being banned by the Berlin police, Käthe saw. It so deeply moved her that she devoted the next five years to creating a series of six pictures reflecting the event. Much to her surprise, this series brought her instant fame.

In 1919, German women were given the right to vote. At about the same time, a women's association separate though related to the Social Democratic Party was formed. This new organization, made up of mainly working-class socialist women, was predicated on the belief that women's low status and exploitation in society were results of sexism. Käthe was too shy to become active in the organization, but she supported the struggle in other ways, by creating inexpensive posters that were widely distributed and designed for consciousness-raising. On one poster, which referred to the problem of poor housing, she inscribed: "600,000 Berliners live in apartments in which five or more persons are living. Some hundred thousand children live in tenement housing without playgrounds."

As a child, Käthe had been shy, serious, and prone to

stomachaches and emotional outbursts that would last for hours. Her mother, who devoted herself to the family, was stoic and distant, perhaps due to the early deaths of three of her seven children.

Käthe's father, educated in law, disagreed so strongly with the authoritarian Prussian government that he gave up his profession and developed a building materials business instead. One of her childhood pleasures was playing on piles of bricks with her siblings and neighborhood children and listening to political discussions.

Käthe's talent was encouraged at home. Her mother was a better-than-average painter, and their house was full of copies she had made of many great paintings. Her father saw that Käthe had good art teachers and encouraged her craft. He also tried, however, to tell her what to paint. Moreover, he opposed her getting married, not believing that a woman could be a mother, wife, and artist.

In rebellion against her father and to prove she could successfully balance those roles, Käthe at last decided to marry physician Karl Kollwitz after a seven-year engagement and much ambivalence on her part. Throughout their marriage, Karl shared an unfaltering love with her as well as a devotion to many of the same social concerns. For fifty years they lived in the same working-class-district apartment house in Berlin. There he maintained his busy but poorly paid medical practice, while she established a small studio.

Käthe, uninterested in housework, had a housekeeper to help her, yet she often interrupted her work to be with her two sons, Hans and Peter. Like her mother, Käthe was not physically affectionate, but she involved herself with her children during their play, their studies, and long walks in the country.

Both her father, an ardent socialist, and the Social Democratic Party had profound influences on Käthe's political beliefs. Many socialist concerns, such as the debilitating poverty of working-class people, were poignantly portrayed in her etchings and lithographs. In her diary she wrote that middle-class people held no appeal for her, but the proletariat, she said, had "a grandness of manner, a breadth to their lives."

In addition to growing up in a politically oriented home, Käthe was greatly influenced by reading about the French Revolution and Charles Dickens's *A Tale of Two Cities*. She began to see that women actually had the power to revolt against tyranny. This belief became another important theme in her work. Until this time, women were usually pictured as romantic figures or as fighting defensively to protect themselves and their families. Käthe showed women as leading revolutionaries, both in the French Revolution and in the German peasant wars. As her children grew older and no longer needed her as much, Käthe turned more intently to her work, saying that it alone was always stimulating, rejuvenating, exciting, and satisfying.

Karl continued to support her ideas and work, despite the fact that so much of his time and energy was poured into his medical practice. Generally nondemonstrative toward him, Käthe nevertheless valued her husband greatly, revealing the depth of her caring in an uncharacteristic burst of gratitude in a note to him on their twenty-fifth anniversary:

> I have never been without your love, and because of it we are now so firmly linked after twenty-five years. Karl, my dear, thank you. I have so rarely told you in words what you have been and are to me. Today I want to do so, this once. I thank you for all you have given me out of your love and kindness.

When World War I broke out, both sons, Hans and Peter, enlisted. Peter, then eighteen, was killed while Hans was still at the front. Käthe's grief was overpowering. In an effort to cope with it, she worked for seven years on a series of woodcuts reflecting death and war as she experienced them from 1914 to 1918. She also created a war memorial for Peter dedicated to other grieving parents.

When this large sculpture was completed and put in place overlooking the cemetery where Peter was buried, the face of the grieving mother was Käthe's own. As she stood there studying it with Karl, her emotions at last emerged: "I looked at her [the statue], my own face, and I wept and stroked her cheeks. Karl stood close behind me—I did not even realize it. I heard him whisper, 'Yes, yes.' How close we were to one another then!"

But this was not to be the end of Käthe's grief. In 1930, the National Socialist Party (Nazis) came into power, romanticizing motherhood and war. Because she was against the Nazis, Käthe had to resign her professorship at the art academy, which provided a small but steady income and valuable work space.

She was also threatened with deportation to a concentration camp when she refused to disclose the name of a friend who, with her, had been interviewed for a politically critical magazine article. Although Käthe was not imprisoned, both she and Karl feared for their safety and carried poison with them to be swallowed if they were taken by the Nazis.

Her work was banned from government-endorsed academy art shows. Karl was forced to close his medical practice and died after a long illness. From that time on, the grieving Käthe used a cane for support. World War II erupted, and her grandson was killed. When the bombing of Berlin brought the war closer, she moved to a friend's house.

Käthe Kollwitz always felt the burden of her work, believing she had no choice but to reveal suffering, especially women's suffering, caused by poverty, hunger, and war. Until her death she remained committed to nonviolence. "Pacifism," she wrote, "is not a matter of calm looking on; it is work, hard work."

FOR LOVE OF HOMELAND

Golda Meir (1898–1978)

Few women take on the grand responsibility of helping to form a nation, sacrificing a marriage out of a strong sense of national duty, as Golda Meir, prime minister of Israel, did. Originally named Goldie Mabovitch, she became Golda Myerson when she was married. Later, David Ben-Gurion insisted that her name be Hebrew, so she changed it to Meir, a Hebrew version of Myerson that means "enlightened."

Golda was born in Kiev in 1898 during a time when many Jews in the surrounding area were being massacred by the Cossacks. Friends and family were always fearful. Doors and windows were boarded up for protection against the bloody, unexpected attacks, and Golda was often deeply afraid. Later, she said: "If there is any logical explanation . . . for the direction which my life has taken . . . [it is] the desire and determination to save Jewish children . . . from a similar experience."

Named after a domineering great-grandmother, Golda grew up in a poor family, always hungry. Because of the terror of the Cossacks and the unremitting poverty, her father, a skilled carpenter, emigrated to the United States with plans for the family to follow.

In the meantime, Golda, her mother, and two sisters moved to Pinsk to live with her aunt, where there was considerable political activity against the czarist regime. Her sister, Shana, who was nine years older, became involved in politics and served as a model for Golda's later involvement. At fourteen, Shana was a revolutionary, in constant danger from anti–Semitism and the counteraction of the rising Zionist movement, a worldwide effort dedicated to establishing a Jewish homeland.

In Pinsk, Golda's family lived next door to the police station, through whose thin walls they could hear people being interrogated and beaten. When this happened, as it did frequently, Golda would lie in bed shaking in fear for Shana; could it be she next door this time? Once, to escape police who were breaking into a secret meeting, Shana jumped off the roof of the building being raided. It was clear to their mother that serious trouble was inevitable if Shana persisted in these pursuits, so in 1906 the family left Russia to join Golda's father in Milwaukee.

In the new land they had their first ride in an automobile, their first new, colorful clothes, and a two-room apartment that was attached to an empty store. Golda's mother determined to stock this store as a market and run it herself, and Golda, at age nine, was obligated to work there—a task she resented, as it often made her late for school. Nonetheless, she got to class enough to receive good grades.

Golda's first political work began when, at age eleven, she called a public meeting to raise money for books for the poor children who could not afford to buy their own. At this time, schools did not provide free books, and Golda thought this discrimination against the poor was unfair. She and a friend printed announcements, rented a hall, made successful speeches, and received publicity on the front page of the local newspaper. When her mother found out about this meeting, she was furious; but Golda had established her power to sway audiences.

Golda's friendly, affectionate parents were more concerned with her working in the store and winning a husband than in her education. When she was fourteen, her mother suggested that she become engaged to a man who shopped in their store and had proposed marriage. Golda, incensed over this advice, wrote to Shana, then living in Denver with her husband, that the man was "an old man, twice my age!" In desperation, Golda ran away and joined her sister in order to continue her studies.

There, along with studying and part-time work, Golda became educated in Zionism and other political philosophies by listening to the passionate discussions in Yiddish, often held at Shana's home, and by dating young men who were involved in these debates.

Eventually, she met Morris Myerson, a shy, well-educated sign painter with very little money, whom Golda described as not very handsome but with a beautiful soul. They fell deeply in love. But Golda's father entreated her to return to Milwaukee, assuring her that she could continue her high school education there. Her parents, who had softened their demands and were more involved in community work, moreover held a constant open house for local Zionists and for people who came from Palestine to enlist others in the movement.

When Golda returned to her parent's home, her romance with Morris, who had remained in Denver, continued by mail. At the same time, her involvement in Israel intensified. Morris, however, as much in love with Golda's beauty and happy smile as he was, was not a Zionist. He told her that he thought the idea of Palestine as a homeland for the Jews was ridiculous, that Jews' suffering was inevitable. He wrote: "The other day I received a notice to attend one of the meetings . . .but since I do not care particularly as to whether the Jews are going to suffer in Russia or in the Holy Land, I did not go."

Golda determined that she must go to Palestine, and when Morris refused to accompany her, their engagement was broken. But they had a problem: They were still in love. At last, he told her that he would—albeit reluctantly—go anywhere in the world she wanted to go, so in 1917 they were married and set off for Tel Aviv, where she started teaching English. This was not, however, her idea of deep involvement in Zionism. She wanted to live and work in a kibbutz, so that was their next move. The work was hard and the food terrible. In her oral autobiography Golda described it: "I forced myself to eat every kind of food or dish, even if it was hard to look at, let alone swallow. The food generally had a most unpleasant taste because of the oil . . . kept in leather bags and bitter as gall."

Morris became so ill when living in the kibbutz that it was necessary for them to leave. They moved to Jerusalem, where they had two children, Menachem and Sarah. Money was scarce. Golda tried to devote herself entirely to Morris and their children and even took in washing so that she could stay home and pay the bills, and when this was not successful, she found an office job. But then Sarah, six, became seriously ill with a kidney disease, so Golda took both children to the United States in 1932 for Sarah's treatment. They stayed two years. During that time Golda worked hard, speaking to many groups to elicit support and money for Zionism. At last, once Sarah was well, they returned to Palestine.

Although Golda stayed married for thirty years, until Morris's death, their marriage was not happy; he simply could not share her passion for Zionism. They separated in 1938 although Golda once said it was a great love that lasted until he died.

A recent biography, based on numerous interviews with people who knew her well, claims that Golda had long affairs with several very brilliant, powerful men. One of them was David Remez, who was directing sorely needed road construction when they first met. As they became more involved in politics, he helped shaped her ideas and the style of her speeches. Deeply attached to each other, they maintained a close relationship until his death, long after they ceased being lovers.

Another brilliant man in Golda's private and public life was Shneur Zalman Rubashov, known as Shazar. He loved poetry and philosophy, Zionism, women, and the applause of audiences. This relationship also continued throughout their lives.

Zalman Aranne, secretary of the Labor Council, was the next important lover in her life, a self-educated, fun-loving, powerful man who had helped plan the kibbutz organization.

She was forty-one years old when she first met him in 1939, and few people knew of this relationship, nor of the intimate one she had with Yaacov Hazan. One of her friends said Golda loved Hazan the most, although they disagreed politically, as he preferred Russia to the United States.

Throughout her life, Golda had the capacity to attract highly intelligent men and hold their interest—in both her love and her causes. Highly discreet, she only briefly commented about her romances: "I am not a nun," she said once. And another time: "There are people who generally don't talk about their intimate affairs, and I am one of them."

More frequently, Golda claimed that it was her passion for her people and the forming of Israel that most interfered with a happy home life. Her jobs required her to travel so much that she did not have enough time for her husband and their children, and she believed that she had no choice except to do what she thought was necessary for love of her country. In her autobiography Golda writes, "It isn't enough to believe in something; you have to have the stamina to meet obstacles and overcome them, to struggle."

Golda often struggled. Although she felt as if she had no choice, she also felt guilty for not being a full-time mother. Her sister and mother added to her guilt with frequent criticism. Once, when a public vote was being held about a political activity, she noticed that her children were unexpectedly there to vote, and that they voted their approval of her position. This was an important moment for her: "It was the most reassuring vote of confidence I ever got, but it didn't keep me from feeling that being able to vote for your mother is not nearly as good or as important as having her at home when you get back from school."

Throughout her life, Golda gave her priority to Zionist affairs, to the labor movement, and to the need to unify labor factions for the good of Israel. Elected to the first Knesset (parliament), she held many labor and government positions.

After David Ben-Gurion came into power, he appointed

Golda in 1956 to serve as minister of foreign affairs. She remembered him as one of the "least approachable men I had ever met." He called her "the best man in my cabinet." Among her many assignments under him, she served as Israel's first minister to Russia, where she had experienced so much terror as a child.

Twice in her sixties, Golda retired to have time with her friends, children, and grandchildren. But she was called back to serve and became increasingly physically and emotionally tired. Years of heavy negotiation and battles with such powerful people as Ben-Gurion had taken their toll. As she explained, "I do want to be able to read a book without feeling guilty or go to a concert on the spur of the moment, and I don't want to see another airport for several years."

At age seventy and against her wishes, Golda was made Prime Minister. The prevailing argument was that she was desperately needed, that she was the only Israeli who could do the job. Golda often worked sixteen-hour days for the next five years as she tried to negotiate peace with the Arabs. For this she was ridiculed by a Jordanian newspaper, which sarcastically claimed she might be willing to go to Cairo to try to find peaceful settlements but that she would never be invited. Furthermore, continued the newspaper, "She believes that one fine day a world without guns will emerge in the Middle East. Golda Meir is behaving like a grandmother telling bedtime stories to her grandchildren."

Golda suffered great inner conflict between her commitment to her family and her commitment to a homeland. According to the United Nations declaration, both are human rights, and her longings for both were never fully satisfied.

> The inner struggles and the despairs of the mother who goes to work are without parallel in human experience. . . . There is a type of woman who . . . cannot divorce herself from the larger social life. And for such a woman, there is no rest.

LEGALIZING HUMAN RIGHTS

Eleanor Roosevelt (1884–1962)

A shy and insecure woman whose husband was president of the United States and unfaithful to her for years, Eleanor Roosevelt was nevertheless able to eventually establish her identity as a powerful political force. Best known for her humanitarian work, she became one of this country's most admired women and "first lady" of the United Nations. Yet throughout her marriage she remained "second lady" to Franklin Roosevelt, whose passions rested elsewhere.

In spite of her unhappiness over this, Eleanor became the single leading force in legalizing human rights worldwide. But even this accomplishment came to pass only after her powerful husband died. It was then that she could fully express her own strong personality and become a social activist, writer, lecturer, diplomat, and U.S. representative to the United Nations.

For most of her life, Eleanor worked hard to overcome the extreme shyness of her childhood, due in part to lonely and painful early years as, in her own words, an "ugly duckling." Her mother, a socially popular beauty, would often introduce her daughter with, "She's such a funny child—so old-fashioned that we call her granny." Eleanor felt like a grave misfit in this wealthy, politically distinguished family.

Eleanor's father was a sportsman whom she adored. Her interest in human rights began when he and her uncle would take her during holidays to visit the newsboy clubhouses and the crippled children in orthopedic hospitals. Eleanor had a special empathy for the crippled children, because she too wore a strong steel brace; hers was to correct a spinal curvature. She was tenderhearted in many ways. At five years old, when riding a donkey rented by her father in Sorrento, Italy, she noted that the boy leading the donkey was bare-

footed and that stones were cutting his feet. Eleanor prompt-
ly got off the donkey and insisted that the boy take her place.

Eleanor's father was an alcoholic, and during one episode
of hospitalization for this, Eleanor's mother fell ill and died
of diphtheria. Because her father was considered too irre-
sponsible to be trusted with children, Eleanor was sent to
live in New York with her maternal grandmother and two
aunts and uncles. For the rest of his life, Eleanor dreamed of
becoming reunited with her idolized, absent father, who had
encouraged her to believe that someday they would live together, and that she would be the lady of his house. But this
never happened; Eleanor's father died when she was ten.

Eleanor did not attend school when she was young; she
had tutors. Without friends her own age, she spent many
solitary hours reading. Her grandmother discouraged contact
with her father's family, whom she visited only at Christ-
mastime.

Her adolescence proved no more happy. A high point
came when, at a family party in her early teens, she met her
distant cousin Franklin Roosevelt. He was flirtatious, cava-
lier, and sports-minded like her father. Feeling sorry for
Eleanor, he asked her for a heart-stopping dance, a long-
remembered, treasured memory for one who had felt
doomed to a life as a wallflower.

At the age of fifteen, Eleanor was sent off to a French
boarding school outside of London, along with a discreet
request by her grandmother that she be taught social skills.
Under the caring guidance of the headmistress this happened,
and Eleanor's world opened up a little.

After three years, she returned to America for her debut
in society, as required by her grandmother. Slowly she began
to make friends, become active in volunteer social work, and
see more of Franklin Roosevelt. But the weekends she spent
on Long Island with her aunt playing bridge and attending
tea parties were filled with frustrating trivia. She wrote to

him, "If you ever find me leading this type of life, stop me, for it's not the way to happiness."

When Franklin proposed, despite his mother's opposition to the match, Eleanor hesitated before accepting, uncertain whether she could look directly into the face of that formidable woman's disapproval. Nonetheless, Eleanor and Franklin went ahead with their wedding, during which the guests seemed more interested in Franklin's uncle, President Theodore Roosevelt, than in the newlyweds.

On their extended, romantic European honeymoon, each wrote long letters daily to Franklin's mother, Sara; Eleanor quickly came completely under her influence. Sara made all their decisions, and Eleanor gave in, hoping this capitulation would help create the kind of happy family she had missed as a child.

But the domination only served to further undermine Eleanor's already considerable insecurity. She doubted, for example, her ability to have children, and even after she had produced five, she left the caring of them to nurses, so fearful was she of "doing something wrong." In reading her biography, one gets a sense that she had to work very hard just to cope with everyday life. Often, for example, she did not feel well during pregnancy but would not give in. The effects of this denial are found in a passage in her autobiography: "I never let anything physical prevent my doing what needs to be done. . . . This is pretty hard discipline . . . what it really does, I think, is to kill a certain amount of the power of enjoyment."

Eleanor, extremely self-disciplined, was also the disciplinarian with their children, because Franklin refused to be. What enjoyment she experienced was continually dampened by her intolerant, jealous mother-in-law, who not only interfered with her relationships but tried to influence her grandchildren against their mother. A family friend wrote that Sara, with all her charm and distinction, "hides a prim-

itive jealousy of her daughter-in-law which is sometimes star-
tling in its crudity."

Eleanor's gradual evolution from shyness to assertive-
ness began in 1918, when she and Franklin were living in
Hyde Park, New York. He was a lawyer at the time when
she discovered he was having an affair with her social secretary, Lucy Page, later to become Lucy Page Mercer. The
affair constituted a double betrayal, involving as it did both
her secretary and her husband. Moreover, it became clear
that Sara herself preferred Lucy to Eleanor.

Eleanor asked for a divorce. Franklin refused, for several
reasons: first, because his mother threatened to cut him off
if he divorced; second, because it would affect both his children and his political career in negative ways; and third, because Lucy was Catholic and unwilling to marry a divorced
man with five children. Denied a divorce, Eleanor struggled
out of submissiveness and began to develop a career of her
own. Some years later, she wrote, "The bottom dropped out
of my own particular world. . . . I faced myself, my surroundings, my world, honestly for the first time. I really
grew up that year."

Although Franklin promised to give up his relationship
with Lucy, it continued. Later, Eleanor would discover that
the two of them had maintained their romance, up to and
including the moment of his death in Warm Springs, Georgia,
of a cerebral stroke in 1945.

Franklin's physical difficulties began in 1920 when he
was stricken with polio, which left him partly paralyzed.
Later, as governor of New York, he had more stress when
faced with serious public problems. Prohibition was an issue.
Protestants were in favor of it; Roman Catholics were against
it. Another statewide issue was the extremely high cost of
electricity. Franklin, as governor, was able to reduce this cost.

Then he became President just before the Great Depression hit the country, and the stock market collapsed, along
with agricultural prices. Banks closed, and unemployment

reached 25 percent. His New Deal, to engender economic recovery, was instated, and Eleanor became his eyes, ears, and legs as she traveled extensively to gather firsthand information on the problems of unemployment. In 1934 Hitler claimed, "Eleanor Roosevelt is America's real ruler."

By this time, any romance between Eleanor and Franklin was over, but she nonetheless opted to help him by becoming more involved in politics. Franklin's assistant, Louis Howe, encouraged her to make speeches and taught her how to analyze political affairs. After the president got polio, Louis lived with them, and he and Eleanor often took turns massaging Roosevelt's useless legs.

One of Eleanor's early concerns was for the poverty-stricken coal miners of West Virginia. Another was a New Deal program for youth employment. She prodded the president to appoint women to high posts and worked for racial equality and desegregation in the armed forces. When noted black singer Marian Anderson was denied the use of the Constitution Hall in Washington, D.C., which was owned by the Daughters of the American Revolution, Eleanor resigned from that organization. She wrote of her resignation in the newspaper in the hope of raising the consciousness of others regarding the unacceptability of segregation.

As the president's wife living in the White House for twelve years, Eleanor held many press conferences and presided over a great deal of political entertainment. She also learned to control her feelings, especially her passions. Her autobiography, written most factually, contains many details of where she went and who she saw, but seldom mentions how she felt. Noted for her dignity and commitment, Eleanor claimed she often felt lost. Evaluating her early years in the White House, she wrote:

> On the whole . . . I think I lived those years very impersonally. It was almost as though I had erected someone a little outside of myself who was the President's wife. I was lost somewhere

deep down inside myself. That is the way I felt and worked until I left the White House.

Perhaps Eleanor's feeling lost was partly a result of her husband's infidelity with Lucy Page Mercer. Surely it had many ramifications, not the least of which was the rift it indirectly created between Eleanor and her daughter, Anna. When Eleanor discovered that Lucy had been with Franklin at Warm Springs when he died, and that she had also been with Franklin on numerous occasions at the White House, Eleanor discovered, on questioning her daughter, that Anna had known of the secret meetings. From this time forth, Eleanor became silent on the subject. And Anna concluded that her mother never forgave her for knowing what she did and for doing nothing to stop it.

Despite her domestic unhappiness, Eleanor was fiercely committed to human rights concerns, and she worked whether she was sick or well. She believed that when a person ceases to make a contribution, that person begins to die. At age seventy-five and still working, she wrote, "I think it is a necessity to be doing something which you feel is useful in order to grow old gracefully and contentedly."

Although Eleanor lost her love for Franklin, her belief in his social goals remained, and she supported his programs in many ways. When Harry Truman became president, Eleanor, at his request, became chairperson of the United Nations commission that drafted and secured the approval of the Universal Declaration of Human Rights in 1948. Resolutions about a peaceful world and the dignity of persons are included in this document. But, as Eleanor pointed out in her last words, resolutions are good only if people really want to keep them: "This I believe with all my heart. If we want a free and peaceful world, if we want to make the deserts bloom and man grow to greater dignity as a human being— *we can do it!*"

THE NEED FOR COURAGE

Women who feel the need to be actively involved in social issues often become powerful even though they may not become famous. They stand by their commitments regardless of the cost, acting with courage and refusing to live by the myths that surround them. These myths, frequently based on prejudicial thinking, often perpetuate the idea that women are not competent or courageous enough to change the social, political, or military status quo. The fallacy of this thinking is exposed by every woman in this chapter.

The word *courage* comes from the French word *coeur*, which means "heart." Courage to strive for human rights usually comes from the desire for freedom. It comes from the inner core of the self and is activated by crisis situations. Each of these women, in her own unique way, courageously and effectively fought against cultural inequities. The worldwide myth that women do not have as much courage as men is indisputably false. Any reading in history that takes note of women shows the error of this thinking.

Women who are deeply committed to social concerns often struggle with their priorities and ongoing decisions on how to use their time. Alexandra Kollontai, who fought against war and authoritarian rule, confronted the political establishment as a controversial popular writer. Deeply concerned about poverty, class struggle, and sexual inequalities, she became a major force in Russia under both Lenin and Stalin. Although she had romances, her commitment to liberation always came first. As she wrote in one of her stories, *Love of Worker Bees*, "You have to have leisure to fall in love . . . and I just don't have time."

Like Alexandra Kollontai, Golda Meir's political action, resulting from her desire for peace and a homeland, required so much dedication that it came in direct conflict with her desire for love and a stable marriage. Yet she fought against

the belief that women who have children should not be involved in political action and should not take risks.

Käthe Kollwitz was one such woman. She had children
and a passion for peace, which did not actually conflict with
her marriage because her loving husband shared her values.
Even when the Nazis considered her antiwar sculptures an
act of treason and both their lives were threatened, he stood
by her.

Two more common myths are that women who are
active in politics are aggressive and strongly anti-men, especially if they feel betrayed. These myths must also be discarded in the light of what is known about all the women in
this chapter. Eleanor Roosevelt, for example, although in-
credibly shy, took a courageous stand by speaking out publicly against social injustice and negotiating human-rights
agreements between nations. Even when her husband remained involved with another woman for many years, she
supported his political and social values through her work.
Was Eleanor disappointed in him as a husband? Definitely
yes. Was she a vengeful and aggressive man-hater? Definitely
no. Neither did Golda Meir live by the myth that it is necessary to hate men to effect political change. She was asser-
tive, fought hard for her social concerns, and often disagreed
with her male coworkers and associates. Yet she also sought
harmony with her husband (even after their divorce), her
male colleagues, and the representatives of other nations.

Eleanor Roosevelt and Golda Meir are not the only
women who dispelled such myths. Many others who have
been personally active in political affairs often are effective at
what has been designated "men's work" and, at the same
time, have also supported men's interests. However, it is a
myth that women cannot be effective without a man's support, as Harriet Tubman demonstrated. Passionately dedicated to freedom, she faced her challenge alone. Without the
encouragement of a husband or lover, she often put her life
at stake in leading slaves to freedom.

The myth that men will not emotionally support women who are committed to social change can also be discarded. In her writings, Mary Wollstonecraft expressed her feelings against the ownership of women by men. This vindication was instrumental to the early development of the women's movement. Furthermore, her husband's love and admiration helped her give up the pathological jealousy that hindered her growth. He did not live by the myth that a man must lead and a woman must follow, and continued to support her work even after her death.

Obedience to a man, whether to a national ruler or to a father or husband, has been expected of most women since the beginning of history. This has perpetuated the myth that women's place is in the home. Yet great women of courage do not think in these terms. They are not homebound but they do not turn away from their children either. They are able to manage their lives so that they can stay in the public arena where decisions are made about life and death.

Most women want both romance and peace; choosing between them, if necessary, may be painful. The achievement of human rights is never easy when ignorance or prejudice rules. Yet, in spite of difficulties, there is no end to the desire for love, no end to the desire for human rights, and no end to the willingness to fight for both.

CHAPTER FOUR

LOVE AND
TRADITION

TRADITIONAL ROLES

Until recently, the most common role for women has had a
domestic focus, as wife, mother, or "the woman behind the
man." As such, women have been expected to be subordinate
to men and also grateful for their place in society. Sometimes
men have been blamed for this and called oppressors; sometimes women have been blamed for accepting their lesser
roles. More often it has been seen as "natural" for women
to be in a subordinate role, a socially sanctioned phenomenon
chalked up to "biology."

Whatever the source, the traditional role of the woman
behind the man most often has been considered to be the
only appropriate one for "nice" women. And if it should
happen that a woman had a professional interest, either inside
or outside the home, that interest was supposed to be secondary to a man's goals and desires.

This value system led to the common assumption that
women will work in the home, and men will work away
from home. A woman raised in this tradition would hardly
be expected to become the wife of a president, the mother
of another president, and also fostered a long line of famous
writers. Yet that is what happened to Abigail Adams.

Nor would a poor woman, traditionally raised to marry a husband chosen by her father, expect to become an empress, especially if she was unsophisticated and not very intelligent. Yet that was Josephine Bonaparte's experience.

Both of these women accepted two other traditional roles: They became skillful and competent hostesses who provided their husbands with social environments that enhanced their work; and they were doting mothers and grandmothers, active in their offsprings' lives.

But they were different in other ways. Josephine Bonaparte, who became empress of France, lived in a sexually open culture and could spend money freely. In contrast, Abigail Adams lived by the Puritan ethic of colonial America and lived frugally.

If alive today, Abigail would fall into the category of superwoman. She was a farmer who planted and sold produce to make ends meet. She kept the farm running, her children happy, and her husband interested in her, even when he was away for a year, before he became the President of the United States. In addition, she confronted her husband with her opinion that unless American women had a political voice, they would eventually revolt. And she was right; they did.

Abigail was concerned with issues and questions startlingly similar to those faced by women today: how to reconcile different cultural backgrounds; how to cope with work (in her case, farming); how to care for children when a husband is often away for months and money is scarce; how to handle political disagreements (especially before the founding of America); what role to play in one's husband's professional life; and how to maintain conjugal interest and love.

In an essay, E. B. White described Abigail as "simply a woman whose claim to immortality is based on a flair for independence, a gift for knowledge, extraordinary intellect, and the capacity to love."

Josephine Bonaparte, born twenty years after Abigail Adams, had a very different personality and lifestyle but also chose the traditional public role of the woman behind the man. Josephine was not an intellectual, but—as is the case with many great women—she had extraordinary interpersonal skills that were genuine and not manipulative. This special intelligence surely contributed to Napoleon's fame.

First divorced, then widowed, Josephine's desire to provide for her children furnished much of the impetus to marry Napoleon, whose passion she originally was fearful of. For her, the fire burned brighter for her children than for anyone else. But like many women today, she wanted a man who was trustworthy and caring, and Napoleon remained so for the whole of their time together.

Sometimes the traditional role assigned to women has been to be subordinate to a father rather than to a husband, captive emotionally if not physically. These parents have encouraged their daughters to remain single in order to stay at home and care for them in their old age. The daughters of such families are not likely to have children of their own. Such was the case with Beatrix Potter, who did not escape her parents' domination until she was almost fifty years old. Yet her love and compassion for children was the motivation for the twenty-six books she wrote. After her eventual marriage, she became a farmer and very much the woman behind the man, insisting on being known only as Mrs. William Heelis.

Anne Morrow Lindbergh always deferred to her husband's decisions, yet was able to maintain a stable relationship. She did this out of love and traditional values based on three important interests in her life: to be a partner in her husband's flying career; to be a mother; and to be independently known as a writer. In spite of overwhelming grief when her child was kidnapped and brutally murdered, she was able to continue pursuing her goals.

Until very recently, women in Japan traditionally walked three steps behind men. They performed all the menial tasks at home and work, cared for children and elder relatives, and knew little about the world outside. Any objection they might have to the militaristic policy of their government would be considered treason. Thus, popular antiwar poet Akiko Yosano posed a multisided threat to the emperor and the military establishment of her country when she made her mark around the turn of this century.

Japan had just survived a difficult political and economic period under the shogunate, which had depleted the national treasury and kept the country secluded from the rest of the world. Under the new Meiji government, which took over at about the same time as Akiko's birth, the Restoration was launched, promoting *minken*, or "the rights of the people." At this time, the first constitution was written, and feudalism was abolished. However, parents still expected traditional homage and obedience from their children. The independent, strong-willed Akiko did not give in to her parents, although she cared for her own husband and children in very traditional ways.

Like actors and actresses on stage, each of us is assigned a gender role that we may enjoy or resist or even change as circumstances change. Some roles we learn early in childhood, some are taught to us as we grow older, and still others are self-selected. The roles and romances in the lives of each of these women reveal some of the timeless problems faced by women who have hearts on fire and take on the cultural role of "the woman behind the man."

WITH LOVING THREATS

Abigail Adams (1744–1818)

Many years before the women's movement started in the United States—in fact, before there was a United States—a woman who was a wife, mother, and farmer wrote to her husband that the day would come when women would revolt unless they had a voice in the government. This was at a time when women's rights themselves were considered nothing less than ludicrous. Yet Abigail Adams, a farming woman and mother of six children, tried to influence the course of history by speaking out to a husband who radically disagreed with her.

Abigail Adams was one of the first women in the United States to argue for the equal rights of women and for the liberation of slaves. Although Mary Wollstonecraft is often given credit for starting the women's rights movement, Abigail Adams's writing actually preceded Mary's work.

Whereas women authors today would be more likely to write essays, novels, or nonfiction, Abigail Adams was an astoundingly prolific letter writer. Writing straight from the heart, she also had analytical, informed opinions on politics, education, slavery, women's rights, and love.

One of the customs of intellectuals at that time was to enter into a formal agreement to correspond regularly with certain people about political or social affairs. Although the writers who agreed to do this also commented on their personal lives, it is their correspondence on other matters that contributes much to our understanding of history.

A brilliant and self-educated woman, Abigail wrote letters daily, and more than two thousand of them were published by her grandson twenty years after her death. During her lifetime, people thought Abigail's letters important enough to save, so well-informed was she, so open in expressing her ideas and willing to discuss controversial issues.

But as well versed as she might have been in the classics, Abigail was not nearly so comfortable with the rules of grammar, spelling, or punctuation. Consequently, when she learned that her daughter was saving letters to pass on to her own daughter, Abigail implored her to desist, claiming that the letters were "unworthy of preservation or perpetuity." Terrified at the idea of her letters being published, she also entreated her husband to destroy her half of their correspondence. To a friend she lamented, "Heedless and inaccurate as I am, I have too much vanity to risk my reputation before the public."

As a wife and mother, Abigail was greatly protective of her family, and did not hesitate interceding when she felt some injustice had been done to one of its members. She sharply criticized Thomas Jefferson, for instance, for what she considered unfair behavior when her husband was running for reelection. Then, when Jefferson, after becoming president, removed her son John Quincy from the position of district judge, she protested this action as well. His subsequent apology was accepted with grace. The Adamses had been close to Jefferson for so many years that neither could remain bitter, and their correspondence continued. When Abigail showed a copy of this correspondence to her husband, he added in a postscript that she had written it without his knowledge and had nothing more to say on the subject.

The relationship between Jefferson and John Adams was, with the exception of the election period, that of close and loving brothers. They corresponded, sometimes several times a month, for forty-nine years and always expressed their deep affection for each other. Jefferson's feelings extended to Abigail. During George Washington's presidency, when John Adams was serving as ambassador to England, Jefferson sent his young daughter, Polly, over to Abigail's care while finding a suitable school for her in Paris.

As a child, Abigail had not had such educational opportunities. Frail and self-educated at home, she studied the works of great writers such as Molière and John Locke. Her father was a warm, rather open-minded minister, in whose home were encouraged work, high moral standards, and study. Part of each year was spent with her grandparents, who also encouraged and respected her intellectual capacities. Her grandfather was speaker of the Massachusetts House of Representatives, and she was privy to political discussions.

The romance between Abigail and John Adams began

during his visits to her father. John, a Harvard graduate, enjoyed their conversations and was entranced by both Abigail's modesty and her ability to handle her opinionated and controlling mother. Abigail's intellectual keenness occasionally took him aback, so that once, when he found her reading John Locke's *Human Understanding*, he patronizingly commented, "A big book for such a little head." Abigail responded with, "Girls are not to know anything, I am told, beyond kitchen and parlour. Yet girls too may have their curiosity. And even a little head, Mr. Adams, may possess a longing for knowledge, or at least for understanding." This moved him greatly. The next time he called, it was with an apology and a book, *The Independent Whig*, which she had been forbidden to read because of its liberalism.

When Abigail's father told him of her knowledge of sheep, John studied these animals so as to be able to converse with her on the subject, and also so that he could lure her out of the house for a walk to gaze at some.

Abigail was twenty years old when she married John Adams after a two-year engagement, which her mother tried to prolong indefinitely. He had inherited ten acres from his father, and with her dowry they bought another thirty acres to farm. Abigail, needless to say, ran it most efficiently.

John was then a twenty-nine-year-old attorney, a political radical who kept his office in their home. Abigail sometimes disagreed with him. When he believed the colonists were being treated as slaves by Britain, she maintained a loyalty to Britain and the king. Later, of course, she changed her mind.

Abigail and John established a pattern in the early years of their marriage. Each day he would put his fees into her purse, and she managed the family finances. They were very poor; but with the little he earned and the produce she raised and sold, they managed. Both enjoyed the farm and discussing politics—in which Abigail was becoming more and more interested. In mixed company she often sat with the men instead of chatting with their wives.

The couple also expressed their emotions freely. Warm and romantic, they were also prone to outbursts of temper over politics. In his efforts to make more money through his law practice, John had to widely travel by horse or buggy. After he became more involved in politics was often away for extended periods on various assignments.

Four years after they were married, and with two young children, they moved to Boston. There a third child was born but died when fourteen months old. British soldiers were then close, and political tension was high. When Abigail was pregnant with her fourth child, a massacre occurred in the city, prompting the family to move back to their farm in Braintree, from where John would commute to Boston. Once more Abigail ran the family farm, only now she also maintained her extensive correspondence and cared for their children, educating them herself.

Abigail, self-taught as a child, taught herself Latin and ancient history as an adult in order to pass these subjects on to her children. Altogether, she created an atmosphere for them filled with love and warmth. After her death, one of her sons said: "While she lived, whenever I returned to the paternal roof I felt as if the joys and charms of childhood returned to make me happy. All was kindness and affection."

After a year and a half, the commuting became too great a physical burden on John, so they returned to Boston, now with four children. Abigail was twenty-eight, John was thirty-seven, their oldest child was seven, and they were almost penniless.

It was in 1775, during the fight against the Stamp Act, that John became well known as a political figure. England had imposed a tax on the American colonies, and its House of Commons would not accept petitions objecting to what colonial leaders saw as "taxation without representation."

Women also objected to the tax. As it rose, so did the prices of imported goods such as tea and coffee. To protest against the tax on tea, three hundred women bound themselves together and pledged not to drink "foreign tea, which was one of the pleasures of life." They took even more drastic steps with the coffee tax. Over a hundred women with carts and trunks marched to a coffee warehouse and demanded the keys. When the warehouse man refused to give them up, one of the women seized him and tossed him into the cart. At this point, according to Abigail, he surrendered the keys. The women released him, opened the warehouse, took the coffee themselves, put it into the trunks, and drove off.

On March 31, 1776, John Adams attended the Continental Congress in Philadelphia, where the Declaration of Independence was being drafted—in part to protest the paying of taxes to England when colonists had no representation.

Abigail protested in similar ways by pleading that women's rights be included in the new code of laws:

> Remember the ladies and be more generous and favorable to them than your ancestors. Do not put such unlimited power into the hands of the husbands. Remember, all men would be tyrants if they could. If particular care and attention is not paid to the ladies, we are determined to foment a rebellion, and will not hold ourselves bound by any laws in which we have no voice or representation.

The male sex, she insisted, while being naturally tyrannical, needed to give up its harsh title of master for the more endearing one of friend.

Her husband wrote back that he laughed at her letter and her sauciness and concluded that, if men gave up the name of master, they would be completely under the despotism of the petticoat. She, in return, chided him for preaching peace and goodwill to all nations while upholding men's absolute power over wives.

For all his laughter, John Adams greatly respected Abigail's advice. He boasted to a friend, "There is a Lady at the foot of Pens Hill, who obliges me, from Time to Time with clearer and fuller Intelligence, than I can get from a whole Committee of Gentlemen." He did agree with her that slaves should be freed, but could not bring himself to share her views on the need to liberate women.

When the new nation was finally formed, with George Washington as its first president, John Adams was sent to France and then to England as ambassador. Once more, Abigail cared for the farm, educated the children, and wrote him long, newsy letters to lift his spirits as he tried to establish relationships in countries not very friendly to the causes of the new nation. During this three-year separation she often declared her love, her interest in women's rights, and her desire for more frequent letters. "Give me the man I love," she wrote. You are neither of an age or temper to be allured by the splendor of a court or the smiles of princesses. I have a right to your whole heart, because my own never knew another lord."

Finally, John begged her to join him, and she did. Then forty years old, she had never been farther from home than forty miles. Although she did not care for the cold climate or frosty reception received in England, which resented the revolution against it, she became a fine hostess. This graciousness carried over into her years when John became the second president of the young United States.

Throughout their fifty-four years of marriage, Abigail burned to establish equal rights for women—in politics, in marriage, and in educational institutions. She maintained as well that slaves should be freed, and that education should be made available to them. In fact, she regularly invited a black boy into her home and taught him to read and write. Massachusetts, her home state, freed its slaves at a much earlier date than did many other states.

When Abigail was dying of typhoid at age seventy-four,

her husband lamented to Jefferson "the dear Partner of my Life for fifty-four years as a Wife and for many Years more as a Lover."

John Quincy Adams, who became sixth president of the United States, carried on his mother's commitment to women's rights and freedom for slaves. To elicit sympathy, he told the House of Representatives about a slave woman with four children who was put into a dungeon, and who killed two of her children and tried to kill the others rather than have them put on a chain gang. He also made an impassioned speech about women: "The mere departure of women from the duties of the domestic circle, far from being a reproach to her, is virtue of the highest order, when it is done from purity of purpose, by appropriate means, and the purpose good."

Abigail Adams was sometimes sharply criticized for being as outspoken as she was regarding political affairs; but the traditional role of silent, noncomplaining wife and mother was simply not the style of this most bright and independent thinker.

A WOMAN TO HER FINGERTIPS

Josephine Bonaparte (1763–1814)

Poorly educated, married at sixteen, imprisoned during the French Revolution, charming, sweet but not book-smart, Josephine was a widow with two young children when she attracted the attention of Napoleon Bonaparte, one of the greatest military geniuses of all time, and assumed the traditional role of military wife. He lavished love and power on both her and her children. In return, he insisted on her adoration, which he also extracted from numerous other women. Authoritarian and ambitious, he instigated and received a divorce from her, but he could never let her go.

Josephine's greatness manifested itself in her political support of Napoleon and her talent for calming important political and military figures as they balked at changes in the government. She participated in all of her husband's strategic meetings when, as first consul, he set about transforming the entire French government from a monarchy into a republic. Often able to mollify those who attended the explosive meetings, she was a good listener who seldom interrupted and always remembered a face. She was, in other words, the perfect hostess for Napoleon; she managed to remember something positive about everyone. Her ways were gentle; her kindness was never-ending. Charming and submissive, she was always ready to do anyone a favor and constantly placated Napoleon.

All through her enormous fame and popularity, Josephine remained an adoring mother whose children continued to be dear and close to her and to each other throughout life. Even Napoleon made her children a major focus in his life, and they remained important to him until his death.

Josephine was born Marie-Rose, a Creole on the French Caribbean island of Martinique. (It was Napoleon who, many years later, began calling her Josephine, and the name stayed with her.) For years she lived with her family upstairs over a sugar mill because their house had been demolished in a hurricane and they were too poor to rebuild it. At age fifteen, with the equivalent of only a primary school education, she was taken to Paris for a marriage arranged by her aunt and father. She wed Alexandre de Beauharnois, an eighteen-year-old French viscount and a well-known rake, who already had three illegitimate children by other women.

Her new husband considered Josephine sweet, but he also called her awkward and ignorant, not fit for the Parisian culture in which he was so popular. He suggested that she become educated in philosophy, but she was not attracted to study. A typical teenage bride, she wanted his undivided attention and was jealous when it was denied her.

Although they had two children, Eugene and Hortense, Alexandre spent little time with either them or his wife. Preferring the company of other women, he was often sarcastic and frequently ridiculed or threatened Josephine in public. He would leave her for months at a time without saying good-bye or telling her where he was going. Yet Josephine never criticized him to their children. Eventually, the marriage became so painful that Josephine returned to Martinique—just in time to find herself in the midst of a slave revolt. Concerned for the safety of her children, Josephine went back to France and attempted a reconciliation.

By this time it was the eve of the French Revolution, and aristocratic Alexandre was under suspicion. Among other offenses, he had manipulated the political situation so that he could be made a general, but he was so incompetent even at this that he was forced to resign and was later arrested. When she spoke out on his behalf, writing and pleading for his release, Josephine was also arrested. Although she had hidden Eugene and Hortense with friends, she agonized over being separated from them.

Josephine and Alexandre were both jailed in one of the worst prisons of the Revolution, and he was finally executed. In her memoirs, Hortense recalls that once she and her brother stood outside the prison and saw their parents standing at a window with their arms outstretched to them. That was the last time she saw her father before the guillotine fell.

When it looked as if the guillotine would also be Josephine's fate, she comforted herself by recalling a childhood fortune-teller who had prophesied that one day she would be greater than a queen. Sharing the same prison were others of high rank, one of whom, General Lazare Hoche of Germany, Josephine briefly became involved with. When they were released in 1794, he gave her some financial help, though not enough to keep her from poverty. And though she was able to recoup some of her husband's properties that had been confiscated during the Revolution, that too did not suffice for herself and her children. She soon became one of three mistresses to Paul Barras, who had overthrown the hated Robespierre to become the powerful new director of France.

It was through Paul Barras that Josephine met Napoleon Bonaparte at a party. Bonaparte, from the island of Corsica, was little known until he succeeded in putting down a riot at Barras's request. At the celebration dinner, while Josephine's two lovers, Barras and Hoche, remained tantalized and jealous, Napoleon fell, deeply and irrevocably, in love. He found Josephine's genuine sweetness, charm, and deference irresistible. Napoleon urged her to marry him. According to Barras's memoirs, Josephine, who was also highly seductive, assured him that her upcoming marriage to "the little general" would not interfere with their relationship.

Neither Josephine nor Napoleon had money, but he was infatuated and also thought her to be wealthy. Throughout the courtship they exchanged many love letters. Hers were sweet and endearing: "Come to breakfast with me tomorrow; I must see you and talk with you about your interests. Goodnight, my friend, I embrace you." But the morning after the first night that they became lovers, Napoleon's declarations were considerably more passionate:

> I awaken full of you. Between your portrait and the memory of our intoxicating night, my senses have had no respite. Sweet and incomparable Josephine, what is this bizarre effect you have upon my heart? What if you were to be angry? What if I were to be angry? What if I were to see you sad or troubled? Then my soul would be shattered by distress.

Napoleon was most outspoken in his dislike for intellectual women. Having an enormous ego, he preferred to receive adoration—but, to be fair, he was fully capable of returning it as well. His letters were always more prolific and romantic than hers. Calling her "beautiful," "enchanting," "tender and kind," he proclaimed that his desire was "to strip

from your body the last film of chiffon, your slippers, everything." The hours that they were apart from each other tormented him: "I will see you in three hours' time: Till then,
mio dulce amor, a million kisses—but give me none in return,
for they set my blood on fire."

Although Josephine admired Napoleon's courage and
brilliance, she was intimidated by his passion. She wavered
about marrying him, and her children feared they would lose
first place in her affections. They needn't have worried, however. Josephine's devotion as a mother, and later a grandmother, was steadfast; her children always came first.

But meanwhile, she was a widow, with no way to support them. Few women worked at that time, and those who
did had menial jobs with little pay. As Josephine preferred
the stability of marriage to being a mistress, she opted to
proceed with Napoleon's matrimonial plans. It was a wise
choice. Napoleon, throughout his life, remained utterly devoted to her children, keeping closer to them than to his
own, writing to them often and sending many presents.

When they married, Josephine was thirty-three and Napoleon twenty-six. Although the hour had been arranged for
their quiet civil ceremony, he was so busy studying maps of
Italy that he kept her waiting two hours. Two days later,
Napoleon was made commander in chief of the army in Italy
and was transferred south.

Although he won many victories, he also languished
with love, begging her to write more often to lift the perpetual nightmare of his life. "Forgive me, my darling. The
love you have inspired in me robs me of my reason; I shall
never regain it." He goes on to say that he is nothing without
her and wants to give her "a thousand kisses upon your lips,
upon your tongue."

Soon Napoleon begged her to join him in Milan; at that
time, battles were not fought daily and were usually confined
to specific areas. But Josephine preferred life in Paris with
her children, friends, and other diversions. So great were her

charms that even Napoleon's lieutenant, who delivered his letters, fell under her spell and became her lover.

When Napoleon ordered her to join him at his head-quarters on the Riviera, she could hardly bear to leave this new lover. Yet, always compliant, she did so. Their reunion was brief, followed by more of his military traveling and further reunions. Josephine began to complain to friends that she was beginning to tire of his worship, much as she rejoiced in his love for her children. His rough-and-ready public affection often embarrassed her, lacking as it did the finesse that she preferred.

Napoleon slowly began to recognize that Josephine's sexual passion did not match his. In spite of her charm and sweetness, she was sometimes indifferent. Although it was common in France at that time for men to openly take mistresses and for women to openly take lovers, both became wildly jealous when this occurred. As rumors spread and jealousy increased, their marriage tottered on shaky ground.

During this time, Napoleon became a powerful first consul, and her social duties increased. Gracious with everyone, she taught Napoleon the value of remembering names until he became skilled at this, even with his soldiers. With women he continued to be rude and crude, provoking in Josephine a mixture of embarrassment and jealousy.

Their lifestyle became more opulent when they were living in Tuileries Palace, and she also had the joy of having the country home for which she had longed. Malmaison, a three-story house surrounded by a garden, reminded her of her childhood in Martinique. Josephine so loved flowers that she became something of a botanist, learning the scientific names and wanting only the best plants around her.

When the time came for Napoleon to be made emperor, Josephine's future role became uncertain; their marriage had, after all, been only a civil one, not blessed by the pope. Napoleon thought she deserved to have the role of empress, and Josephine charmed the pope into performing a religious marriage ceremony the day before his coronation. She was thus also crowned. All the pomp and ceremony previously addressed to royalty—and supposedly discarded in the days of the Republic—was reinstated in court.

A major crisis ensued when Napoleon left her again, this time to fight Admiral Nelson and the British navy. A letter accusing her of infidelity was captured by the British and published. In retaliation against her, Napoleon took the wife of one of his lieutenants as mistress and threatened Josephine with a divorce. It was the turning point in their relationship.

With tears and pleading, Josephine begged for a reconciliation, but he refused. Eugene and Hortense, horrified by the situation, interceded on their mother's behalf. Napoleon finally relented and forgave her and the many debts she had incurred. But, from this point on, the marriage was clearly on his terms, not hers.

Meanwhile, Napoleon had many short-term, superficial affairs, plus a more serious one with Maria Walewska, the wife of an elderly Polish nobleman. Although at first she was not as interested in Napoleon himself as she was concerned that he might make good on his threat to destroy Poland unless his passion for her was returned, she eventually changed heart. In time, she fell in love with him and bore him a son.

Meanwhile, Josephine remained important to him as a woman and a partner. No one could serve him as she did, and no one could equal her as a charming hostess capable of also establishing a firm, sorely needed court etiquette. Her great tact and boundless kindness was noted by all. Even Napoleon's valet was enchanted: "She made everyone around her happy; no woman was ever more loved by those near her, or more deserved to be."

Although Napoleon did not respect women and was often contemptuous of them, his stepdaughter, Hortense, remained an exception. She not only gave him advice but could also serve as peacemaker in the stormy domestic scenes with Josephine, which were often brought on by her extravagances. One time he was so angry with his wife's high laundry bills that he declared the palace sheets could be changed only once a month. Josephine, as usual, was able to placate him, and fresh sheets continued to be available each week.

When Napoleon traveled long distances, Josephine often accompanied him. When she did not, they continued to exchange love letters: "Everything in this world must come to an end: beauty, wit, sentiment, the sun itself; but that which has no term is the happiness I find with you—the ineffable goodness and sweetness of my Josephine."

Despite his adoration and Josephine's desire to remain in the union, trouble arose when she bore Napoleon no children. The lack of a legitimate heir became a serious issue, politically as well as personally. Time after time, Napoleon's family accused Josephine of being at fault. In an attempt to establish harmony, Josephine arranged for Hortense to marry Louis Bonaparte, Napoleon's younger brother. Neither Hortense nor Louis wanted this, but they were too afraid to complain.

From the beginning it was a most unhappy marriage, made worse by the vicious rumor started by the Bonapartes that Napoleon was the father of Hortense's son, who was named Napoleon-Charles. Napoleon tried to adopt him to settle the issue of a legal heir, but Louis refused.

Meanwhile, although Napoleon was inextricably tied to Josephine, he also resented her and continued his affairs with other women, justifying himself with, "The laws of morality and of society are not applicable to me. I have the right to answer all your objections with an eternal I." Josephine, in her jealousy, sometimes intervened directly and broke up the affairs but did not remain angry at the women involved. These episodes were often followed by passionate reconciliations and the exchange of even more love letters. Gradually, Josephine became more subservient to Napoleon's demands, while he became more egocentric.

As a loving stepfather, Napoleon not only adopted Eugene and treated him as a lifetime confidant, he made his charge his aide-de-camp, and then a prince and viceroy of Italy. Three of Eugene's children gained thrones in Sweden, Portugal, and Brazil. Hortense, sweet and submissive like her mother—though vastly better educated—became queen of Holland, and her son became emperor of France.

Josephine's own pleasure in her traditional roles of lover and hostess did not last and Napoleon continued his affairs and fathered two children by two of his mistresses. Finally, after thirteen years of marriage, he demanded a divorce so that he could marry the Archduchess Marie Louise of Austria and thus strengthen political ties by having a direct heir. Josephine was forty-six at the time and he was thirty-eight; he believed it was his duty to produce an heir to his throne.

This was an agonizing time for Josephine, especially when Eugene had to present the request for the divorce to the senators for their approval. When the divorce was granted, she was allowed to remain empress, with all honors and with an annual income of two million francs from the state treasury.

Although a son was born of Napoleon's new marriage, the union proved one of political convenience only. Napoleon often visited Josephine secretly, and they continued to exchange letters. He also tried to cheer her up, as well as keep her out of the spotlight. Nonetheless, she became depressed and continued her excessive spending. When she asked to meet Marie Louise, Napoleon protested: "Today she believes you are old and does not think about you. If she saw you with all your charms you might make her anxious, and she would ask me to send you away. I should have to do it. You are all right as you are. Keep quiet."

Military battles continued to separate them. As the empire began to fall, Josephine's concern grew for Napoleon as well as her children and grandchildren. Treason, loss of power, and Napoleon's capitulation to the czar followed. Through it all, Josephine stood up for him both publicly and privately. When England and other parts of the empire turned against him, Napoleon abdicated and was exiled to the island of Elba. The last letter Josephine received from him included a tender request for her to visit him. "Never forget him who has never forgotten you and will never forget you. . . . I shall await news of you at Elba."

Josephine, meanwhile, had apparently lost her will to live. Usually subservient, she refused at this time to follow her physician's orders and, already fighting a cold with fever, deliberately subjected herself to further cold and died in the arms of her children at the age of fifty-one, not knowing that in the future her beloved grandson would rule France as Napoleon III, instead of Napoleon's own son.

When Napoleon returned from Elba a year later, he walked with Hortense through Malmaison, Josephine's cherished home with its beautiful gardens and bittersweet memories. Then he returned to war, lost the decisive battle of Waterloo, abdicated again, and was exiled to St. Helena, where he died six years later. Before his death he described his never-ending attraction to Josephine: "I truly loved her . . . she had a certain something that was irresistible. She was a woman to her very fingertips.

UNMARRIED CAPTIVE

Beatrix Potter (1861–1943)

Although children's writer Beatrix Potter lived more than a hundred years after Abigail and Josephine, when it would seem as though women would "naturally" have more freedom, she and many like her still lived very much within the confines of traditional orders. In Beatrix's case, it was the very different traditional role of unmarried captive that was assigned her by parents who, only once she was in her twenties, allowed her out of the house without themselves or a governess in attendance—and then only in the company of her brother. She did not travel anywhere alone until she was almost thirty years old—and then it was to visit a cousin who was a feminist and a socialist.

Beatrix Potter started a new literary tradition of drawing and writing for children. At the age of twenty-seven she began to write stories of Peter Rabbit and other animals that have remained best-sellers for eighty years. The effort to escape is a theme in all of her writings, which often focus on small animals trying to find their way out of various traps. Nineteen of her books explore this theme in one way or another; Peter Rabbit, for instance, narrowly escapes with his life from Mr. McGregor, and Jemima Puddle-Duck complains that the farmer's wife does not allow her even to hatch her own eggs.

Born in London to parents of independent wealth, Beatrix was raised primarily by a Scottish nurse who, according to the author, "had a firm belief in witches, fairies, and the creed of the terrible John Calvin (the creed rubbed off, but the fairies remained)." In addition to fairy stories, her nurse read her *Uncle Tom's Cabin*. Meanwhile, Beatrix taught herself to read with the Waverly novels. She had a governess and never went to school. As a child, she was often sick. During one of those illnesses she wrote in her diary that she could not move in bed without screaming in pain.

At a very early age, Beatrix was encouraged to draw and paint, and she fell in love with the illustrations in Lewis Carroll's books. Her passion for drawing was so great that she sometimes smuggled animals such as frogs, newts, and even a snake into the house to draw. Her brother, five years younger, had a similar enthusiasm. They sometimes boiled dead animals and sketched pictures of their skeletons.

As she began to grow up, her father, an attorney with no practice and no need to work, but possessing a keen interest in art and photography, often took Beatrix to art galleries, and she enjoyed spending long hours at the British Museum (Natural History). Gradually, her drawings became more scientifically correct and aesthetically pleasing. Although her mother was also artistic, occasionally transcribing books into Braille, she was much more interested in making formal calls to friends than in spending time with Beatrix. Their relationship was difficult.

Each summer the family would rent a country house, often near a pond where her father could fish and where Beatrix delighted in getting to know the many mice, squirrels, and rabbits and seriously studied fungi. One of her illustrated scientific papers on this last subject was so highly thought of it was later used by other scientists.

Beatrix had no friends, and when she was about fourteen she began to keep a journal with a secret writing code that no one might decipher. It contained hymns and records of conversations. Her writing was so small that a magnifying glass was required to read it—in fact, Beatrix herself could not read it. The code was finally deciphered in 1958 by Leslie Linder after more than nine years of work. One of her biographers says that in her early years she was "as quiet as the tame mouse washing its whiskers in her sleeve, or the hedgehog curled up behind the coal-scuttle."

Beatrix Potter's career began in the midst of pain, during one of her frequent illnesses. A friend's sick child, Noel, had asked for a letter from her. "My dear Noel," Beatrix responded, "I don't know what to write about, so I shall tell you a story of four little rabbits whose names were Flopsy, Mopsy, Cotton-tail, and Peter."

Along with her letter, Beatrix sent Noel a page of drawings of four little rabbits. The Peter Rabbit that children cherish to this day, named after her own pet, was born in this first letter and appeared in her first book, *The Tale of*

Peter Rabbit, one of the favorite children's books of all time. At first it was courteously rejected by the English publisher Frederick Warne and by at least six other firms. One said it smelled like rotten carrots. Others considered it too short to be a whole book. To solve the problem, Beatrix took her own savings and published the book herself in 1901, printing a very modest 250 copies. She concluded, "The publisher is a gentleman who prints books, and he wants a bigger book than he has got money to pay for."

The Tale of Peter Rabbit sold so well that Frederick Warne reconsidered his earlier decision and took over publication. The two became friends, and while visiting him Beatrix became acquainted with his shy and gentle son. Although he had helped her plan some of her books, he was so shy that he proposed marriage to her by letter. Beatrix, thirty-nine and still living at home, was encouraged by her parents to turn him down. Nonetheless, and against their wishes, she became engaged to Norman Warne.

Although both of them were approaching forty, she looked forward to a new and happy life. Tragically, however, Norman died of leukemia only a few months after their romance began, and before they could be married. Grief-stricken, Beatrix worked hard to accept this tragedy. Finally she was able to write, "He did not live long, but he fulfilled a useful, happy life. I must try to make a fresh beginning next year."

As the popularity of her books grew, Beatrix's parents began to object, and she was not permitted to see or even write to her publisher. Eventually, however, she was allowed to renew her professional correspondence—this time with Harold Warne, Norman's brother, who was her new editor. Over the next thirty years, despite frequent disagreements about details, Warne published more than twenty of her little books with illustrations. Today, more than ninety years later, they are still in print.

With a small inheritance she had received from her aunt,

Beatrix bought her first farm in the country she adored and left home in an effort to escape the confines of her restrictive parents. Always having preferred the country to the city, Beatrix loved to spend long hours studying and drawing plants, insects, and animals. Then, with additional money that came in from her books, Beatrix bought a larger property.

William Heelis, the attorney who arranged for her to make this purchase, became attracted to her. At age forty-seven, she found romance again and married him. William, very different from her attorney father, loved the country as much as Beatrix. Tall and relaxed, he had many practical skills. But even this happy marriage chafed against her parents' wishes, and Beatrix's children's stories continued to reflect her efforts to overturn this particular domination. In the last line of *The Story of Miss Moppet*, for example, Beatrix clearly was referring to herself when she wrote about the mouse escaping the cat: "He has wriggled out and run away—and he is dancing a jig on the top of the cupboard!"

William encouraged her interests. He helped her select large land holdings to buy with her royalties and, like Beatrix, believed they should be kept in trust in their natural state for the convenience of the small wild animals that lived there. She devoted herself particularly to the practical concerns of the wife of a solicitor, sheep farmer, and landowner, displaying an old-fashioned, gentle deference to her husband and a deep respect for his way of life.

For themselves, Beatrix and William bought a farm and lived there for nearly thirty years—the rest of their lives. Animals and farming became more interesting to her than writing. Yet she captured the peace and beauty of both the farm and her marriage in many delightful illustrations. She had, in fact, dedicated her *Mr. Tod* to William just before their wedding and wrote to a friend: "The portrait of two pigs arm-in-arm-looking at the sunrise is not a portrait of me and Mr. Heelis, though it is a view of where we used to

Elizabeth Browning

Mary Ann Evans   (George Eliot)

Clara Schumann

Katharine Hepburn

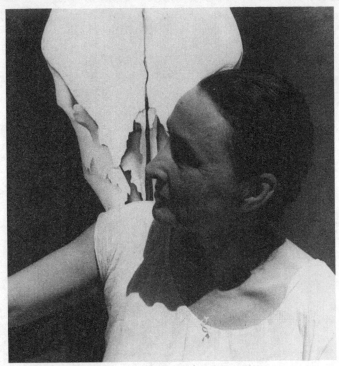

Georgia O'Keeffe

Margaret Mead

Catherine the Great

Beryl Markham

Frida Kahlo

Simone de Beauvoir

Mary Wollstonecraft

Alexandra Kollantai

Sarah Bernhardt

Harriet Tubman

Käthe Kollwitz

Golda Meir

Eleanor Roosevelt

Abigail Adams

Josephine Bonaparte

Beatrix Potter

Anne Morrow Lindbergh

Akiko Yosano

Margaret Sanger

Aurore Dupin (George Sand)

Elsa Lanchester

Gertrude Stein

Mary Leakey

Karen Horney

Charlotte Brontë

Emilie du Châtelet

Queen Victoria

Marie Curie

Helen Hayes

walk on Sunday afternoons! When I want to put William into a book, it will have to be some very tall thin animal."

Professionally very successful, Beatrix nonetheless accepted traditional roles and always looked up to the three men in her life: her father, whom she loved and feared; her fiancé, whom she loved and trusted; and her husband, who encouraged her love of the land and its creatures, and who protected her from intruders when she became famous. With William, at last, came a union as loving and respectful as it was traditional. They were a hand-holding couple until her death.

THE WOMAN BEHIND THE MAN

Anne Morrow Lindbergh (1906–)

Shy and self-deprecating, Anne Morrow Lindbergh was also complicated and introspective, and she attracted and married the most famous and sought-out man of the time. The phrase "the woman behind the man" usually applies to a mate who emotionally supports, encourages, follows, and sometimes directs a usually prominent man. Anne was such a woman, but without the desire to direct him—an ideal partner for Charles A. Lindbergh.

Because both of them were painfully shy, a major problem they shared throughout their lives concerned avoiding the crowds of reporters and others who constantly sought Charles out. He dreaded publicity so much that Anne edited his name out of many of her letters, which were sometimes opened by servants or others who then publicized their contents. In correspondence with her own family, Anne often used the pseudonym "Boyd" for her husband, although in her diaries she always referred to him as Colonel L. or Colonel Lindbergh. "Life in the air," she wrote, "was beautiful, limitless, and free—if often hazardous—but life on the ground married to a public hero was a full cry between the hunter and the hunted. We were the quarry."

A writer, mother of six, pilot and navigator, Anne stayed at her husband's side, both in and out of the cockpit. She followed him everywhere; he was as much her hero as he was the rest of the world's. Throughout their crisis and grief when their baby son was kidnapped and murdered, and throughout the overwhelming publicity accompanying almost every move around them, Anne remained romantically enthralled and deeply devoted.

Anne grew up in a small town in New Jersey in a family that prized family closeness, education, ambition, and hard work. Her father became ambassador to Mexico, then a senator representing New Jersey; at heart, however, he was a teacher and a lifelong student. Her mother had similar values. She campaigned for equal educational opportunities for women in the days when few women had them, and as a trustee at Smith College was profoundly committed to furthering education.

Anne described herself as "an ordinary person who lived an extraordinary life." Anne's family included two sisters and a brother, and as a family they traveled extensively. These travels were more like educational seminars, with her parents opening her eyes to the history and culture of each place they visited.

In this close-knit family, voluminous letter writing between the women was enjoyed and expected. She kept diaries so that she could savor an experience, "make it more real, more visible and palpable, than in actual life." Even as a young girl, Anne wanted to be a writer. It was what she called her "ultimate longing."

Charles Lindbergh was independent, modest, and committed to his family and personal privacy. An adventuresome man who loved flying and frequently risked death, he recounts how this began with his first flight when he "lost all conscious connection with the past . . . in this strange, un-

mortal space, crowded with beauty, pierced with danger."
This mixing of beauty with danger continued with his first
parachute jump, for which he was paid twenty-five dollars.
He explained jumping: "[It is] where life meets death on an
equal plane; where man is more than man, and existence is
both supreme and valueless at the same instant."

Lindbergh was twenty-five years old when he flew the
first nonstop solo flight from New York to Paris on May
20–21, 1927, in thirty-three hours in a monoplane and became
a hero overnight. On his flight he computed the weight of
everything so carefully that he substituted a wicker seat for
the usual, heavier arrangement. He also went without a radio,
had special lightweight shoes, and even cut out spare pages
from his notebook to save additional ounces. When Charles
landed, the press and souvenir hunters overwhelmed him,
even tearing out pieces of fabric from the plane for souvenirs.
When he returned to New York, four million people greeted
him. From then on, he was always in the spotlight.

Anne, who was attending Smith College at this time,
soon met Lindbergh in Mexico City, where her father, then
ambassador to Mexico, had invited him to strengthen United
States–Mexico relations. She was not, however, particularly
interested in the meeting; she thought the pomp and ceremony surrounding him was odious, "public hero stuff breaking into our family party."

But when they did meet, her customary shyness was
greater even than this tall, silent man's, embarrassed as he
was by the attention of the crowds. Each tried to avoid the
other. Envious of her sisters, who could speak to him with
ease, Anne was overwhelmed when he took them all up for
a plane ride. In those days, long before jet planes were invented and filled the skies, such an event was nothing short
of dazzling. For Anne, certainly, it was beautiful, intense,
never to be forgotten—like the feelings she was developing
for the young pilot himself.

When Lindbergh phoned and asked to take her out, Anne

panicked. She believed he would be embarrassed and bored with her, that he preferred her sisters and had only asked for her out of a sense of duty to the family. She was also afraid she would be a "bother" to him. But on their first date, when he took her up in a small plane with an open cockpit, she discovered she could be natural in his presence. She fell in love with both him and with the air during this first flying lesson.

When they were planning to marry, she wrote to a friend and asked her not to wish her "conventional happiness"; it was so much more than that. To avoid publicity, the date and place of the 1929 wedding were kept secret. Even the invited guests did not know what was scheduled ahead of time.

Anne earned a pilot's license, passed a radio operators' exam, and served as copilot and navigator for Lindbergh for many flights throughout the world. She loved flying and her free life with her husband. "Charles is life itself," she wrote, "pure life force, like sunlight—and it is for this I married him and this that holds him to me—caring always, caring desperately what happens to him and whatever he is involved in."

Early one evening in 1932, a kidnapper put a ladder up to their nineteen-month-old son, Charles Jr.'s, room on the second floor, took him, and left a ransom note instructing them to await word regarding the payment. Under no circumstances were they to involve the police. There were many false alarms, and a ransom was paid, but about two months after the kidnapping, the baby was found in a shallow grave, killed with a blow to his head. The tragedy was constant front page news, and although the Lindberghs pleaded with both the public and press for privacy, they did not receive it. Their home was constantly surrounded by the curious. Four years later, Bruno Hauptmann was brought to trial and executed for this act.

Anne's first book, *North to the Orient*, published that same

year, in 1935, was written to help her deal with the pain. In
it she told of their pioneering flight across Canada, Alaska,
and Siberia to Japan and China. When she first took it to her
publisher she was so afraid it was too short that she carried
the book under her coat.

As is customary, the publisher said he would let her
know. She went through all the agony that new authors
experience while waiting, and to keep up her self-esteem
would talk to herself about the importance of being a wife
and mother and about how wonderful it would be to have
more children. Suddenly the phone rang, and Mr. Harcourt,
the publisher, congratulated her and asked to see her and
Charles the next day to tie up the contract.

To Anne it was a moment of joy, a moment of power
and affirmation. "I fit into this world," she wrote. "There
is a place for me. There is some reason for my living. I can
hold my head up." It was especially reassuring that the publisher requested that she also use her maiden name, Morrow,
along with Lindbergh.

When she was home, Anne was a devoted mother who
worried about how Charles's fame and the publicity from
the earlier murder would affect the other children. Her hope
for her next son, Jon, was that he would be kind, appreciative,
and independent, and she left him alone to fight out his early
quarrels so that he could become a self-directed, courageous
man who was not afraid of life. Later, there would be four
more children, for whom she had equal concern.

Anne had been pregnant with Jon at the time of the
kidnapping and fought to keep her emotions in check, in
order to protect her unborn baby from unnecessary trauma.
After the birth, when Anne and Charles went on trips, he
was left with a nursemaid in the well-guarded estate of her
mother. Yet threats were made against his life also, and this
danger precipitated their moving to Europe.

The publicity surrounding the case was so distasteful that

the Lindberghs remained in Europe for several years. Charles visited German centers of aviation and warned the United States against their growing air power. He also recommended that the United States remain neutral in World War II. Highly criticized for this, Lindbergh resigned his commission in the Air Force Reserves. He continued, however, to help the Department of Defense fly combat missions, and he assisted several aircraft corporations as well.

Anne and Charles were sometimes separated because of his government assignments, and when together they were forced to move many times to avoid publicity. Anne did not complain, for she believed it was a man's right to determine where his family should live. One of their homes was in France, and had neither heat, electricity, nor plumbing.

Although as wife and mother she was very traditional, as a modern woman she was not. Anne wanted to be a person in her own right, beyond "the woman behind the man." She wrote poetry, novels, and essays. Her most well known book, *Gift from the Sea*, which contains short essays about nature and life, has remained popular since 1955 and has given strength to many thousands of readers.

Some forty years after the murder of her first child, Anne was finally able to read what she had written during that crisis when she strove to be self-disciplined and maintain a "stiff upper lip." She had tried many false roads: stoicism, pride, remorse, self-pity, clinging to scraps of memories— but none of these had healed her. What was necessary was mourning and facing the truth with loving friends and family. Her journey out of this suffering took many years. Finally she decided to publish some of her memories about the kidnapping, because "although suffering is individual, it is also universal."

Through the pain and the joy, Anne remained a romantic. In 1944, when flying from Chicago to San Francisco to meet Charles, she wrote with the same flavor found in many

of her letters to him: "I have been overcome by the beauty
and richness of this country I have flown over so many times
with you. And overcome with the beauty and richness of our
life together."

DEFYING AUTHORITY

Akiko Yosano (1878–1942)

From a traditional Japanese family, where the father is the
sole means of support, Akiko Yosano learned to support
herself, her eleven children, and her husband by writing poetry and social essays speaking out for the rights of women.
This would be a remarkable achievement at any time, for
only the rarest of poets have been able to make a living writing
poetry. Usually they are financially supported by others or
work at something else for income.

But poetry was important in Japan at the beginning of
this century. It was a custom for lovers, after a night of love,
to exchange poems. An unconventional writer, Akiko Yosano founded a famous progressive school of art, Bunka Ga-
kuin, and wrote poetry that touched the heart.

As a social critic, Akiko took a stand for equal rights for
women in voting and in education, and decried the military
establishment and cultural expectation that men should go
willingly to war. Military power in Japan was exalted, and
the cultural tradition was that men would without question
die for the emperor.

Akiko became a powerful threat to this Japanese tradition, and was publicly accused of opposing the emperor
and the military establishment. This accusation was based
on a poem she published that was considered to be revolutionary. Addressed to her brother during the Sino-Russian
war in 1894, it implores him not to go to war, even for the
emperor:

Please do not die, my beloved brother
His Majesty would not go to war himself
because His mind is benevolent. He would not
order blood to run and death in a way of an animal.
He would not consider death an honor.

When Akiko wrote this poem, her husband was engaged in producing his own very popular poetry glorifying war and denouncing "effeminate" poetry in favor of the more "manly" tiger-and-sword style. Akiko's poetry advocating peace, then, was considered nothing less than outrageous; it was both insubordination to her husband and treason to her militaristic government. Only because of her place in the society, her mastery of poetry, and her pioneering work for women's education and the establishment of schools did she survive attacks from all fronts.

Born in 1878 in the city of Osaka, Akiko was the daughter of Soushich Hou, a well-to-do merchant who ran a confectionery. He was so angry when she was born a girl that, against her mother's wishes, he sent Akiko to live with her aunt for three years. After a boy was born she was allowed to return home and was finally accepted by her father and given a good education. He was a member of the local council and widely read in the Chinese classics, and Akiko's interest in classical literature came early. At the age of twelve she was reading the works of Confucius and the classic *Tale of Genji*. But after Akiko graduated from high school she was not allowed to leave the house unattended, and she was obligated to mind the confectionery store for her parents. She secretly continued to read the classics, managing to "leave the house" in another way.

When she was eighteen, Akiko's first poetry was published. At twenty-two she became a member of a prestigious literary circle that published the journal *Myojo*, or "Morning Star." Its chief editor, the famous poet Tekkan (Hiroshi) Yosano, later became her husband.

Akiko's first book of poetry was well received. The poems were in the tanka form, an important traditional style of short poetry with rhyming lines, and with a specific number of words stipulated for each line. The book's title, *Midaregami*, or "disarrayed hair," came from a poem her husband had written in which he called her "the lady of the restless mind and disarrayed hair."

In Japan, women's hair is seldom disarrayed. It is long, straight, black, and carefully coiffed. If a woman does not keep her hair in that manner, she is likely to be accused of being a prostitute. On the other hand, if only a few strands escape, she is considered sexy. When Akiko used the word *tangled* twice, as "tangled tangled hair," she hinted at sexual freedom that would do more than merely unsettle a few hair strands.

When Akiko first fell in love with Tekkan, she had to give up her parents to be with him. She left them a poem that in essence said, "Please forgive me, dear parents. I do not think I can be the woman you expect me to be. I am intoxicated with sweet wine of love now. Therefore, please think of me as nonexisting."

This was almost unheard of. Traditionally, families arranged marriages for their sons and daughters, as well as jobs for their sons. Marriage was a union of not only individuals but their families as well. Hard work was expected, but never disobedience to family rules and traditions.

Tekkan Yosano came from a very different background than Akiko. He was the fourth son of the poverty-stricken family of a Buddhist priest. Throughout his life he had money problems and often secured funds from women. Before marrying Akiko, for example, he had been married to two wealthy women, who had both divorced him at the insistence of their fathers.

In the case of his second marriage, he had refused to take his wife's name. Traditionally, if a wife's parents had no sons, the son-in-law often agreed to take her family name. But although Tekkan had agreed to take the name Hayashi to please his second wife, once he had a son of his own he changed his mind. For this her father insisted they get a divorce, which was granted. Tekkan had used the dowry from this second wife, Takino Hayashi, to pay the rent and create the journal *Morning Star*. But even after their divorce he continued to exchange love letters, visits, and get money from her long after he married Akiko.

Tekkan often had several women simultaneously. At one time, Akiko and one of his other women, also a poet, entered into a triangle relationship that lasted nine years. The details of this threesome are unknown and can only be guessed at from a tanka that Akiko wrote when the other woman died at the age of twenty-nine.

That secret
We sealed in a jar,
The three of us,
My husband, myself,
And the dead one.

In 1908, the *Morning Star* was discontinued after its hundredth issue. Although Akiko lost the home base for publishing her works, she vigorously continued to write, primarily poetry, social essays, and a few short stories.

It was a widespread custom in Japan at that time for women to care for their husbands as though they were children. Not surprisingly, Akiko became the sole breadwinner of the family. This became more and more difficult as the size of her family continued to grow. Four of her eleven children were born before she was thirty years old, and like most Japanese children, they were dearly loved and greatly indulged.

Meanwhile, Tekkan, who was becoming increasingly depressed as he observed his fame waning, managed to raise the money for a trip to Europe. Later, Akiko joined him there and was greatly affected by the artists and intellectuals who were interested in social issues and philosophy. In fact, she named a daughter after Ellen Kay, a Swedish feminist, and one of her sons after sculptor Auguste Rodin. Her fascination with the French sculptor, however, was temporary:

> *Only the sculptor's fame*
> *Attracted me*
> *When young,*
> *But how exquisite now*
> *The Buddha's face!*

After returning to Japan, Akiko expressed her new social awareness in essays in various journals, continually calling upon women to respond. By 1911, her voice was strengthening, as she compared the power of the women's movement to the power of a mountain: "The mountain-moving day is coming. . . . All sleeping women now awake and move."

In one of her essays she questions the reader with, "How do we women educate ourselves to get out of these miserable circumstances and catch up with men and fortify ourselves to have equal life with men in the future?" In answer, she advises women to read books, periodicals written for men, to integrate the information into their lives, and to respond with the head and not only the heart:

> If women get in the habit of thinking seriously, even on trivial matters, they will not just act on a feeling level, but the eyes of intellect will open up and she will be able to criticize and understand by expanding her abilities and integrate thoughts, feeling, and behavior with less chance of disintegration.

A courageous woman and financial supporter of her large family, Akiko died in 1942, at the age of sixty-four. By that time, one of her adolescent dreams had come true. When young, the only places in which she could study were a very small kitchen corner or a storage shed where the wind blew through the cracks. There she dreamed of the day when she could "sit at a desk and read books as ordinary people are doing." It took many years before she had a desk "like ordinary people," but Akiko Yosano herself never came close to being merely ordinary.

ROLES AND ROMANCE

In every century, there have been women who have put much energy into their careers as well as their intimate relationships. Some have done so out of necessity, others by choice. There has been a major shift in the roles women take because of the rapidly increasing number who are choosing careers outside of the home. This has dispelled the common myth that a woman cannot combine the two roles successfully and still maintain a traditional yet romantic marriage. All the women in this chapter balanced romance, marriage, and career. The belief that marriage will inevitably interfere with self-actualization was not the experience of these women. Traditional to the core, they were very independent in their words and actions.

Women have often felt trapped by the popular myth that they are members of the "weaker sex." The women in this book show that while they may not be as physically strong as men, they are certainly not weaker emotionally or mentally. It is only the cultural myths about women's roles that encourage them to accept subordination.

Abigail Adams did not do so. She spent most of her married life alone, supporting a family through farming while deeply involved in political letter writing. For her, life was difficult in the 1700s but not impossible, even when her husband was away for months or sometimes years at a time. In her outspoken, direct, and loving letters she demanded political rights for women and educational rights for black children, when such ideas were new and different. Her life reveals another false myth: that men don't like women who give them advice. Abigail continued to advise and influence her husband and son before and after each became president. She also gave advice to other great political leaders such as Thomas Jefferson.

Josephine Bonaparte demonstrated similar strengths. Although their personalities and situations were different, she and Abigail Adams shared traditional marriages and exerted great influence over their husbands. Josephine, the epitome of romantic femininity and the ideal hostess for a busy man, did not live according to the myth of women as the weaker sex. She rose to power from a poor and unlettered family to become a well-educated and competent woman. Her knowledge of botany was extraordinary for that time, and her interpersonal skills with political leaders served as a powerful aid to her husband.

An accompanying myth that powerful women do not love nor are loved by their children is also false. Josephine's charm, amiable personality, and sincere concern elicited lifelong loyalty and love. Her biographers agree that her personality was neither artificial nor manipulative but deeply affectionate. In fact, before she met Napoleon, when she was in prison during the French Revolution, she was adored by other prisoners for her shining qualities. She expected to be beheaded, but, at the end of the revolution, when her name was on the first list of those to be released, all the prisoners cheered.

It has also been proven false that women cannot take rejection or negative criticism. This is demonstrated by the life of Beatrix Potter. She was confident of her writing and drawing abilities and her awareness of what children would enjoy, even though she had no children of her own. When publishers refused to recognize the value of her story *Peter Rabbit*, she published it herself. Beatrix did not marry until she was forty-nine years old, shattering the belief that unless a woman marries young she will never marry at all.

There are other myths to which Beatrix did not conform. One is that to be successful, a person must devote a lifetime to a particular interest. She had two careers: first as a writer, second as a farmer who was concerned about wildlife. So great was her commitment that she put her farm, purchased with royalties from her book sales, into a national trust so that small animals could live there without being disturbed.

Competition for power is assumed to be characteristic of spouses who work together. This myth is discredited by Anne Morrow Lindbergh, who had two successful careers, one as a writer and one as a copilot with her famous husband. In their traditional marriage there was no power struggle. They were partners who shared love of each other and their children, grief when one was murdered, and devout passion for flying.

Akiko Yosano, who lived in a highly traditional culture in which women constantly conformed to men's desires, belies the myth that women are not able to confront the political and military establishment. Fighting for what she believed in did not diminish her role as a caring and dedicated mother.

Today many great women who enjoy traditional values also enjoy their freedom. They are never ordinary. Time and again their lives confirm others who have hearts on fire and are willing to take responsibility for living by their own values. Great men are also never ordinary. Many recognize women's intellectual and emotional capacities to both embrace and break with tradition.

CHAPTER FIVE

VARIETY IN
SEXUAL CHOICES

IN HER OWN WAY

In most prehistoric and historic cultures, women were not allowed their own choices of mates, values, or the direction of their own lives. The chattel of their fathers or husbands, they were bought and sold as property. This practice has changed slowly—and in some countries, such as Moslem nations, even slower than slowly. The change involves increasing options for women and has sometimes been called a sexual revolution, but it would be more accurately called a sexual evolution.

Today, of course, more women are making their own choices involving both work and family, living the lifestyles they choose, in their own way. Sometimes these ways are traditional and culturally approved; sometimes they are not. Yet many women are willing to pay the price of social disapproval in exchange for their own integrity. It no longer makes sense to them to pretend to uphold values they no longer hold sacred.

As women become more aware of the sexual choices available to them, they are more inclined to speak openly of their sexual needs and to act on them as well. As a result, new sexual patterns have emerged. Teens have become more sexually active, and premarital sex has become more open. Virginity, sometimes revered and even faked in an earlier era, has also become less important. Extramarital sex has increased, and a lifetime of marriage to one person is seen by some women as incompatible with their sexual and emotional proclivities. Serial marriage and long-term single lifestyles have become genuine options. Homosexual and lesbian lifestyles are also more common. In Denmark and Sweden, marriages between same-sex couples are legal, with all the obligations and privileges, such as the right to inherit, that accompany a heterosexual marriage.

Furthermore, as economic patterns have changed and the job market has opened up, women have discovered they can support themselves and do not need to be subservient to men in order to survive. Educational opportunities have created a new kind of self-determination. In addition, women are no longer stigmatized by terms such as *old maid* or *spinster*. Living as a single independent woman has become an acceptable and respectable choice.

In the past two hundred years, women have become increasingly "liberated" in making their own sexual choices. This liberation is due to a combination of self-determination, social and political opportunities, timing, consensus, institutional change, and personal interaction with people who are themselves liberated. It has also to do with breakthroughs in birth control, which allow women to be freer to choose whether or not to have children and how many to have.

In every century women have been concerned with their sexual choices. A few, personally liberated from some of the cultural restrictions imposed on their sexuality, have committed themselves to helping others win the same gains.

Margaret Sanger is one of these women. She cared enough to fight for a woman's right to birth control and was willing to go to prison for presenting this information publicly. She had a major impact on three nations, won the respect and friendship of many women, and was also able to keep her husband fascinated in both her and her cause.

This kind of woman, who fights for the rights of other women, sees the difference between sexual choices and gender roles. She knows that sex is a biological reality, but that gender roles are either assigned or chosen and are influenced by family and culture.

Author Aurore Dupin, who wrote under the name of George Sand, also believed in the need to speak out and protest against beliefs about women that were assumed by men. She severed her relationship with the great composer Chopin, her lover of ten years, when he was flirtatious with her daughter.

The poet Gertrude Stein, who lived in Paris for much of her life, chose an open, long-term lesbian relationship. She was an eccentric, avant-garde genius, and her writing was unusual and obscure to many readers. It was not until she published what she called an "autobiography" of her lover —really about herself—that she became well known.

Elsa Lanchester, an exceptional British actress, chose to give up sex and romance to remain with her husband, who was homosexual, and live in her own way. Theirs became a long-term intellectual companionship based on a common commitment to the theater. Today, with more people admitting to homosexuality and with the tragic spread of AIDS, this kind of marriage presents new problems to those involved.

Traditional values and roles can change with circumstances. Anthropologist Mary Leakey was married to a brilliant, egotistical man who was so hungry for fame that he compromised himself personally and professionally; as a result, their love died. It is not unusual for women who may enjoy the role of being subordinate to men to make a turnaround when they feel betrayed either sexually or professionally. In such cases, a woman may discard her traditional role, give up the dream of a romantic relationship, and focus her attention on her work.

Psychoanalyst Karen Horney raised many people's awareness of the variety of women's choices. When she began teaching publicly about the psychology of women's sexuality, her work went against traditional psychoanalytic theory, which claimed women had "penis envy." Instead, she believed women were likely to be more envious of men's culturally sanctioned freedom. When she was a mother of three daughters, the disintegration of her marriage prompted her to establish many close friendships—and some romances—with her professional colleagues and students.

In her own way, each of the women in this chapter demonstrates the variety of sexual choices open to all women. Historically and even in some arenas today, woman's biology has been called her destiny. These great women show us that this widespread belief is on shaky ground. Women have the capacities to control the use of their bodies and to make their own sexual choices.

THE WOMAN REBEL

Margaret Sanger (1883–1966)

One woman's commitment to the cause of birth control affected the population of the world. Condemned by the medical profession for distributing such information, Margaret Sanger was jailed eight times. Yet the great historian H. G. Wells, who was one of her lovers, predicted that within one hundred years the movement she started would be the most influential in controlling human destiny on earth.

H. G. Wells was prescient. The movement took hold about fifty years ago, when birth control was legalized in the United States, Japan, and India. This change was due largely to Margaret Sanger's initiative and lifelong commitment to fight for women's rights to have choices in childbearing. Margaret once commented that one could tell a person's age by his or her attitude toward birth control, and that only the young accepted birth control as fact.

Before becoming involved in what was to be her life's work, Margaret Higgins first became interested in socialism and labor unions, as was her father. But her work as a nurse on New York's Lower East Side focused her concern more specifically on the problems of maternal and infant mortality among poor women who could not afford more children. It became increasingly clear to her that self-induced abortions were not only common but disabling and often fatal, and that preventative measures were needed. It was necessary, she decided, to learn the "secrets" of preventing unwanted pregnancy. This decision changed the sex lives of millions of people and the patterns of world population growth.

Margaret's determination and commitment are not surprising. She was born in Corning, New York, to a gentle, loving, often frail Irish mother who had eighteen pregnancies. Seven ended in miscarriages, and Margaret was the sixth of the eleven children who lived. Her mother, always busy caring for the family, died at an early age of cervical cancer. Margaret blamed her father with an angry accusation: "Dammit, you killed my mother. She was only forty-nine when she died. But those eighteen pregnancies didn't hurt you a bit. You—you'll live forever!"

Years later her father read the magazine she published, *The Woman Rebel*, and agreed that her mother would have lived longer if they had had information on birth control. He apologized. And most likely Margaret accepted his apology, because she loved him dearly. A Civil War veteran, he was also an intelligent man, a rebel, an Irishman, and an artist who carved angels with expressive faces for tombstones. Although he sometimes drank too much, he also had a passion for socialism, free education, libraries, and freedom of speech, and she appreciated that kind of openness. At one time he sponsored a controversial atheist, Robert Ingersoll, to speak at the town hall, and took the older children in the family to hear him. Margaret's education about the penalties of being outspoken began that day, as she observed tomatoes and other vegetables being thrown at the speaker by those who did not share his views.

Margaret's personality resembled her father's, with his openness and willingness to fight for freedom of choices. But after her mother died her many chores became so burdensome, and her father so tyrannical, that she escaped into books and entered nurses' training. There she was confronted with sick women either dying in childbirth or else so poor that neither they nor their children could be healthy. Margaret became convinced then that women desperately needed more options in forestalling pregnancy.

While still in nursing school, Margaret was ardently wooed by William Sanger, an architect, who tricked her into marriage before she was ready. The feelings she expressed about this to her sister were ambivalent:

> That beast of a man William took me out for a drive last Monday and drove me to a minister's residence and married me. I wept with anger and would not look at him, for it was so unexpected. I had an old blue dress on, and I looked horrid. He is the loveliest of men, but I am mad at him. I am sure I could not have a better husband—he is my ideal in many ways but I wanted to wait.

Their initial happiness did not last. Margaret, weakened by tubercular symptoms, had great difficulty and pain delivering the first of their three children. They moved to the suburbs for better air, but their carefully designed new house caught fire, and their financial difficulties drove them back to New York. In the city, William's mother was eager to help and soon took over their lives. This actually allowed Margaret the freedom she longed for; she had found life in the suburbs boring and superficial after the life-and-death drama of nursing poor women in the city slums.

In 1913, Margaret accompanied her husband and children to France so that he could further his study of architecture and she could study the many methods of birth control then readily available in Europe. At that time, condoms were not manufactured in the United States, although they were imported for men wanting to avoid venereal diseases. Women's health, emotional desires, and need for protection against pregnancy—or against diseases contracted from men—were not considered. William, who did not share her interest, remained in France for some time after Margaret returned to the United States with a plan to challenge the laws forbidding the sale or free distribution of information about birth control.

In 1917, just before the United States got involved in World War II, Margaret was arrested, taken to court, and accused of two violations against the State of New York for dissemination of birth control information and for "maintaining a public nuisance"—in this case, the first planned-parenthood clinic in the country. When she was sentenced to thirty days in jail with many women criminals who were illiterate, she helped them to learn to read and wrote letters for them.

Like her father, Margaret spoke out for what she believed. This was courageous, even dangerous at a time when euphemisms were used to refer to anything even remotely related to sex and childbearing. When she began to lecture publicly and use sexually technical words, many people were horrified. To escape a trial on charges of obscenity, she fled the country. Her commitment to making birth control information available to all women was more important to her than anything else. It was not important to William, however; he remained married to his architecture.

Once more Margaret felt compelled to gather more information on birth control and on the importance of using only licensed physicians if abortions were necessary. She went to England and became involved with the British birth control movement, known as the Malthusian League. In 1915 she met Havelock Ellis, who had written seven books on the psychology of sex and had an important influence on her. Before meeting him, Margaret's primary interest had been in reducing the number of unwanted children and in saving women whose lives were threatened either by continued pregnancy or by self-induced abortions. But after meeting him, she became aware that another advantage of birth control was that it liberated women from their fear of pregnancy so that they could enjoy sex more fully.

As a mentor, Havelock deepened her understanding of sex. They met twice a week at the British Museum and he directed her reading about the many techniques used to avoid pregnancy in various cultures since ancient times. As she learned about how freedom from fear of pregnancy contributed to the liberation of women, she came to realize sex was more than procreation; it also had a play function. This was a new concept for women, who had been for countless generations indoctrinated against the joy of sex.

Margaret became so liberated herself that, like many men, she took as many as three lovers at a time, including the famous author H. G. Wells. Although multiple sexual relationships always had been common for men, they were not then common for women—and it was generally the fear of pregnancy that prevented them.

It has been hypothesized that Havelock Ellis also became Margaret's lover, but there is no real evidence for this. What is clear, however, is that she greatly admired him: "[Ellis] belongs to all mankind. I define him as one who radiates truth, energy, and beauty. I see him in a realm above and beyond the shouting and the tumult."

Margaret was highly esteemed by others, including

Françoise Delisle, Ellis's lover for almost twenty years. A book she wrote about their relationship was dedicated to Margaret, for "Margaret's love of Havelock."

Margaret divorced William in 1920. She kept his name and blamed the marriage's failure on his having pressured her into it before she was ready, on his being a spendthrift, and on the fact that they had grown apart in their interests. Indeed, she was moving in other intellectual circles. When she first went to Japan to lecture, for example, her cospeakers were Albert Einstein, Bertrand Russell, and H. G. Wells.

Two years after her divorce, which William fought bitterly, Margaret married J. Noah Slee, a wealthy advertising promoter who, among other things, invented the concept of painting advertisements on country barns. He was sixty-four, she was forty-three; and she insisted upon a prenuptial agreement allowing her to live her own life with no questions asked. Margaret had a private apartment in their home, and her husband was required to phone her even for a dinner date. Fully aware that everything else took second place in her life, he encouraged her work and often provided financial backing for her clinics and conferences on birth control.

Margaret created the phrase *birth control* and opened many birth control clinics, which were often closed by authorities. Time and again she was imprisoned for distributing information and then released. Eventually the climate began to shift toward acceptance. Family planning received some positive attention, and worldwide conferences were held.

In 1923 Margaret organized the Clinical Research Bureau to dispense information and contraceptives. She also organized the American Birth Control League and published numerous books and journals, including *The Birth Control Review* and *The Woman Rebel*. She advised women: "Look the world in the face with a go-to-hell look in the eyes." She believed strongly that with an important idea it was absolutely necessary to speak and act in defiance of convention.

This rebel with a cause lived by her own advice until she died at the age of eighty-seven.

Margaret was frequently asked, "How do you fit birth control into a world in which dictators are clamoring for more and more people?" She answered by using the metaphor of a relay race in which each member of a team runs part of the distance. In Ancient Greece, where the Olympic games began about 700 B.C., each runner had to carry a torch and deliver it undimmed to his successor. Margaret saw herself as this kind of a torch bearer, running a race against time with others on her "team" who were concerned about personal health, family well-being, and, in the final analysis, the welfare of the community at large.

When asked why she had taken on so much responsibility herself, when physicians and scientists had more knowledge, she replied, "I found myself in the position of one who had discovered a house was on fire, and it was up to me to shout the warning."

Margaret's lifelong commitment to her cause may have made her controversial, but it did not make her less attractive to men. In spite of her proclivity for multiple lovers, J. Noah Slee praised her: "She is the adventure of my life. Nothing interesting ever happened to me before."

WHAT'S IN A NAME?

Aurore Lucie Dupin, a.k.a. George Sand (1804–1876)

A prolific writer who wore men's clothes, used a man's name, and had many lovers, including composer Frédéric Chopin, George Sand was acclaimed as one who helped begin the human revolution as many of her heroes were peasants or workmen. Along with her desire for equality for women, she wanted to expand people's economic options in a society divided by "haves" and "have-nots."

An unconventional woman, she lived life fully, as few people do. She explained: "I never asked myself why I wanted this or that. The inner me always proudly answered: Because I want it. That said everything."

Her decision to become a professional writer was the practical result of a failed marriage; she wanted to support herself. Her fluent pen produced over one hundred plays and novels, many of which were idealized and erotic romances. She also wrote over a thousand letters, usually many pages long. By the time she was thirty-two, twenty-four volumes of her works had been published. Less than twenty years later, the collection had grown to one hundred and twelve volumes. The task of collecting her letters is still ongoing. Aurore seldom needed to correct or revise. "I write," she said, "as others might do gardening."

Born Amandine Aurore Lucie Dupin, she became famous using the masculine pseudonym George Sand on her novel, *Indiana*, which carried the message that women should not remain in unhappy marriages. At that time, using a female name would have doomed her to obscurity, so she coauthored a novel with one of her many lovers, Jules Sandeau. When their relationship broke up, she borrowed part of his last name to create her own new pen name.

George somehow fit Aurore, who left her first husband out of boredom and enjoyed shocking French country society by smoking cigars in public and occasionally appearing in pants and a top hat. In Paris, wearing men's clothing at that time was not as quixotic as it might seem, for it was impossible to keep long gowns clean in the dirty streets. She was also safer when walking the streets alone disguised as a man. Furthermore, she could get inexpensive theater seats in sections where women were not allowed to sit.

Aurore learned independence in childhood in a country house at Nohant, 180 miles south of Paris. This house belonged to her grandmother, an enlightened aristocrat who allowed her great freedom. Her father was a French army officer who was seldom home and who died suddenly at age thirty when flung from a horse. At the time, Aurore was only four. Her mother, Sophie, was impetuous, uneducated, and disliked by Aurore's grandmother because of her lower-class background.

To support herself, Sophie had gone to Paris to become a dressmaker and signed papers that gave her mother-in-law custody of Aurore. Although Sophie visited her daughter monthly—sometimes weekly—she was never welcomed by her mother-in-law. Aurore remained torn between her love for both. As the older woman lay dying after a stroke, she bound Aurore to her with her last words: "You are losing your best friend."

In some sense that was true; her grandmother encouraged her to think for herself and provided excellent tutors. By the age of four, Aurore could read; by five, she could write and never stopped writing. When she attended a convent school in Paris, she fantasized about becoming a nun but was so rebellious that she was not encouraged to take up this vocation. Studying Rousseau, she became more liberal, trying to make sense out of her Catholic background and her intellectual quest.

After her grandmother's death, Aurore made a marriage of convenience to establish some stability and to avoid living with her mother. But matrimony with Casimir Dudevant, a robust man who preferred hunting to intelligent conversation, was dull and unsatisfying. Out of sheer boredom, she became infatuated with a romantic intellectual, Aurélian de Sèze. In deference to the strict moral codes they adhered to, they wrote many passionate, idealistic letters, intending for their relationship to go no further. But one day passion took over, and Aurore's husband found her in Aurélian's arms.

To placate her husband she signed an eighteen-page document, pledging to keep her relationship with Aurélian entirely platonic. In exchange for this pledge, she asked her husband to become better educated, to study philosophy and languages, to read books she recommended and to discuss their theories. She also asked him to listen to her when she played the piano.

Their marriage survived for several years under this unusual arrangement, until Aurore found a letter that was supposed to be opened only after her husband's death and discovered how enraged he continued to be over the situation. Later he pulled out a gun and, in front of their children and guests, threatened to kill her. Eventually, she left him. After all, she wrote, "To live with a man who neither respects nor trusts me is as useless as trying to bring a corpse back to life."

The separation was most unpleasant, and numerous times they went to court about money, property, and the custody of their children, Maurice and Solange, whom she loved dearly and who were often in boarding schools or with nurses. Finally, her husband was awarded half of her inherited income, while Aurore was able to keep her grandmother's country estate at Nohant, where she had spent much of her youth. This legal process was so painful that Aurore vowed never to marry again. Like her mother, she had to support herself, so she went to Paris.

Her first job as a journalist required that she be concise instead of lavish with words, as she preferred. Frustrated with this restriction, Aurore went her own way. Later, when she became famous, her autobiography, *Story of My Life*, was published in column form—though not in journalistic style —in one hundred and thirty-eight installments in a Paris newspaper.

Throughout her career, her writing was often controversial. *Indiana*, her first novel was a plea for women's rights, a scandalous idea at the time. *Lelia*, an allegorical novel, brought her more fame, as it reflected the widespread spiritual search of the time to find God and the truth. The church banned it; the public loved it.

The premise of many of her novels was that of a competent woman attracted to a less than competent man—in many ways her own story. Aurore was, after all, constantly attracted to intellectuals who appeared to need nurturing.

At an early period in her life, Aurore had an important relationship with Marie Dorval, a well-known actress. It may have been the equivalent of an adolescent crush, or it may have been a lesbian relationship. Whichever it was, it was possessive and lasted for years, with many effusive love letters exchanged.

> I feel that I love you with a heart made young again by you. If it is a dream, as everything else I have desired in life, do not wake me from it too quickly. It does me so much good! Good-bye, great and beautiful one, no matter what, I will see you this evening.

These kinds of letters, however, made Marie's lover jealous. He claimed that even if the relationship wasn't sexual it could easily become so, and he finally forbade Marie to have further contact with Aurore.

In spite of her idealization of Marie and extravagant expression of distress when they could not be together, Aurore had other lovers. One was poet Alfred de Musset, her first lover to summon her maternal instincts by declaring that he loved her like a child loves a mother. This appeal so endeared him to Aurore that she was overwhelmed with grief when he later rejected her in favor of gambling and other women. She begged him to continue their romance: "I will suffer as much as you wish, but let me go to you sometimes, if only once a week, for the sake of the tears, the kisses, which bring me back to life."

Despite her despair, Aurore at this time not only had

another lover but was also working at reconciliation with her husband for the sake of their children. Each of these relationships failed.

Aurore, now well known as George, lived in a hotel that served as a center for many artists, writers, and musicians. It was through composer Franz Liszt and his mistress that Aurore was invited to meet Frédéric Chopin. Chopin was not eager to meet George Sand; her reputation had put him off. He was twenty-six, fastidious, conventional, and frail, with a constant cough. George was thirty-two, avant-garde, and decidedly eccentric. When they first met at a party, her conversation was philosophically oriented, while his tended toward light chitchat.

At their second meeting, however, she fell under his spell, cast no doubt by the music he and Liszt played together. Although she smoked cigars throughout the evening, she also wore a highly becoming Turkish dress. Chopin remained unimpressed. George, meanwhile, as usual had another lover.

When their relationship finally took hold, it grew slowly. Chopin insisted that they keep their passion hidden because of his strong sense of propriety. In fact, even when they lived together in Nohant, her large country mansion, it was with the pretense of his being a houseguest. Eventually, his constant ill health helped cause the relationship to evolve into one more of mother and child. George, in fact, often spoke of him in those terms.

Unlike others, Chopin called her Aurore and not George, and she gradually gave up some of her boisterousness and her custom of traveling in men's clothes. When in Paris, they maintained separate apartments in the same block, although they spent much of their time together and were mutually helpful. He listened to and commented on her writing, and she did the same with his music. For three months of each year they would return to Nohant, where they could concentrate more intensely on their work than in Paris, where both were interrupted by a steady stream of visitors.

Chopin composed spontaneously, then analyzed his work over and over again, pacing the floor, weeping, smashing pens, rewriting, sometimes spending six weeks on a single page. In contrast, Aurore was more easily satisfied, often with her first draft. In one evening she could complete some eight or ten pages.

During her ten years with Chopin, Aurore became deeply interested in politics, in the working class, and in the revolution of 1848, which brought the overthrow of the constitutional monarchy. She was also attracted to a liberal priest whose theories served as a foundation for her own philosophy of equality of the sexes. While this priest had no objection to her using his ideas, he became utterly horrified when she extrapolated from them to affirm divorce as a sensible solution to an unhappy marriage. He became even more offended when she called a current lover, Pierre Leroux, "a new Plato, a new Christ."

When Aurore's novels began to take a metaphysical vein, they were not as well received as her earlier romantic novels. This disturbed both Aurore and her publisher, who then suggested she write a play. *Cosima*, her first, was loudly booed. Without royalties, problems concerning time, energy, and money increased. As Aurore's income dropped along with her book sales, Chopin's grew with each concert. So did his craving for luxuries and adulation. He became greatly jealous of Aurore's other lovers and the time she spent with them, despite the fact that she served more as a mother than a lover to him.

Contributing to their problems were Chopin's deteriorating health and the fact that their separate apartments in Paris consumed not only money but time and energy as they traveled back and forth. Staying at sprawling Nohant would have been even more costly, requiring as it did a relatively large number of servants to manage it when they were in residence. The relationship became strained; their work suffered. But the coup de grace came when Chopin was found flirting with Aurore's daughter. He defended it as "light family behavior," but Maurice, Aurore's son, protested; it was undermining the family. Their attachment, much to Chopin's distress, was severed.

Meanwhile, Aurore had begun to read and write social history, which was not warmly received. Her writing reflected her sympathy for the poor, her love for the countryside around her grandmother's estate, and her belief that love could overcome obstacles of social convention and class. George had became so radical and outspoken that she was in physical danger. Her publisher decided not to publish anything further that had themes of the working class versus the bourgeoisie. Instead, he persuaded her to continue writing the kinds of novels that had first made her famous—and that had made them both money. When she did this, she regained her popularity. In addition to her novels, she wrote ten plays in the next ten years, six of which were successful. Aurore also took yet another lover and became a very affectionate grandmother.

To the working class she was the "Goddess of the Poor," arguing as she did for their right to free education and the opportunity to work. In her honor it was written. "She still fights triumphantly against the retrograde ideas of the past. We align ourselves anew with her in the name of liberty."

George Sand's lifetime commitment to women's independence and other social issues brought a touching eulogy at her death, especially when Victor Hugo claimed the issues surrounding women's rights were proved by her genius. Because of this, he said, the problems that contributed to the French Revolution could be considered finally finished, and the human revolution could begin—equality between the sexes was coming to the fore. He then added: "A great woman was needed. A woman had to prove that she could have all our manly qualities without losing her angelic ones: that she could be strong without ceasing to be gentle: George Sand is that proof."

WHEN ONE IS GAY

Elsa Lanchester (1902–1986)

Many women have known heartbreak in marriage and have chosen to stay married in spite of it. The union of actor Charles Laughton, perhaps best known for his Henry VIII, and eminent actress Elsa Lanchester, best known for her role in *The Bride of Frankenstein*, lasted thirty-five years—despite the fact that he was homosexual. It lasted, she said, because there was "loyalty to the idea of marriage, there was mutual protection, and tolerance and respect."

Elsa was a brilliant actress, comedienne, and dancer, much acclaimed by critics; and her stage and film career continued for almost seventy years.

In private life, Elsa and Charles always had a deep friendship. They enjoyed art, country living, frequent long walks, and quiet dinners together. Both were totally committed to the theater and often performed together. Their marriage of minds was based on mutual interests, not on romance and sex. She had lovers, all of whom were men. He too had lovers, all of whom were also men. Elsa protected him carefully, and few knew of his sexual proclivities, only that he was an actor of genius.

Much of Elsa's life was marked by a strong spirit of independence. She came by this trait quite naturally, as her parents, Edith Lanchester and James Sullivan, were radical socialists. Her father was an outspoken Irish policeman; her mother was well educated and secretary to the daughter of Karl Marx. When young Edith had announced her intention of living with James outside the bounds of matrimony, her father (Elsa's grandfather) had her dragged to an asylum and committed as insane. The cause: "over-education"! It soon became clear, however, that Edith was fully sane, despite being well educated, so she was released.

Elsa retained the same independent spirit as her parents.

Her childhood with them was exciting, to say the least, as they deliberately confronted and antagonized authorities on many occasions. They often moved in the middle of the night to avoid legal entanglements, such as those resulting from nonpayment of rent. Sometimes, when camping illicitly on private property, they had to move before sunrise so they would not be apprehended. Six of their moves were made to avoid having Elsa vaccinated; her mother believed that government-ordered vaccination intruded on a family's free choice.

As a child, Elsa's unmarried parents along with her flaming red hair, deeply dimpled chin, short blunt nose, and poorly homemade clothes often brought her ridicule. But this did not deter her. At age eleven she won a scholarship to study dance with Isadora Duncan in Paris.

Later, back in England, she served as a teacher's assistant, then supported herself teaching dance to poor children and helping them perform some of the children's classics in what was called the Children's Theatre. This endeavor almost became self-supporting until it was closed by officials who accused Elsa of exploiting the children financially.

Next, Elsa opened a nightclub, the Cave of Harmony, with several friends. This group became known for their impromptu parodies, and Elsa began to receive considerable positive attention from drama critics. Well-known artists and writers as Aldous Huxley and Evelyn Waugh began to frequent the club, and H. G. Wells wrote three plays especially for her.

Because her acting did not bring in enough money to pay the rent, Elsa also modeled for painters. During this period she had numerous sexual affairs, none of which brought about much involvement. Her advice to herself at this time: "Keep each person separate in your heart. Don't have two sex partners going at the same time. And don't ever join a conversation about something you know nothing about."

Elsa described herself as being cerebral, resilient, and survival oriented. She also had many close, lifetime friends.

Charles Laughton came into her life when she was twenty-five and they were rehearsing a play together. He was twenty-eight, plump, shy, and unattractive, but he also had the reputation of being a genius. Overweight, insecure, and homely even as a child, in the theater he came into his magnificent own. English born, trained at the Royal Academy of Dramatic Art, he could play exceedingly diverse roles on stage or in film. Anyone who has seen him as Captain Bligh in *Mutiny on the Bounty* or as Henry VIII in *The Private Life of Henry VIII* cannot help but recall his magnetism and power.

Elsa and Charles's first dates were simple, often consisting of very long walks in the country in almost total silence. One evening on the way home after a party, they suddenly recognized their mutual attraction. Elsa recalls the moment: "When it came time to say goodnight, we awkwardly and embarrassingly kissed in a rather conventional way. Then, staring at each other in utter surprise, we clung together."

They would have preferred to live together without marriage, as her parents had. That, however, would have embarrassed his mother, who was very ambitious for Charles and thought it would interfere with his success. So they got married—and his mother and brother both accompanied them on their honeymoon.

Elsa and Charles had been married only two years when he tearfully confessed that he was homosexual, attracted to many young men and deeply ashamed about it. This confession was precipitated by the arrest of a young man for loitering around their apartment. The youth told the police he was there to collect the money Charles had promised him on the previous night for sexual favors.

On hearing this news, Elsa became emotionally numb and psychosomatically deaf. For a week she "couldn't hear anything more"; the information was simply too painful. When her hearing returned, they never discussed that particular episode again.

Although they enjoyed their intellectual and professional lives together, Charles also told Elsa he was socially comfortable only with his "own kind," and he continued to see a series of men. Marriage protected him from the public censure of that time, when homosexuality was considered to be a crime. Instead of a life of romance, then, their partnership segued into a lifelong friendship, a meeting of two brilliant minds. Over the years Elsa gradually accepted his male lovers, though Charles continued to feel guilty about them. She explained their adjustment: "Charles needed his own kind of freedom and had a certain amount of it through the protection of our marriage. . . . I enjoyed freedom, too. So, in a way we both had what we wanted."

Sadly for Elsa, Charles's self-centeredness resulted in his usually putting his own interests first. For example, an avid and discriminating art collector, he considered his taste to be above reproach. Once Elsa bought herself a mask of a warrior's head, which she treasured greatly. But when she was on tour, Charles sold it without permission, in order to buy some terra-cotta figures he fancied. Elsa never quite forgave him this presumption. She eventually got over her anger, but never recovered from the hurt. In the interests of self-protection, she vowed to never again fall in love with an object so much that its possession would be critical.

One of the key figures in Elsa and Charles's marriage was Paul Gregory, who became Charles's manager. He booked Charles for innumerable "readings," usually of the classics. These one-man shows became a new form of entertainment. Those who listened to his readings of Shakespeare, Charles Dickens, and Walt Whitman did not forget them. And the way he read the Bible aloud was soul-shaking.

As manager, Paul handled the publicity and collected the

money for these performances. He insisted on collecting it during intermission, in case Charles's sponsor reneged on his financial obligations. Although he also booked Elsa on some tours and appreciated her great talent, it was Charles who completely mesmerized him.

Both Elsa and Paul supervised Charles's "road men" lovers, and she often became upset if the "road men" did not sufficiently cater to Charles's inclinations, making it clear in no uncertain terms what was expected of them. Although Paul was not one of Charles's lovers, he and Elsa were often in conflict, and eventually the two men parted in anger.

Throughout their long, unusual marriage, this extraordinary pair whenever possible lived in a house in the country so they could walk. Their dearly loved first house, for instance, had four trees growing through the roof and was set on thirty-two acres. They also continued to help each other in the development of their theatrical roles and in rehearsing them.

In addition to acting on stage and in films for many years, Elsa loved to sing and dance so much that even in dirty, poorly lit theatres it made her feel alive and clean, "like a butterfly coming out of a dirty old chrysalis." She particularly favored the sophisticated Turnabout Theatre in Hollywood.

In exchange for her acting, the more than fifty songs that were written for her by composer Forman Brown became her property. She also played unique characters developed specifically for her talents. Three popular roles were without glamour—a kitchen maid, a sleazy housewife, and a slum brat. Others were more glamorous, many comical. All of them delighted her audiences.

Charles's guilt about his homosexuality persisted until his death. Toward the end, he became both psychologically and physically ill, and eventually he died of cancer. Widowed at sixty, Elsa sold their huge art collection and started to build a new life. In her eighties, she was still intellectual, resilient, and a survivor, living in a house with a lovely garden in Santa Monica, California. She died of pneumonia at age eighty-four.

   With the kind of relationship Elsa had with Charles, one might wonder, did she love him, or did she just love the excitement of sharing the theater with him? Perhaps the answer is best found in the way she explained the effect of his death on her: "When Charles was alive, I always sang in the bathtub and went upstairs two steps at a time . . . but after Charles died it never did occur to me to dash around the house."

TWO WOMEN IN LOVE

Gertrude Stein (1874–1946)

Gertrude Stein was a successful poet, critic, playwright, and novelist whose unique style established her as one of America's most heady, oft-disputed writers.

   Often described as a genius, she wrote in very unorthodox ways. In exploring the traditional rules of grammar, parts of speech, punctuation, and the sound of words, she developed her own rules and broke through the barriers of convention. Who else, for example, had ever said anything like, "Rose is a rose is a rose is a rose." In this famous, often-quoted line, Gertrude said she "caressed completely caressed and addressed a noun." In addition to her controversial repetition of words for emphasis, much of Gertrude's work was not punctuated except for periods, which, she said, "had a life of their own and could be used almost anywhere in a sentence and be happy."

   Question marks were to her "revolting," and commas "servile." She had a particular antipathy for commas: "A comma by helping you along holding your coat for you and putting on your shoes keeps you from living your life as actively as you should lead it and to me . . . the use of them was positively degrading." She often reacted to overelaboration by oversimplifications and constantly experimented with new ways to use language. After her death, readers and literary critics strongly aligned themselves in opposite camps. Some couldn't stand her; others saw her writing as a language experiment that worried the reader.

Gertrude lived in an open lesbian partnership with Alice B. Toklas, her friend and lover for twenty-nine years. In this unique, same-sex relationship, certain roles were expected and performed. Gertrude most often assumed a traditional male role and Alice that of a traditional female hostess. As a leader in avant-garde literary and art circles in Paris, Gertrude often entertained talented literary and artistic friends, while Alice was designated to talk to their wives.

> The wives of geniuses I have sat with. I have sat with so many. I have sat with wives who were not wives, of geniuses who were not real geniuses. I have sat with real wives of geniuses who were not real geniuses. I have sat with wives of geniuses, of near geniuses, of would-be geniuses, in short I have sat very often and very long with many wives and wives of many geniuses.

Born in Allegheny, Pennsylvania, of German-Jewish parents, Gertrude lived as a young child in Vienna and Paris because her father wanted his children to have broad horizons. The youngest of five, she was greatly indulged. When it developed that Gertrude spoke only French and German, her parents returned to the United States so that their children could learn to speak English without an accent.

Growing up in Oakland, California, Gertrude began to read extensively—everything from Charles Darwin's and

Aldous Huxley's works on evolution to the *Congressional Record*. She wolfed down the works of many of the great British writers and at age eight tried to write a tragedy in the style of Shakespeare. One of her frequent childhood fears was that she might run out of books to read. Later, when studying in the British Museum, she realized this was unlikely to occur.

Most important to Gertrude's childhood was her relationship with her brother, Leo. She followed wherever he went and adored him until well into adult life. In her book *Everybody's Biography*, she described this relationship:

> It is better if you are the youngest girl in the family to have a brother two years older, because that makes everything a pleasure to you, you go everywhere and do everything while he does it all for and with you which is a pleasant way to have everything happen to you.

Gertrude's mother died when she was fourteen, but the most profound effect of this occurrence turned out to be that her father then became "more of a bother than he had been." She was seventeen when he died of severe alcoholism. Always honest, she declared after his death, "Our life without a father began to be a very pleasant one."

An independent scholar all her life, Gertrude never graduated from high school. She attended Radcliffe and studied under William James, the philosopher and psychologist, who had a tremendous influence on her writing, particularly with regard to his theories about stream of consciousness. James was her favorite and most important mentor, and he often praised her independent thinking.

Once, Gertrude was to have taken a written examination for one of James's classes. Instead of doing so, she turned in a paper that was blank except for the comment, "I am so sorry but really I do not feel a bit like an examination today."

He gave her the highest grade in the course and sent her a postcard that read, "Dear Miss Stein, I understand perfectly how you feel, I often feel like that myself."

After graduating from Radcliffe, Gertrude began medical school at Johns Hopkins but became "bored." After two years, when she had not prepared for an examination and was confronted by an instructor about this, she dropped out. By temperament, Gertrude was unwilling to comply with other people's expectations and often chose to be deliberately controversial.

In 1903 she and Leo, who had become an established art critic, set themselves up in an apartment in Paris and started holding Saturday-night open houses. At first Gertrude mainly listened to the interchange of ideas. But later she became the center of attention as her brilliance was recognized. She also sponsored numerous writers such as Ernest Hemingway, F. Scott Fitzgerald, and Sherwood Anderson. Artists of many backgrounds came to the open houses for art displays, literary readings, and discussions. Among the luminaries Gertrude encouraged and became friends with were the modern painters Matisse and Picasso. She exhibited their art, bought their works when no one else would, and encouraged others to do likewise.

Leo became jealous of her popularity and was critical of her writing. He felt justified when her first book, *Three Lives*, was turned down by several publishers. Finally Gertrude self-published it through Grafton Press, a vanity press in New York. But the publisher could not imagine how anyone could write English as she did and sent someone to Paris to determine if she was totally ignorant. She told them not to worry; it was, after all, being published at her own expense. And she kept on writing in her own style.

As Gertrude developed more of her own power and identity and idolized Leo's less, he became threatened, and they finally parted in anger. The art that they had jointly purchased was divided into "his" and "hers," after which they severed all connection. Once, when passing each other on the street, they acknowledged each other with only a single formal nod.

Gertrude's intimate relationship with Alice B. Toklas had begun in 1907, while she and Leo still lived together. Alice described their first meeting:

> She held my complete attention, as she did for all the many years I knew her until her death, and all the empty ones since. She was a golden brown presence, burned by the Tuscan sun and with a golden glint in her warm brown hair.

After Leo and Gertrude separated, the two women shared an apartment until Gertrude's death. Like many romantic couples, they praised each other extravagantly, worried about whether their partner's love would last, and called each other by private endearing names. To Alice, Gertrude was "Baby Woojums," and to Gertrude, Alice was "little dove" and "dear wife."

Both wore loose-fitting suits with long skirts that were comfortable but certainly not flattering. Gertrude's one delight in dressing was a collection of some thirty hand-embroidered vests that were once exhibited in the Museum of Modern Art. During World War I she drove back and forth to the front lines to give food and gifts to the wounded and hospitalized. One of her great appeals to the soldiers was her hearty laughter. Even during World War II, when the Nazis occupied Paris and she had to walk seven miles every other day to get food, she maintained her joy of life.

The *Autobiography of Alice B. Toklas* was Gertrude's first popular piece. Originally she had encouraged Alice to write her own autobiography, but Alice delayed and delayed, so Gertrude stepped in. Actually, it is more an autobiography of Gertrude than of Alice, not withstanding the title. Gertrude explained this by drawing comparisons to Defoe, who invented the autobiography of Robinson Crusoe. Gertrude's other writings included seventy-seven plays, which she said were to be performed, not read silently. Hardly understandable if read to oneself, they magically came alive on stage through the human voice. Once asked why she didn't write the way she talked, Gertrude responded, "Why should I? Do you think that Shakespeare talked in blank verse?"

Alice was the quieter of the two, involved in all of Gertrude's activities, editing her books and often responsible for planning their regular open houses. Once when hosting a group of painters, Alice arranged for each to be seated opposite his own painting. The group was a happy one, and no one noticed how this pleasure had been arranged until Matisse remarked on it when leaving. He told Alice it was proof that she was wicked, and they had a good laugh.

Gertrude's death came suddenly from cancer. Although she was given no hope, she insisted upon surgery. On her way to the operating room her last words were, "What is the answer?" When no one responded, she asked, "Then what is the question?" Gertrude never came out of anesthesia, and Alice remained alone for the next twenty years.

In one of Gertrude's plays, "The Five Georges," which includes an abstract conversation among five people all named George, someone says, "Forget me as well as forget me not." Alice did not forget. So that others would also remember, she wrote *Going on Alone*, in which she affirmed, "The past is not gone—nor is Gertrude."

Throughout her life, Gertrude saved thousands of letters from friends. Many were addressed to Gertrude and Alice in recognition of their relationship as friends and lovers. One sent to Alice on Gertrude's death recalled Gertrude's personality and deep integrity: "She has been one of the few authentic experiences in my life. . . . Everything was alive in her, her soul, her mind, her heart, her senses. Those fits of laughter . . . swept away all nonsense and all sadness—all silly ideas and dull objections."

IN SEARCH OF PREHISTORY
Mary Leakey (1913–)

While studying human origins through cave art, fossils, and
skeletons, Mary Leakey fell deeply in love with another ar-
chaeologist, Louis Leakey, who sought out and demanded
the spotlight, even when it rightfully belonged to her.

In 1959 in Tanzania, Mary found a hominid skull that
became known as "the missing link" in the *New York Times*.
On finding the highly significant fossil, she shouted, "I've
found him—found our man!" In addition to this extraordinary discovery and newspaper publicity, Mary contributed
to many scientific journals as a leading authority on prehistoric cultures. Yet much of the credit for these accomplishments went to Louis, because of his charismatic, flamboyant
style.

Even when Mary was desperately unhappy and her marriage to Louis was falling apart, she revealed little about it.
What was known was that her love for him died when he
had a series of affairs with very young women, and that her
betrayal was heightened and her respect shattered when
Louis, excavating in the Mojave Desert of California, sought
to promote himself along with carelessly made, erroneous,
unscientific conclusions.

As a child, Mary lived a happy and stimulating life. Her
father and grandfather were both successful landscape painters. Mary's extensive traveling in early years was due to her
father's annual painting trips, and she claims her remarkable
drawing skill was genetically inherited. Although one of her
ancestors on her mother's side was famous in the field of
prehistoric archeology and her cousin was a professor in the
field, Mary attributed her interest not to genetics but to the
fact that she simply enjoyed it. She also appreciated the family
willingness to express new, sometimes unwelcome views.

Her father, who was particularly interested in Egypt,

lived there on a houseboat for four years until Mary's birth, after which the family returned to England. Mary's mother also enjoyed art and travel and was fluent in several languages. Her linguistic ease helped greatly in their travels and encouraged Mary to also become fluent.

It was in France, traveling with her father, that she first was attracted to archeology, as she viewed the famous prehistoric cave paintings from the Cro-Magnon period. She was only eleven, but this experience with cave art and with those who taught her to understand it were focal points of her education. So were her trips to Stonehenge and the Neolithic excavations near her home in England.

At thirteen, her adored father died, and her mother became more active in her life. Money was scarce. Mary spent many hours observing animals in the wild, as well as caring for their many house pets. Formal education was neither interesting nor particularly useful, and she had little success in either of the two convent schools she attended, despite her brilliance. When Mary decided she wanted to study archeology at Oxford, she was turned down because of her educational deficiencies. She wrote: "I never passed a single school exam, and clearly never would, and there was accordingly no way in which I could become a candidate for entrance to any university to study archeology or anything else."

Being rejected by the university did not quench the fire in Mary's heart for archeology, so she creatively designed her own way to study it. She attended lectures, assisted in the excavation of archeological sites, and produced technical illustrations of the objects that were uncovered. It was her skilled drawing that attracted Louis Leakey to her and led to their romance and marriage. She was twenty; he was ten years older. It was not love at first sight. He was a well-known archeologist and author and was already married, albeit unhappily. He was also a conceited womanizer and accused—by even his parents—of self-glorification and love of the limelight.

Initially, he was interested in Mary solely as a potential illustrator for his book, *Adam's Ancestors*. But as they met more frequently, discussing his book and her illustrations, their intellectual and physical attraction grew. Mary, warned against getting romantically involved with Louis by both her mother and one of his close professional friends, nonetheless plunged ahead. An intense attraction flared between them as they worked together at various archeological sites in England.

When he returned to Africa, Mary followed him, once more against her mother's advice. Louis loved Africa. Born of missionary parents in Kenya and educated in England, he returned there every chance he got and often spoke of himself as a "white African."

At age thirteen Louis had been initiated into the Kiskuyu tribe, a warlike people. He had then built a three-room Kiskuyu hut and had gone home only for meals. After reading paleontology of the Neolithic period, he decided archeology was to be his life's work, and he went to England to prepare for it. In England he was criticized for his affection toward the Kenyans, although in Africa he was applauded for speaking the Kiskuyu language and being able to "think black."

From the first moment Mary saw Kenya, there were two loves in her life: Louis, from whom she would tolerate almost anything; and East Africa, with its wildness and beauty. Being chased by a rhino when she first arrived only intensified this love, and she began to study the animals and the cave paintings abounding there.

Louis and Mary returned to England, where his bitter divorce became final. (Afterward, he did not see his children for many years.) In spite of widespread disapproval he married Mary, and the two repaired to Kenya, where they established their home base. In time, their relationship evolved into more of a warm, professional partnership than a continuing romance. During their thirty years together they excavated many sites, and discovered art, prehistoric household objects, ancient fossils, and skeletons. They worked hard but were usually short of money for even the simplest necessities of life.

In 1948 Mary made her first major discovery of bone fragments that she thought was the skull of a human-like creature who had lived about 17 million years ago. She named it Pro-Consul. The "consul" part of the name referred to a chimp at the London zoo; the prefix "pro" was by way of saying that it preceded the apes. Originally, the pro-consul was thought to be some kind of hominid, a primate of the family Hominidac of which the modern Homo sapiens is the only extant species.

However, the skull Mary found turned out to be more like that of an ape. To date, the relationship of the pro-consul to the early, upright apes of four million years ago is not known. But finding this skull was a major event in paleontology, so Mary and Louis celebrated the finding by conceiving their fourth and last child.

Of their four children, one, a daughter, died at only three months. The boys, Jonathan, Richard, and Philip, always accompanied their parents on their excavations. They enjoyed themselves as children do, playing, swimming, and fishing, but as time went on they had periods of estrangement. During one such period, Richard and Philip did not speak to each other for ten years. Yet when Richard required a kidney transplant, Philip donated one of his, putting his own life at risk.

As Mary had done in her youth, her children collected many pets—including antelopes that would lie under their beds; eagle owls that would bring them small mice and snakes that Philip would pretend to eat; and genets, small nocturnal animals that would jump on their sleeping keepers in order to be fed. The Leakey children also had a cheetah and often some hyraxes, small furry animals that, like guinea pigs, are affectionate and like to sleep curled around their owners' necks, preferring to use their owners' toilets but not needing training to do so.

Throughout their years together, the Leakeys built their houses to accommodate their dogs' comings and goings. Mary was particularly fond of Dalmatians, to whom she dedicated her autobiography.

Violence became part of their life in the early 1950s with the brutal Mau Mau uprising in Kenya against the British. It lasted for four years, and the Leakeys were often in danger. The Kiskuyu tribe, to which Louis belonged, would not join the Mau Maus. Many were murdered, including Louis's cousin, who was buried alive.

Both at home and in camps, wild animals were also a threat. In her letters Mary mentions that she counted fifty-five rhinos on one occasion; at other times, leopards and lions often came uncomfortably close. To scare the rhinos and lions away, Mary would sometimes throw firecrackers; to frighten the leopards, she would beat on tin cans. At one time lions were so prolific around Nairobi that they disrupted a women's championship match by taking up residence in the Karen Country Golf Course.

For some years Louis was in charge of the museum in Nairobi, capital of Kenya. Part of the local folklore of the Luo group was that a whisker from a dead lion or lioness would protect women from the pain of childbirth. Understandably, the whiskers of lions in the museum were often secretly removed. Louis just as secretly would replace them with nylon whiskers, which were also removed from time to time.

Their work was given great impetus when, in 1959, Mary and Louis discovered a skull in the 30-mile Olduvai Gorge in Tanzania. They named the skull "Zinji." After this discovery, the National Geographic Society became financially involved in supporting and recording their discoveries of other hominids, including one that had been able to craft stone tools. In addition, Louis made popular yearly lecture trips to the United States to educate people and seek additional funding.

By 1968, Mary and Louis's marriage was disintegrating. Originally a couple who loved each other, their work, and their children, they became miserably unhappy. Each traveled in different directions, he to the United States and she to new archeological sites. Louis became increasingly arthritic, irritable, and irrational. He perceived his son Richard as a competitive threat for simply proceeding on his own course. At first Richard did not want to be in the same field as his parents and instead became a safari guide. However, when he found an Australopithecine jaw in 1963 while exploring northeast Tanzania, he decided to become an anthropologist. Since that time Richard has made numerous important discoveries in human evolution.

While Louis traveled, Mary usually remained at Olduvai, the center of their most important excavations, which by 1968 was becoming popular with tourists. Louis continued to travel, raise funds, and try to elicit hero worship. He also returned to his earlier sexual escapades, some with very young women, and not always discreetly. But despite the loss of romance, love, and respect, Mary would occasionally meet with him in family and professional contexts. She was capable of letting go of a dream and settling for reality.

Louis's health deteriorated. He suffered two heart attacks, several falls, and other physical problems. At the time of his last heart attack, he was being cared for in London by an old friend, the mother of Jane Goodall, who was well known for her study of chimpanzees and had once been Louis's secretary.

After his death, Mary went to Laetoli, thirty miles south of Olduvai Gorge, and continued her excavations. There she found footprints and trails of three hominids, plus a three-toed horse that had lived three-and-one-half million years ago. She was awarded an honorary doctorate at Oxford University, where she had once been rejected.

Her important discoveries revealed details of animals and the way people lived in the late Stone Age, including their clothes, jewelry, hairstyles, and bows and arrows. With her talent and skills in art, she recorded cave paintings at 186 different sites and greatly added to our knowledge of prehistoric times. Mary's greatness lay in her professionalism, her personal style of enjoying life and work, and her ability to cope with unhappiness and humiliation borne of her husband's behavior.

CONFRONTING A FREUDIAN MYTH

Karen Horney (1885–1952)

One of the first psychoanalysts to challenge Freudian theory and question the entire psychoanalytical establishment, Karen Horney objected to many of Freud's theories, including his idea that women have penis envy. Freud argued that girls "naturally" felt inferior and scarred without such a protuberance. Horney disagreed and said that that his argument stemmed from male narcissism. As a teaching analyst, she insisted on the need to explore the cultural determinants of a patient's life that may affect the development of personality, as well as the parental determinants. As she set about developing her own theory in the early 1900s, a new type of woman was emerging, one who sought freedom from the responsibilities of large families by having fewer children. This "new woman" was seeking educational opportunities, becoming more involved in social concerns, and beginning to move toward an independent career. Like Karen Horney, she was freer sexually and often chose to have affairs that did not interfere with her other interests.

As she observed her clients and other middle-class women, Karen concluded that a woman's primary inner conflict was between society's expectations of her to adore and serve men and the opportunities that were opening up for independence and careers. Early in her writings she made the point that culturally the male is always considered to be more important than the female, and this value system leads women to develop a sense of inferiority and a belief in the necessity to adapt to men's wishes. She also saw that women were beginning to rebel against this belief—directly, with the rejection of "feminine" roles; or indirectly, with frigidity, resentment, and envy.

Her insights into the social subordination of women were an important factor in that part of the feminist movement concerned with female psychology; her work started the liberation process of women from the psychoanalytical, restrictive, and sexist point of view. This liberation proceeded in spite of the psychoanalytical community, which stood firmly against her.

Like all theorists, Freud, the originator of psychoanalysis, was affected by his time and culture, and his perspective was rooted in studying hysteria in women. In contrast, Karen Horney's perspective developed in her study of character disorders. Understandably, in a new field without previous reference points, the early studies of each of these thinkers influenced their later theories. Karen disagreed with Freud's view that personality was essentially negative, that people were driven by sex, greed, and the death instinct. Her own view was that people were self-healing, especially if raised in a healthy environment, and that they have an innate drive toward growth and goodness despite their capacity for evil.

Karen was born near Hamburg, Germany, as Karen Danielson. She was the daughter of a rigidly religious, authoritarian Norwegian sea captain often gone for months at a time. When he married her mother, he was seventeen years her senior and a widower with four teenage children. Karen's mother, from an upper-class German-Dutch family, was very beautiful and well educated, but also narcissistic, emotionally dependent, and easily depressed and irritable.

Karen was a typical adolescent. She began keeping a diary at age thirteen and addressed it as if it were a friend, "Kitten." In it she expressed her religious doubts and her desire not to be hypocritical with prayer. She also criticized herself for having adolescent "crushes" on teachers. At the age of fourteen, she decided that she wanted to become a doctor, despite the fact that her father did not believe in education for women.

Even before she studied psychology, Karen employed self-analysis. She enjoyed reading erotic poetry and confided her sexual fantasies to her diary. At sixteen she wrote: "In my own imagination there is no spot on me that has not been kissed by a burning mouth. In my own imagination there is no depravity I have not tasted, to the dregs."

Seven years later she was told by her male psycho-analyst—no doubt after revealing the contents of her diary —that she really wanted to be a prostitute. After this, and with a certain amount of struggle, she terminated analysis.

Part of Karen's Horney's early interest in sex and sexual politics came from the frequent lengthy public debates on the subject of prostitution that she heard during her growing-up years in Hamburg, where prostitution was legal and protected by the police. The countermovement against it, however, was strong, and these opposing points of view, coupled with the rise of the "new morality" of women's freedom, impressed Karen so much that she determined that there were only two preeminent moral laws: "The first is 'Thou shalt not lie.' The second is 'Thou shalt free thyself from convention, from everyday morality.'"

At age eighteen Karen fell romantically in love for the first time. It lasted only two days, until she became aware that the object of her love was actually indifferent to her. Her second romance was with a poor music student whom her

family rejected because he was Jewish. Their meetings had to be clandestine, and they did not become sexually involved, since premarital sex was not acceptable in Germany at that time. Besides, she said, he didn't kiss well. During this time she became infatuated with yet another young man and felt pulled in opposite directions by the two of them. But the problem of whom to choose disappeared as she prepared to take the examinations for medical school. With little time or energy for either man, the romances burned out.

In 1906, Karen entered medical school at the University of Freiburg, where she first met Oskar Horney, or "Hornvich," who later become her husband. As one of the first women to study medicine, she was greatly discriminated against. (Of the 2,350 students at the university, only 58 were women.) A typical point of view, as expressed by her anatomy professor, was that women were physically weaker and had smaller hearts than men, were nervous and hysterical and therefore not fit to study medicine. Another critic claimed that if a woman knew about anatomy and could talk of sex without blushing, she would repel men altogether or at least leave them cold.

Despite this widespread cultural prejudice against educated women, Karen began to seriously consider women's emancipation and the various roles she played with different people, and to question who she really was if she didn't play those roles. In her letters to Oskar, who was away working on his Ph.D. in political science, she raised many questions about this. Open-minded and reliable, he supported her thinking. A man such as this who could understand her would, Karen thought, make a good husband: "*Because* you understand the good in me, I have a burning wish that you should know me wholly, wholly. Why is it so unutterably beneficial, the thought that somebody besides myself knows me?"

They married and settled in Berlin, the center of medicine for much of Europe. Karen decided to become a psy-

chiatrist and began her psychoanalysis with Karl Abraham. The experience was not satisfying and contributed to her independent thinking. This was at about the same time that two other famous analysts, Alfred Adler and Carl Jung, were breaking with the precepts of Freud.

Karen's real break from traditional Freudian thinking came after having three daughters within four years. She had enjoyed being pregnant and giving birth and began to argue that women may very well be not the least bit envious of men's penises, as Freud declared. Instead, she believed that penis worship was behind Freud's view of women and was a "reflection of the boy's narcissistic self-absorption when he first sees the naked female body." At this time in history, women were thought to be too "spiritual" to have sexual drives or, if they had them, were "above" expressing them Most people believed that women belonged in the home, where they would not threaten men in the marketplace or become independent of men's control or benevolence. At home, a woman was expected to be an indulgent, self-sacrificing wife who would humbly rely on her husband for making intellectual decisions. Karen disagreed with this set of values, and her disagreement prompted a major step in the development of the social psychology of women.

Karen saw women differently than other analysts and was not in any way inclined to conform to the cultural or psychological beliefs she did not share with them. She recognized the potential for uniqueness: "There is nothing more unbearable than the thought of disappearing quietly in the great mass of the average, nothing more fatal than the reproach of being told one is a nice, friendly, average person."

The marriage she and Oskar had was certainly not average. Throughout it they lived comfortably together but without much excitement between them, and both partners were sexually active with others.

Then postwar inflation hit Germany, and Oskar went bankrupt. He had a habit of making careless investments, and

she got tired of supporting them. They separated on friendly terms, but were not divorced until some years later.

At that time, Karen, forty years old with three daughters, had a heart on fire less for love than for her work at the Berlin Psychoanalytic Institute. The early analysts believed so strongly in their work that they sometimes paid their patients' streetcar fare to keep them coming.

Considering her many years engaging in self-analysis when writing in her diary, it seemed natural that Karen would begin to write for publication and to use her own experiences as part of her data. "The Problem of the Monogamous Ideal," the first of six papers on marital problems was no doubt stimulated by the failure of her own marriage. This paper was the beginning of her extensive writing on female psychology and issues of sexism.

In her early writings she supported Freud's theory that females have different instincts than males. Later she rejected this in favor of focusing on the cultural determinants that shape the "female" and "male" characters. Thus she became one of the first social psychologists to see personality disorders as responses to an unhealthy and repressive culture— a belief very different from that held by Freud.

She also perceived that infants needed care, love, and protection, and not only self-gratification. She believed a child's need for safety and satisfaction was more important than its desire for pleasure.

In 1932, Karen left Berlin to become assistant director of the Psychoanalytic Institute in Chicago, where she continued to develop her theory about anxiety being the genesis of neuroses. In *The Neurotic Personality of Our Time,* published in 1939, she claimed that when people feel anxious they either withdraw from others, move toward them, or move against them, and that all three are natural responses that can be integrated into the total personality.

Next, Karen moved to New York and became part of the New York Psychoanalytic Society. She also became in-

volved with many of the intellectuals from the New School
for Social Research and lectured to other professionals and
lay people who were seeking to understand themselves better.
Her audiences were intrigued by her direct style, in which
she presented information in a way that encouraged self-
therapy at a time when this was unheard of.

When her second book, *New Ways in Psychoanalysis,* was
published, it created an uproar, and the schism that had been
developing in the New York Psychoanalytic Society for some
time finally came into full effect. The title of the book inferred
moving beyond traditional Freudian theory, and this was not
acceptable to many colleagues. The rivalry and discord intensified; the faculty and student body split. Karen was discredited not only because she challenged some of Freud's basic
beliefs but also because she believed that students should have
some freedom in making their own choices within the academic curriculum. A few other faculty and students resigned
in protest against the action taken against her. With Karen
Horney as leader, the Association for the Advancement of
Psychoanalysis was established, as well as the American Institute of Psychoanalysis.

Further controversy grew over her work, and a small
study group formed composed of theorists interested in cultural determinants of personality. Among its members were
Erich Fromm, Margaret Mead, Ruth Benedict, and John Dol-
lard. Each week they met to discuss cultural issues and the
differences between individual traits and those common to
individuals in a particular culture.

Erich Fromm, as a member of this group, was allowed
to train and supervise analytic students. Some of the group
objected to this on the grounds that he was "only a lay analyst," having as he did no medical degree. Fromm resented
this devaluing of his work. As a result, the new association
split apart. This was a painful process, because he and Karen
had had a longtime intimate relationship—sexually and
intellectually—that dissolved in bitterness over this issue.

Karen, who did not believe in monogamous relationships, had affairs with a number of men who were highly intelligent and younger than herself. Fromm was her junior by fifteen years. She had known him in Germany when they were both studying psychoanalysis and became sexually involved when they both moved to Chicago and then to New York. Details of their romance are not well known, but the two of them were constantly together on weekends, and the papers and books they wrote at that time reflect their intense interaction.

Another famous man who was attracted to her was theologian Paul Tillich, who also emigrated from Germany to Chicago to New York and was a member of Karen's close-knit group. What few details we have on this relationship came, ironically, from his wife, Hannah, who surmised the two to be lovers (her husband often had affairs, and he and Karen were very close) and moreover harbored no ill feelings about it, since Karen's warmth, caring, and joyful spirit touched even her.

Always a dynamic thinker seeking to understand more of the truth, Karen, toward the end of her life, began to explore Zen Buddhism under the famous D. T. Suzuki. She died at sixty-seven of cancer. In spite of great pain, she did not lose her independent way of thinking, her love of life, and her capacity for happiness. One of her daughters described her as being "like a child in front of a Christmas tree, full of wonder, full of the joy of the moment."

CHOICES OF SEX AND GENDER

Although women's bodies function in similar ways, the choices they make about the ways they express themselves sexually are often different. The women in this chapter demonstrate the wide variety of choices.

It is no longer believed that a woman who is deeply

committed to a social cause will not be attractive to men. Margaret Sanger's social cause was to fight against parenthood by accident, violence, or rape in favor of *planned parenthood*. In countries such as India and Japan, where she journeyed several times as an educator and consultant to national leaders, her work has been essential to international well-being. For example, in overly crowded Japan, the use of birth-control methods resulted in a 50 percent drop in the birth rate within ten years. While controversy raged around her, her marriage to a conservative businessman demonstrated how a man can be so fascinated by a woman activist that he supports her work financially and emotionally.

Many fine women writers had to have a male pseudonyms to be taken seriously. Furthermore, if women dressed like men they were often considered to be too "masculine." So have others refused to wear pants and wear only skirts in order to emphasize their sex and to attract men sexually. The myth that femininity is related to dress or the use of a name is still prevalent. Even today, some women in executive positions use initials in their correspondence to disguise their sex.

George Sand (Aurore Dupin) was a politically active woman with no financial resources except her own work. In a time when it was considered unfashionable, she dressed in pants to avoid the high cleaning costs of skirts, and she used a man's name to get recognition. Even then it was difficult. During explosive times, her publisher refused to print her fiery revolutionary tracts because he feared for her life and his income. But that did not stop her desire for self-expression.

When women choose to be in a primary lesbian relationship, it is widely believed that they dislike men. This was not true for Gertrude Stein. An honest woman, she was not content to hide or deny her relationship with her lover, Alice B. Toklas. At the same time, she enjoyed a life of laughter and joy, surrounded by many men who sought her friendship because of her wily mind, generosity, and interest in anything related to art.

When a husband is homosexual, it is not unusual for his wife to believe his homosexuality is somehow her fault, that she is not attractive enough or is inadequate in some other way. Elsa Lanchester teaches us that when a couple works together, shares common interests, and remains friends but nonsexual partners, they may accept the sexual choices the other partner makes.

The myth that a woman enjoys basking in the admiration lavished on a famous husband is also untrue if the husband displays colossal conceit and desire for attention. It is apparent from the life of Mary Leakey that marriage to such a man is likely to become a great disappointment but need not interfere with the validity and importance of one's own work.

With the advent of psychology it came to be believed that women's motivations are the same as men's, and that women are jealous of men's anatomy. Yet only forty years ago Karen Horney exposed the fallacy of this notion. Women were envious of men's cultural freedom, not their anatomy. Furthermore, she concluded that tension developed in women who were conditioned to remain always grateful and subordinate to men. She showed how women who overvalue love, and love too much, develop a morbid dependency in which the partner becomes the sole reason for existence. Her research led others, including men, to become more aware of women's choices.

Whereas it is often difficult to distinguish between a biological urge for sex, an emotional desire for romance, and a lifelong search for romance and love, the myth that it is impossible to make this distinction is patently false.

CHAPTER SIX

LOVE WITHOUT END

TILL DEATH DO US PART

In today's world, the idea of a never-ending romance is only a daydream to many people who fall madly in love and just as madly fall out of it. Love often has a hint of madness about it. Spanish philosopher Ortega y Gassett called it a temporary state of imbecility because of the manic-depressive mood swings that so often go along with romance.

Divorce statistics are so high that many couples who marry change the traditional words of their marriage vows. Instead of committing themselves to loving and remaining together "until death do us part," they make promises to "stay together as long as both of us are growing in the relationship."

This indicates a widespread expectation that neither romance nor personal growth nor commitment can be expected to last. Promises given during the period of infatuation are often broken. The initial powerful attraction may never become a true romance, much less love.

Yet despite the reality, the dream remains in our conscious or subconscious minds that many-splendored love will come and will have no end. The women in this chapter are embodiments of the realization of this dream. Great in their professional accomplishments, they were also great in their capacity to maintain never-ending love.

Never-ending love is not the same as romance, which, like infatuation, often fades. But true love can continue, even after the romance subsides. The women in this chapter managed to find both, and their love was enduring and bore many things. It was not jealous, it was not boastful, arrogant, or rude. And each of these women demonstrated different ways this kind of love could be expressed.

Charlotte Brontë, like many women at any time or place, was an unattractive, self-conscious teenager, made all the more aware of her shortcomings at school. Yet despite both this and extreme poverty, she received several marriage proposals before finally accepting the hand of a suitor and achieved immortality by writing some of the most beloved books of all time.

Physicist Emilie du Châtelet, who lived with the great philosopher Voltaire for fifteen years and was a philosopher in her own right, had many infatuations and romances, but only one great love. That, too, lasted until death. Even when romance retreated, they remained close and loving friends, although she was having a child by another man.

Queen Victoria was deeply infatuated, romantic, and in love with Albert, her husband, and this love never ended. The Victorian era may have been named for her, but she was no prude and never lost her high vitality or love of life. Although he died young and she lived into old age, Victoria was a sexually passionate woman, as well as one committed to ruling an empire as wisely as she could.

A very different type of woman in a different line of work is Helen Hayes. Although many who live in the spotlight, on stage or in film, "put on an act" in their private lives, Helen Hayes was not one of them. Her authenticity and capacity to love made her great. In a world in which strong social action is called for, the contrast of living and loving now—in the present and with the greatest enjoyment—is a major contribution of Helen Hayes to the public.

Marie Curie, winner of two Nobel Prizes, has been a role model for many women, especially those interested in physics. Yet her love for her husband, who died when she was young, lasted for the rest of her life. This one man, her daughters, and her work formed the true focus of her existence.

These five women from England, France, Poland, and the United States were great women who dared to love greatly.

THE BEAUTY OF PLAIN JANE

Charlotte Brontë (1816–1855)

The author of *Jane Eyre* lived most of her life in a secluded country parsonage in northern England with her siblings and dictatorial father, an Irish clergyman. The childhood home was dismal, set in the corner of a graveyard between wild and windy moors and rolling hills. It was at the edge of Haworth, an industrial town in Yorkshire, where many children worked in the factories and died before the age of fourteen. On their death certificates, the cause of death was often listed as "worn out."

During these times, when it was customary to list only a father's name on a birth certificate, many baby girls were not even recorded when born. Yet Charlotte Brontë's father, though extremely authoritaritan, was somewhat advanced in his thought and included his wife's name as well as his own on their children's records.

He had brought his wife and six children, born within seven years, to live in Haworth, by the church and graveyard, after having served in several other parishes. Charlotte first experienced the pain of immediate death when she was five years old and her mother died of cancer. Her father, twenty-nine at the time, tried to find another wife but was turned down. He was very poor, very politically minded, and strongly anti-Catholic.

He also expected his daughters to be perfectly obedient and dutiful in caring for him. After their mother's death, the oldest, twelve-year-old Maria, died of tuberculosis, as did her next sister, Elizabeth. This left Branwell, the favorite and only son, Charlotte, Emily, and Anne. Finally, the father persuaded his sister-in-law to come live with them in the cold, damp parsonage and help supervise the children. Her sternness did not enliven matters.

So it was that within three years of Charlotte's mother's death, two of her sisters died of illness contracted in the Cowan Bridge boarding school. Charlotte, who went to the same school, was removed after their deaths. She disliked the place intensely, blamed it for their deaths, and vividly portrayed an institution like it in *Jane Eyre.*

The Bronte children, all insecure, had no childhood friends except each other. In defense, they became imaginative and prolific writers, creating the fantasy kingdoms of Angria and Gondal, where people lived with horror and tragedy. It was only when Charlotte left home to attend Roe Head School that she had her first friends. But even then, she was handicapped by her appearance:

> Unattractive—thin, stunted, meager; sallow of complexion with dry, frizzy-looking hair screwed up in tight ugly curls. Her dresses were old, rusty, dark, and mended. Extreme near-sightedness and her refusal to wear glasses imprisoned her in a narrow world from which she peered anxiously and shyly.

At nineteen Charlotte tried being a governess at her alma mater, but she detested it. With her aunt's financial help (her father was far too poor), she left for Brussels to learn how to be a teacher. Twenty-six years old by now, she hoped to open a school with Emily and Anne, so that the sisters could be self-supporting.

In Brussels, Charlotte fell head over heels in love with Pensionnat Heger, the head of the school, who was married and had five children. Joined by Emily, Charlotte worked on her writing skills and also learned French, but then their aunt died, and all pursuits romantic and scholastic were suspended when they were called home. Emily remained to run the house for her father, while Charlotte returned to Brussels, seemingly to teach English but actually to follow her heart. When her infatuation began to interfere with Heger's marriage, she was encouraged to leave. In her last letter to him she wrote: "To forbid me to write to you, to refuse to answer me, would be to tear from me my only joy on earth, to deprive me of my last privilege—a privilege I shall never consent willingly to surrender."

It was only after Charlotte's death that a bundle of letters was found that she had written but never sent. Others, which she had sent and he had torn up, had been pieced together by his wife. These are now in the British Museum.

Throughout her life Charlotte maintained an active correspondence with her family and friends, in which she did not hesitate to exchange encouragement and advice, often about love and duty. Yet letters did not fill her life. Charlotte, along with two of her sisters, became a famous writer; among them they wrote seven novels. Each used a masculine pen name (Charlotte adopted Mr. Currer Bell), because women writers were ridiculed at the time. Even Robert Southey, the poet laureate, strongly cautioned Charlotte against writing, which was, he said, no profession for a woman.

Charlotte had many sorrows to cope with. Branwell died, of alcohol and opium, at thirty-one years of age, and was closely followed by Emily two months later at the age of thirty, and Anne next at twenty-nine, both of tuberculosis.

Charlotte's first published novel, *Jane Eyre*, contained a

great deal of autobiographical, plain-Jane material, along with highly entertaining fictional plot lines. The book created a furor, dealing as it did with a woman's inner conflict between what society expected and her natural sexual desires. It included the drama of the heroine's narrow escape from a bigamous marriage with her employer and the death of his insane wife by fire.

Elizabeth Barrett Browning, who had been restricted by her father, deplored the story as "half savage and half freethinking writing." In contrast, Queen Victoria declared it to be wonderful, powerful, and thrilling, even though it was "peculiar in parts." The famous critic-publisher G. H. Lewes applauded it with: "This indeed is a book after my own heart . . . The story is not only of singular interest, naturally evolved, unflagging to the last, but fastens itself upon your attention and will not leave you."

Like *Jane Eyre* her heroine, Charlotte considered herself to be very plain. She sometimes drew portraits of herself as an ugly duckling and was deeply ashamed of her size, which was so small she was obligated to wear children's underwear. Although proposed to by several curates who knew her father, she did not believe any of them could possibly care for her. At the same time she was also critical of them and their clerical roles: "They regard me as an old maid, and I regard them, one and all, as highly uninteresting, narrow, and unattractive specimens of the coarser sex."

Yet even while rejecting proposals of marriage, Charlotte admitted to being lonely. To her friend Ellen she wrote, "The evils that now and then wring a groan in my heart [are] not that I am a *single* woman and likely to remain a *single* woman but because I am a *lonely woman* and likely to remain *lonely*."

Loneliness was one of the forces that led Charlotte into marriage with one of her father's curates, Arthur Bell Nicholls. For years Arthur had been deeply attracted to her, and he had proposed several times, only to be rejected. But suddenly a clearer reason emerged for marrying him. One day, he came to see her after being forbidden to do so by her father:

> He entered—he stood before me . . . never can I forget it. Shaking from head to foot, looking deadly pale, speaking low, vehemently yet with difficulty—he made me for the first time feel what it costs a man to declare affection where he doubts response.

On the basis of her new awareness of how difficult it is for some men to ask for what they want, Charlotte began to fall in love with this man who had shown such resolve and courage. The relationship flowered because Arthur was intelligent and moreover genuinely enjoyed reading what she wrote. When reading *Shirley*, in which she said she was trying to be "as unromantic as Monday morning," he discovered himself there, only thinly disguised. So delighted was he by this that he suddenly burst out laughing, clapped his hands, and stamped on the floor.

This kind of animation brought new life to Charlotte and spurred her interest in Arthur. Yet her father was totally against the marriage, permitting it only when it became clear that his own financial straits were so dire that he was obliged to accept Arthur's promise of financial assistance and life-long care in the parsonage. Even so, when the wedding day came, her father suddenly wavered in giving the bride away. He went to bed, and the ceremony continued without him.

Tragically, the marriage was brief. Charlotte became pregnant and very ill with an extreme case of morning sickness, which in those days was untreatable. When six months pregnant, she anticipated her death, and her dying words were, "Oh I'm not going to die, am I? He will not separate us—we have been so happy."

A plain woman, only four feet, nine inches tall, Charlotte, in both her writing and romance, became a woman of great stature in spite of the omnipresence of death in her family.

"JUST LIKE A MAN"

Emilie du Châtelet (1706–1749)

In today's world, the number of women scientists is much fewer than that of men. But Emilie du Châtelet was even more unusual for her time. She was a physicist, mathematician, and philosopher and wanted to be valued for herself and her scholarship, not merely recognized for her association with the famed philosopher Voltaire.

"I am," she claimed, "inferior to no one." Emilie made two major scientific contributions that are still seriously regarded today. She translated Newton's work from Latin into French, including the only remaining French translation of Newton's *Principia*. She also developed an integration of Newton's physics and Leibniz's metaphysics.

In a letter to King Frederick of Prussia, Voltaire, in an acknowledgment that would be considered left-handed at best today, compared her superior thinking to that of a man:

> She was a great man whose only fault was in being a woman. A woman who translated and explained Newton, and who made a free translation of Virgil . . . a woman who never spoke evil of anyone, and who never told a lie; a friend attentive and courageous in friendship—in one word, a very great man.

The two great scholars, Emilie and Voltaire, lived, loved, and worked together for fifteen years, remaining intimate until she died in his arms, even though he was then having an affair with his niece and her death occurred three days after she gave birth to another man's child.

Born Gabrielle-Emile Le Tonnelier de Bretruil in Paris, Emilie was a precocious child, always outspoken and demanding. Her mother was from the nobility and raised her daughter in a large house surrounded by gardens and subdivided, as was common in France, into family apartments. Her father, chief of protocol at the royal court and quite powerful, recognized her intelligence and from her early childhood supplied her with the finest tutors.

His appreciation did not extend itself, however, to her physical charms. Repeatedly her father would tell her she was an ugly duckling who would be unable to find a husband and described her as twice as tall as other girls, very strong, clumsy, with large hands and feet, and skin "as rough as a nutmeg grater." Fortunately, Emilie evidently outgrew her father's negative appraisal, and later lovers declared her very beautiful. She became fluent in five languages, was versed in classical poetry and philosophy, rode horses well, and was also adept at dueling.

At age nineteen, Emile married Florent Claude, the marquis du Châtelet and count of Lomont; he was thirty years old at the time. The marriage was one of convenience. She had a good dowry, and his château at Cirney was run down. He took up a military career, became a regimental colonel, and seldom came home.

Emilie became restless and took her first lover in an overpowering infatuation. It was so intense that when he left her she attempted suicide with poison and wrote him a farewell note, which fortunately he read in time to come and save her. In court Emilie was both very popular and, according to the duc de Richelieu—her second lover—exquisite. "No man," he declared, "can resist her natural beauty." He complained, however, of her extravagance, enormous wardrobe, and compulsive gambling. She replied that she was as bored by money as by his complaints. Later Voltaire wrote: "Emilie's tastes are impeccable and she is so covetous that not even the wealthiest of kings could afford to grant her desires. What she sees, she wants, and her eyesight is remarkably keen."

In 1733, at the age of twenty-seven, after the birth of her third child (she had had her first two by her husband), Emilie began the serious study of mathematics and became close friends with Alexis Claude Clairaut, who favored Newton's theories over those of Descartes.

It was at this time that she met Voltaire, who was thirty-nine, and it was love at first sight. He became a brilliant historian, philosopher, playwright, and poet who often wrote against the establishment. Once exiled to England for three years for insulting a young nobleman, he returned to France only to be forced to flee occasionally from the authorities because of his revolutionary writing.

At that time in France, taking a lover was not a scandal but an event worthy of pride. Emilie announced that she was going to live with Voltaire for the rest of her life, and she did.

Since her husband was usually away, he gave permission for them to live together on his estate at Cirey, which Voltaire rebuilt because it was so decrepit. It became a center for intellectuals. The lovers came and went freely, except for those times when Voltaire was obligated to dodge authorities. (Unfortunately, new ideas then were not tolerated as liberally as were new lovers.) Emilie encouraged him to begin his serious study of physics, metaphysics, ethics, and religion. Together they wrote commentaries on the Bible that had to be circulated privately. To do otherwise would have meant putting their lives in jeopardy.

Throughout the years they lived together, Voltaire continued to be greatly influenced by Emilie, whom he called "the divine mistress." At one time they unknowingly competed against each other for a prize to be given by the Academy of Sciences on the nature of fire. Neither won the prize, but her dissertation on fire was so important that it was later published at the Academy's expense. Her name was so associated with Voltaire's that she once wrote to King Frederick of Prussia and requested that he judge her as an individual on the basis of her merits:

> Do not look upon me as a mere appendage to this great general or that renowned scholar, this star that shines at the court of France or that famed author. I am in my own right a whole person, responsible to myself alone for all that I am, all that I say, all that I do.

When writing this, Emilie suspected that the king would send her lavish letters of flattery that he did not mean, as he often did to Voltaire and others. The king, she knew, was emotionally attached to Voltaire, and possessive as well. One time he summoned Voltaire to his estate, where there were always many transvestites and no women. Voltaire avoided going, and his relationship to the king ended unhappily when he wrote of his adoration for Emilie: "I have become a willing slave for the sake of living with the individual near whom all disagreeables disapprove. . . . I ask nothing more than to live [with her] buried in the mountains of Cirey."

Emilie's professional life was devoted to physics and mathematics. She wrote a physics textbook on the historical and philosophical principles of Leibniz, but when Voltaire thought she was wasting her time and should concentrate on Newton, where his own interest lay, her major work became translating Newton from Latin into French and then writing a book of her own commentaries with analytical solutions.

Her personal life was often filled with lovers. When she discovered, at age forty-two, that she was pregnant by a new lover, the marquis de Saint-Lambert, she summoned her husband to visit her at his own estate where she lived with Voltaire. He did so and, after a three-week visit, left imagining that he was to be a new father. Voltaire, for his part, suggested that the child would need to be listed as one of her "miscellaneous works."

Emilie gave birth while sitting at her desk and died unexpectedly a few days later, while in the process of making a full translation of Newton's works. Many mourned her, Voltaire—her deepest love—most of all: "I have not lost merely a mistress, I have lost the half of myself—a soul for which mine was made."

CIRCUMSTANCE WITHOUT POMP

Queen Alexandrina Victoria (1819–1901)

A deeply romantic woman with high energy and a lively sense of humor, Alexandrina Victoria, queen of the United Kingdom and Ireland and empress of India, ruled for sixty three years, from age eighteen until her death at eighty-two. She had nine children and, despite her many duties, was able to build and maintain a close family life. Furthermore, her descendants, including forty grandchildren, married into most of the royal families of Europe.

Her own marriage, which was politically arranged, came to be one of love and passion. Just before she announced her decision to marry Prince Albert, Queen Victoria was seen to be trembling and was asked if she was nervous. "Yes, but I have just done a far more nervous thing," she replied. "I proposed to Prince Albert."

Victoria, an insecure child, had a lonely upbringing. Her father, the duke of Kent, died when she was young, and her mother, then thirty-two, came under the strict control of Captain John Conroy, who had been her father's equerry and was very ambitious. He wanted to be made regent if Victoria succeeded to the throne before she was eighteen and did everything possible to assure this by encouraging Victoria's mother to be totally dependent upon him.

For years Victoria had to live in total seclusion in Kensington Palace, but she was never allowed privacy. At night she was obligated to sleep with her mother or governess; even when walking down stairs, she was required to hold someone's hand. Her strict governess never left Victoria's side and would not permit her to see other members of the royal family.

Although well educated, the seclusion the future queen suffered kept her very naive. At the age of thirteen she began to keep a diary, which she continued throughout her life. Her habit was to write copious journal entries, notes to many people, and also to record minutes of many meetings. In fact, it has been estimated that Victoria wrote at least 2,500 words each day, more than many professional authors.

In 1837 Victoria came of age. Three days later her uncle, William IV, died without an heir, and the lonely Victoria was crowned. Extremely conscientious, she enjoyed her new position and was determined to serve well. The prime minister, Lord Melbourne, and her uncle, King Leopold of Belgium, were her mentors. At this time in history, England was virtually ruled by Germans, who were groomed to marry into the British royalty. Many applied for her hand, but few were attractive to her heart. Albert, her cousin, was the exception. Despite Victoria's initial resistance, after only two meetings she became wildly infatuated, partly because he was such a good dancer and his appearance was so appealing to her. To King Leopold she wrote effusively: "Albert's *beauty is most striking*, and he is so amiable and unaffected—in short, very fascinating, he is excessively admired here . . . such beautiful blue eyes, an exquisite nose, such a pretty mouth with delicate mustachios . . ."

During their engagement their romantic natures flowered. Victoria wrote in her journal that when she signed some papers, he "was so kind as to dry them with blotting paper for me. Oh! what happiness is this! How I do adore him! I kissed his dear hand. He embraced me again so tenderly."

Three weeks later, when they parted after an evening together, her journal bespoke a typical love-smitten teenager:

I gave Albert a last kiss, and saw him get into the carriage and drive off. I cried much, felt wretched, yet happy to think that we should meet again so soon! Oh! How I love him, how intensely, how devotedly, how ardently! I cried and felt so sad. Wrote my journal. Walked. Cried.

When first married, Victoria would not allow him to direct her in any way. This rankled Albert, who wrote to a friend, "I am only the husband—not the master in the house." However, being "only the husband" did not last long. According to one ancedote, shortly after their marriage they quarreled:

> Albert stalked out of the room and locked himself in his private apartments. Victoria hammered furiously upon the door. "Who's there?" called Albert. "The queen of England, and she demands to be admitted." There was no response and the door remained locked. Victoria hammered at the door again. "Who's there?" The reply was still "The queen of England," and still the door remained shut. More fruitless and furious knocking was followed by a pause. Then there was a gentle tap. "Who's there?" The queen replied, "Your wife, Albert." The prince at once opened the door.

Albert would have preferred to live on his own land with his own intellectual interests, but royal marriage was his duty—along with an allowance, a title, and a strong position in the royal family. Although Victoria adored him and frequently told him so, in the beginning it was she who made all the decisions. Gradually this changed. Albert was a brilliant man, loyal and hard-working. He was also jealous and domineering, arrogant and committed to court etiquette.

But Albert knew above all how to woo her, and her adoration for him became so great that she lost much of her resolve for independent decision-making, turning many of those duties over to him. Her explanation for this to King

Leopold came complete with her characteristically excessive underlining:

> We women are not <u>made</u> for governing—and if we are good women we must <u>dislike</u> these masculine occupations. . . . I am every day more convinced that <u>we women</u> if we are to be <u>good</u> women, <u>feminine</u> and <u>amiable</u> and <u>domestic</u> are <u>not</u> <u>fitted to reign</u>.

Victoria, in love with love, so idolized Albert and was so greatly influenced by his dictatorial manner that, in time, she acted as stern in court as he did. But Victoria's adoration for her husband was not necessarily shared by her countrymen, many of whom found him mean and too fond of money. In poor health from childhood, he died, much to Victoria's despair, at the early age of forty.

Although she had nine children, loved them dearly, and spent a great deal of time playing with them, pregnancy was not one of Victoria's pleasures, and she complained of the "great inconvenience of a <u>large</u> family" and also that "men never think, at least seldom think, what a hard task it is for us women to go through this <u>very often</u>."

As a family, they enjoyed each other, animals, and outdoor picnics even in cold weather. They also had many parties. Victoria, a fine dancer, so loved to pass the time this way that, after teaching the children, she held a young people's ball at Buckingham Palace, complete with engraved invitations.

As a new queen, Victoria had been vulnerable and apprehensive. This gradually disappeared as she became more confident, partly due to the genuine devotion of her first prime minister. Often in conflict with later prime ministers, she occasionally used her power as queen to overrule them, and did so in increasingly outspoken ways.

The Victorian age was named after her, but she could hardly have been called Victorian herself. One of the private forms of entertainment she shared with Albert after their marriage was exchanging nude drawings of each other that they had personally sketched. She was against drinking, but dancing, card playing, and other games were nightly entertainments. She also enjoyed reading novels and poetry, traveling, and the theater, which had fallen into disrepute. Her support of this art form helped it to recover its prestige and enabled it to flourish once again.

Queen Victoria was known to prefer a simple style of living and dressing, except for her habit of wearing rings on each of her fingers and thumbs, which made it difficult for her to use a knife and fork. In her diary she explains that she started doing this in her adolescent years because she thought her hands were ugly. Once, when criticized for the excess of rings, she defended herself by saying she took them off in the morning. Throughout her life, informality and spontaneity were more important to her than pomp and ceremony. When she traveled, the queen often went incognito and delighted in not being recognized. She was short and grew greatly in girth with the years. Yet she was unpretentious and self-confident enough for this not to worry her.

One of Queen Victoria's characteristics, commented on time and time again by her biographers, was her good humor and loud and hearty laugh. Slapstick comedy and jokes were very appealing—but they had to be in good taste, or she would "not be amused." The phrase "I was amused" shows up in her diary when, on her fourteenth birthday, she attended a royal ball given in her honor. It was a favorite expression, occasionally set in a more formal context, as in, "We are *not* amused," when a joke went too far past good taste. This was not always easy to gauge, however, since she so enjoyed laughing heartily and hearing jokes about the foolishness of men.

After Prince Albert died, the queen was heartbroken. To work through her grief she spent more time in Scotland and wrote even more intently in her journal. Included were many personal details about the prince, which she published under the title *Leaves from a Journal of Our Life in the Highlands*. Her style of writing, with its excessive underlining, was sometimes ridiculed, but she didn't care.

John Brown, a Scotsman, became her friend and protector, largely because he was so forthright and honest. Another friend was Benjamin Disraeli, a very different type of man, who often flattered her by referring to her as "Faery Queen." He also appreciated her adoration of Albert. On his deathbed, however, Disraeli, when asked if he wanted Victoria to come and say good-bye, replied, "No, it is better not. She will only ask me to take a message to Albert."

WITH PEANUTS AND EMERALDS

Helen Hayes (1900–)

One of the most popular actresses in the United States during this century, Helen Hayes was honored for her acting by having a theater in New York named after her and having bestowed on her numerous awards in both radio and television. Like Queen Victoria, whom she played on Broadway, Helen Hayes's love for her husband was also without end.

She never planned to be an actress because, from the age of five, she already was one. Neither did she plan to fall in love with an alcoholic, but she knew how to live with one, having been the daughter of an alcoholic mother who sometimes drank herself into oblivion. She didn't expect to be swept off her feet with peanuts and emeralds, but she was. Love without end is often unexpected. No one expected the romance between Helen Hayes and Charles MacArthur to last, even before the tragic death of their daughter. Yet it did—for thirty years, until his death.

It is impossible to write about Helen Hayes without writing about Charles MacArthur, because their lives were so interwoven and their romance so intense and long-lasting. He was a famous playwright who often collaborated with Ben Hecht. Their first success, *The Front Page*, had a major influence on the public's view of the newspaper profession and how newsmen viewed themselves. Other successful collaborations included *Twentieth Century* and a number of popular motion pictures.

They first met at a party, and they immediately fell in love. Charles, a playwright and playboy, offered her a peanut. When she accepted he gave her more, declaring, "I wish they were emeralds." Years later, in memory of this first meeting, Charlie, returning from the eastern theater of World War II, brought her a package of uncut emeralds from India, reversing his earlier quip and making it even more romantic with, "I wish they were peanuts."

In some ways they were very much alike. Both loved the theater, each other, their children, and their friends. Yet Charlie was a trickster and a great wit who often embroidered events lavishly and acted outrageously. Highly gregarious, he enjoyed wine, women, and song. And Helen, in contrast, was a shy, naive "nice girl" who once hid from actor Clark Gable when he made sexual overtures toward her and bit Hollywood producer Louis B. Mayer on the neck when he also tried.

She often described herself as a "walker from way back," insisting on this form of exercise regardless of where she was in the world or how famous she had become. She dreaded, however, being recognized. At the height of her fame, friends or members of her cast often took turns accompanying her as protection from crowds seeking her autograph.

One of her most unpleasant memories about being a celebrity concerns her last performance of *Victoria Regina*. In a rush to catch a train to get home to her family, she did not have time to sign autographs. As she hurried to a cab, a disappointed fan shouted at her again and again, "You stinker! You stinker!"

Helen always thought of herself as a lover of words, a heritage she received from the women in her family, who were all lively, vocal, and enjoyed quoting from the world's great literature. She preferred poets who wrote of lofty ideals and appreciated the vast scheme of life. Helen expressed her admiration for words to her grandchildren: "From your parents you learn love and laughter and how to put one foot before another. But when books are opened you discover you have wings."

Helen was proud of her Irish working-class background, for it taught her the value of work. Born Helen Hayes Brown, she grew up in Washington, D.C., and in her earliest years was cared for by her father, often absent as a traveling salesman, by her cheerful and loving maternal grandmother, and by two doting aunts. Her ambitious, erratic mother wanted to be an actress and from time to time would leave to pursue her dream. When that dream did not materialize, she would return and redirect her ambition onto Helen.

Home was both pleasant and unpleasant. Arguments were frequent between Helen's parents. When they occurred, her father tended to withdraw into silence and her unfulfilled mother into alcohol. But when Helen went to baseball games with her father, he was as noisy and joyful as anyone in the stands; and when she traveled with her mother, who sought roles for Helen to play, the world seemed magical.

By the age of five, Helen was dancing, singing, and captivating people with her gift for impersonating others, an art she learned from her sparkling and energetic mother and grandmother. To pay for Helen's extra tutoring in French, her mother washed lace curtains. In her teens Helen played summer stock. At fourteen, she was called to a New York role that lasted eight weeks in the play *The Prodigal Husband*, with the famous actor John Drew. After this she returned to school, where one of her teachers called her "Mary Sunshine" because of her smiling, dancing eyes, her love of life, and her admiration of the world.

Helen's greatness as an actress began to emerge when she was seventeen and played the lead in *Pollyanna: The Glad Girl*. Despite its popularity, the role of a girl who played games of being glad was obnoxious to Helen, and it was during the run of this play that she discovered and constructed an "ideal woman" for herself. This woman was a mixture of some of Shakespeare's greats—part Rosalind, the young, vulnerable girl in love; part Viola, because of her unrequited passion; part Juliet, because she was so ardent; part Portia, because of her dignity and graciousness; and part Emilia, for some tart contrast. Then, to make the ideal woman more real, she added Constance (from *King John*) as a grieving mother; Cleopatra, whose grief leads to her suicide; and out-spoken Kate, advising women to place their hands under their husband's foot because, "Thy husband is thy lord, thy life, thy keeper, thy head, thy sovereign; one who cares for thee."

Helen and Charlie were in love for some time before he proposed marriage; he wanted to prove that he could succeed as a playwright, as she already had as an actress. But when success came with *The Front Page*, Helen got a "first night" proposal.

Throughout their marriage his care and adoration for Helen was boundless. During her pregnancy, for example, when she was in New York and he was in Hollywood, he phoned her several times each day and did the same with her doctor to implore him to take good care of her. They also became adoring parents when Mary was born and later, be-cause they could not conceive more children, adopted a son, Jamie. Helen worked as hard at being a mother as she worked at her roles in the theater: "I decided that Whistler's Mother was going to seem like Medea when compared with the per-fection of my motherhood. I studied the character and started to draw my portrait—half Olympia and half Mary Cassatt."

For Helen, one success in the theater followed another, as she grew to be one of America's most distinguished ac-tresses. She won many prestigious awards for stage and TV roles, including one for her best-known and triumphant four-and-a-half-year portrayal of the queen in "Victoria Regina." Though not queenly in her private life (she preferred dogs and flowers to pomp and fame), Helen played several rulers, including Mary, Queen of Scotland, said to be the tallest queen in history. Helen, only five feet tall when drawn up to her fullest height, portrayed her majestically.

But life was not only a stage to Helen. Always loyal and conscientious, during World War II she raised strawberries and chickens as a patriotic effort and took eggs to the theater to sell to members of the cast. On her thirty-five-acre farm, the chickens were particularly well cared for. According to actress Tallulah Bankhead, her neighbor, on cold nights Helen would lovingly cover each hen with a silk blanket!

Charlie's tender loving care persisted. On returning from Europe as a lieutenant colonel, he brought her a rose he had picked in Normandy and had tried to keep fresh in a jar of water during the long plane flight home.

The tragedy of their life was the loss of their daughter, Mary, at age nineteen to polio. Each coped with their grief in different ways. He lost his will to live; she lost her will to work. Finally, in desperation, Helen turned back to the church for solace and became active in raising funds to fight polio.

It might at first have been anger that made me dedicate myself to the National Foundation and its crusade to wipe out polio. But then I met one of the medical heads whose own children had been afflicted and who was determined to see that others would not be. I was struck by the fact that, if there is any divinity, it is in man's willingness to help alleviate suffering in others.

In contrast to Helen reaching out to help others from the midst of her grief, Charlie sank into deeper despair and more alcohol. Seven years after his daughter's death, he slipped painfully from life, his body deteriorated from drinking. According to friends, however, he more accurately died of a broken heart. Yet his amazing sense of humor did not leave him, even on his deathbed. When Helen whispered to him, "I love you," he winked and replied, "You should." And Helen wrote, "Laughter is the sound of heaven."

Many years later Helen, at eighty, was asked if she had ever considered remarrying. To this she answered, "I'm still waiting for my reunion with Charlie, waiting eagerly and happily for it."

NOT INTERESTED IN FAME

Marie Curie (1867–1934)

In spite of a life of poverty and the absence of opportunities for higher education in her homeland of Poland, Marie Sklodowska Curie became a role model for scientists, especially women scientists. As a matter of fact, her husband, Pierre, a well-known physicist, gave up his own research in crystals because he was convinced that her pursuits were more important. Later, her fame became so great that she was invited by President Herbert Hoover to stay at the White House when visiting the United States—a most unusual invitation.

Marie and her family were so close to Albert Einstein and his family that the two families sometimes took vacations together. Einstein, who had great respect for her, said she was "the only famous person not corrupted by fame." Her daughter, Eve, described her as an individual who did not know how to be famous.

Marie Curie, often called Manya, was born in 1867 and grew up in Poland when it was under harsh Russian control. Both her parents were poorly paid teachers, and Marie was their fifth child. By the time she was ten years old, her older sister had died of typhus and her mother of tuberculosis.

Although she was impressed with her mother's dedication to religion and mysticism, Marie believed this was in conflict with her father's mathematical approach to life. She thus became an agnostic.

Throughout life she was logical, introspective, and extremely shy—so much so that after becoming famous she often denied who she was if recognized by a stranger. An overly conscientious student, she was blessed from early childhood with a prodigious memory. At age fifteen she collapsed after winning a gold medal on completing her secondary education award. Although there were people who thought this was part of some kind of emotional breakdown, Marie wrote that the collapse was due simply to "the fatigue of growth and study." Throughout a life of overwork, she never gave up her intellectual curiosity and her commitment to education and work.

In Poland at that time, however, it was impossible for her to receive a higher education; women were not admitted to the universities. Furthermore, all education was strictly dictated by Russian authorities. To further her quest for knowledge, then, Marie met secretly with groups of young people to discuss intellectual ideas. These groups were called the Floating University because of their need to meet in various secret places to avoid government interference.

Because Marie's father was poor, at age eighteen she was obliged to take a position as governess in the village of Szczuki to help her sister go to Paris to get an education in medicine. In exchange, her sister would later help her financially. As a governess Marie taught seven hours a day, after which she spent another two to five hours a day doing the same with a class of peasant children, who came to her secretly and despite the Russian law against such activities.

At a time when many young women experience the joy of romance, Marie's heart was not a happy one. She and her employer's son fell in love and wanted to become engaged, but his parents disapproved because of her poverty and their difference in social class. She may have been acceptable as a tutor to their children, but not as a wife to their son. In spite of her deep disappointment, she continued to work as a góverness and kept at her self-education by studying physics and mathematics, all the while sending her salary to her father and siblings. Many years after her death, her first love was often seen walking around her statue in a Warsaw square and sitting on a bench gazing up at it. No doubt he wondered how different his life might have been had he followed the way of his heart.

After three years as a governess, Marie returned to Warsaw, still with a burning desire for more education. Once more she became active in the Floating University, studying chemistry from books while conducting scientific experiments in a secret laboratory. It was not until Marie was twenty-four that she got word that she could finally go to Paris to study. Her sister, newly married, was able to offer her a room in her apartment. Scraping together enough money to cover fourth-class railway fare, Marie set out on her journey to fame, if not to fortune.

After a brief stay with her sister, Marie moved into an old building where poor students lived. She started to attend classes at the Sorbonne. During that time she had little to eat except bread, butter, and tea. Unable to speak French, she found the struggle to get a scientific education difficult and all-consuming. When preparing for final examinations, she was almost petrified by fear that she would not pass, yet she won first place in physics. A year later, she won second place for her studies in mathematics.

Marie was driven by a passion solely for science—until she met Pierre Curie. The first conversation between the twenty-seven-year-old student and the thirty-five-year-old professor was quite technical. A colleague arranged to have them to tea so that Marie could ask Pierre's opinion about some new laboratory equipment she needed for her research. Pierre already had made significant advances in physics because, from their earliest years, Pierre and his brother had studied and practiced science together. They had discovered special electric characteristics of crystals, and Pierre's individual work on crystals has remained fundamental to researchers even today.

From their first meeting, Marie and Pierre were attracted to each other. Yet his first "love letter" to her was only an affectionate greeting scrawled on the front page of his latest publication on electric and magnetic fields.

Marie's original life plan had been to earn her doctorate and return to Poland in order to teach and to participate in political struggles against Russia. So convinced was she of her duty that it took Pierre, with the help of her family, a year to persuade her to stay in Paris. Pierre, recognizing their kindred passion for science, pleaded his case: "It would be a fine thing, in which I hardly dare believe, to pass our lives near each other, hypnotized by our dreams: your patriotic dreams, our humanitarian dream, and our scientific dream."

They were married quietly, with only a few relatives and friends present. When a relative offered to send her a wedding dress, Marie wrote to her, "I have no dress except the one I wear every day. If you are going to be kind enough to give me one, please let it be practical and dark, so that I can put it on afterward to go to the laboratory."

Throughout her life, Marie dressed with extreme simplicity. She usually had no more than three dresses, all most often a serviceable black. Her living quarters were also austere: Simple curtains at the windows, bare walls, a bed, a table at which to eat and work, and plain chairs were all she wanted.

The couple lived and worked together in what seemed to be an ideal relationship. Their conversations were of poetry and physics. During the rare times when they had to be apart, their letters were often full of alternating thoughts—a line of sentiment followed by a line of mathematics or science: "I miss you very much: my soul flew away with you. . . ."

might be followed closely by, "Poincare's book is more difficult than I thought. . . ."

As a student, Marie's work was subordinate to Pierre's. Even when she started to work with him, she often referred to him as her "boss." Neither had good health, which was made worse by the primitive situations in which they had to work. Their laboratory was in the hall of the school where he taught. Later, and for many years, her laboratory was in an unheated greenhouse where water dripped onto her work and the temperature sometimes dropped to forty-four degrees. When Marie started on her doctoral research she chose as her topic the investigation of phenomena to which she would eventually give the name "radioactivity." This seemed so important to Pierre that he gave up his work on crystals and joined her.

From then on they worked even more closely and discovered two new elements, radium and polonium, the latter named after Marie's native Poland. In 1903 the Curies shared the Nobel Prize with Henri Becquerel, another researcher in physics, for their work in radioactivity. That same year, she won her doctorate.

Marie had always known hardship, but deep tragedy entered her life only three years after she and Pierre won their Nobel Prize. While crossing the street he was run over by a horse and cart, and his head was crushed.

She was thirty-nine years old at the time and became suicidal, often walking the streets by herself, seeking a cart to run her down. Her great sadness was overwhelming, although she tried to hide her grief from others. The sun and flowers, which she had always loved, lost their meaning. In desperation she finally burned the passionate love letters they had written to each other, along with his blood-stained clothes. Her children were young at the time, and only the presence of her sister sustained her in this act.

In the struggle to overcome her grief she also began to write a diary addressed to him in which she poured out her

pain. Only small parts of this diary have been opened for others to read. One especially poignant entry describes how she put periwinkles from their garden and a picture of herself in his coffin: "It is the picture that must go with you into the grave, the picture of her who had the happiness of pleasing you enough so that you did not hesitate to offer to share your life with her . . . we were made to live together, and our union had to be."

Ironically, a great professional triumph came to her with Pierre's death. One month later, in an unprecedented move, the administrators of the Sorbonne voted to have her replace Pierre on the faculty. As the first woman to be appointed to any position of higher education in France, she attracted even more attention than she did as a Nobel Prize winner. Her first lecture was heralded as a news event. People crowded the lecture hall and waited for her appearance. Reporters made elaborate guesses about how she would introduce herself and what she might say about Pierre or about her historic appointment. No one, however, predicted what actually occurred: She stepped up to the podium, opened Pierre's notebook, and continued his lecture at exactly the place where he had stopped right before his death.

Some time later Marie was accused of having a romantic involvement with her colleague Paul Langevin, a known womanizer, a genius at research, a popular teacher—and an unhappy husband. He had been one of many lifelong professional friends of the Curies, but his wife accused Marie publicly of being "that illustrious widow" who had been having an affair with her husband for years.

Some newspapers labeled her "husband snatcher"; others said such a thing was impossible for someone with her values. Two editors holding opposite views challenged each other to a duel. At that time in history, duels were more like rituals, intended to prove a point by drawing a small amount of blood but not to kill. Although she was vindicated in the duel and the newspapers and public finally lost interest, both she and

Paul suffered from the accusations. They continued their professional relationship, but they maintained a careful distance as they recognized the destructive power of jealousy. From then on Marie kept her private life even more private, and as far as we know she never allowed a man to get close to her again.

In spite of the stress of the unproven affair and the notoriety, Marie continued to work hard, and in 1911, after being widowed for five years, won the Nobel Prize in chemistry for her preparation of one gram of pure radium, a feat that had taken many years to accomplish. She was the single support of her two daughters, Irène and Eve, and she often took them with her to scientific meetings, lavished attention on them during vacations, and sent them to live with friends for safety when Paris was torn with war. When Irène developed an interest in physics and was away at school, Marie frequently wrote her affectionate notes and often included challenging mathematical problems to solve. In her teens Irène worked with her mother in her laboratory, and together they set up the first X-ray machines in a war zone.

Irène then married one of Marie's assistants, Frederic Joliot. Together, Irène and Frederic Joliot-Curie won a Nobel Prize in chemistry. Eve, her other daughter, became a war correspondent and also wrote a biography of Marie, a loving and detailed story of a great woman with a heart on fire for her work.

As Marie's fame grew, so did the gifts and grants to her work and to her dream of building an institute adjacent to the Pasteur Institute. Gradually, as the uses of radium became more widely known, she was also called a "benefactress of the human race." Marie's later years were spent studying radioactive substances, their medical applications, and the sources for radioactive materials to be used in research in nuclear physics. While still working and traveling to raise money for the institute in Paris, she also became involved in developing international scholarships and a Radium Institute in her beloved Warsaw. In spite of her schedule and interests, she never lost the love of her family and many friends, both men and women.

She did, however, lose most of her sight, hearing, and energy—infirmities that she tried to hide from others as she continued her work. To her, a private life should be kept private. So this great and increasingly frail woman was often accompanied and protected from the public by her daughters. At the age of ninety-six, Marie Curie died as a result of many years of overexposure to radiation in her laboratory research. She had recognized the great power—both positive and negative—that radium possessed and that in the hands of criminals it could be greatly misused. Nevertheless, she wrote, "I am one of those who think like Nobel, that humanity will draw more good than evil from new discoveries."

IMMORTAL LOVE

Immortal love is, by definition, beyond the love of mere mortals. It is the love of the gods, deathless and eternal. Great writers such as Dante and Shakespeare have tried to portray it: Dante through Beatrice, Shakespeare through Romeo and Juliet.

Many people would like to experience a love that feels as though it has been sent by the gods. They yearn to live a childhood story that ends with ". . . and they lived happily ever after." Some romances are that way. There are clues in the lives of the women in this chapter who fought against deep-rooted myths.

One such myth is that people who grow up in depressing environments will never be free of the past. Charlotte Brontë's life shows that in spite of having an unhappy past, happiness can be boundless. Her burning heart, which had been limited to her novels, was released bursting with romance. Her life was short but full.

Always sure of her destiny and her important role in shaping England, Queen Victoria overturns the myth that a woman's power interferes with love. A woman of many contrasts, her reputation for decorum in court was a sharp contrast to the free and flamboyant spirit she displayed to her husband, children, and members of the court. Even in her later years she enjoyed whirling around the dance floor, and she remained romantically attached to her husband until her death.

Helen Hayes and Charlie MacArthur were always delighted by each other's successes. The myth that successful people compete with each other for attention is not true in their case. With tenderness and respect, humor and laughter, their romance never ended. There is another myth that all people want to retire at age sixty-five, if not earlier. Not so with Helen. Her lifetime commitment to work—from early childhood until she was well into her eighties—was another form of love without end. To her, work was necessary, even when it was disappointing or exhausting.

The same holds true for Marie Curie. There was passionate romance but no competition with her brilliant husband, Pierre. They demonstrate how the power to work may be fueled by having a partner with similar interests, even if the woman is judged to be superior in the field. Marie's love of science and her love for Pierre kept her alert and working in spite of her excessive fatigue and failing health in her later years.

The myths that science is men's work and that women are less intelligent than men are obviously false as shown by the lives of both Marie Curie and Emilie du Châtelet. Both are examples of what is possible when encouragement and opportunity are available to a woman with a consuming passion for science. Being authentic in an antagonistic, male-dominated world is often an important step in the evolutionary understanding of women.

Love that seems immortal—coming freely from the

gods—is both a dream and a possibility. It is not a myth. Many great women and men have experienced it, and their lives reveal that romance and sex, work and play, joy and sorrow are natural expressions that can enhance life and liven the heart.

EPILOGUE

When two people come together in love, they may feel such passionate joy that their hearts seemingly catch fire. It is with such fire that Elizabeth Barrett Browning wrote these deeply moving words:

> *The face of all the world is changed, I think,*
> *Since first I heard the footsteps of thy soul . . .*

In such terms, romance seems impossible to explain, even though many writers have attempted to do so. Blaise Pascal, the seventeenth-century scientist and philosopher, claimed: "The heart knows its own reasons which reason does not know," which means that the heart has its own motivation, which the logical mind may not understand. As we have seen, the passion great women have for work and romance is not quenched by societal standards or constraining myths: Great women listen to their minds as well as to their hearts.

NOTES

For more complete publication information, see the Bibliography on page 240.

CHAPTER I: ROMANCE AT ANY AGE

9. "recognizing that the other person" Jane Howard, *Margaret Mead,* 364. **10**. "*How do I love Thee?*" F. B. Browning, *Sonnets from the Portuguese.* **11**. "I love your verses" Betty Miller, *Robert Browning.* **12**. more than 600 letters exchanged V. E. Stach, *How Do I Love Thee.* **13**. accused her of being "more coarsely masculine" Elaine Showalter, *Women in Sexist Society,* 342. **12**. their comparative respect G. B. Taplin, *Life of Elizabeth Barrett Browning.* **13**. "Beautiful" at the time of her death Jonathan Green, *Famous Last Words,* 124. **14**. Their romance, which began Gordon Haight, *George Eliot.* **14**. Her first grief Margaret Crompton, *George Eliot: The Woman.* **14**. she . . . tell for Herbert Spencer Herbert Spencer, *Autobiography.* **15**. Mary Ann met George Henry Lewes Phyllis Rose, *Parallel Lives,* 204–205. **16**. "Few women, I fear" *Revelations: Diaries of Women,* 222. **16**. "easily pronounced word" Crompton, ibid., 123. **17**. judged on its own merits Showalter, op. cit., 327. **19**. Herr Wieck's domination Nancy Reich, *Clara Schumann,* 26–42. **20**. "I beg you" Nancy Reich, *Clara Schumann,* 96. **20**. "My state of mind" Reich, ibid., 97. **20**. Perhaps her father Berthold Litzmann, *Clara Schumann.* **21**. "Ah! if only you" ibid., 140–141. **22**. "My Beloved Clara" ibid., 73. **22**. "I feel called" Reich, op. cit., 287. **23**. "The single most important thing" Christopher Anderson, *Young Kate,* 14. **24**. "I want to tell you" ibid., 166. **25**. "I think Spencer always thought" Larry Swindell, *Spencer Tracy,* xii. **25**. couldn't pass a mirror *New York Times,* June 18, 1967. **25**. "For the independent woman" Ann Edwards, *A Remarkable Woman,* 134. **26**. A fine golfer *Katharine Hepburn,* 84–87. **26**. "There will be no more" Edwards, op. cit., 306. **26**. eccentric in her dress Anderson, op. cit., 13. **27**. "You're rather *short*" Kanina Garson, *Tracy and*

Hepburn, 4.   **27**. "Kate always comes in"   Bill Davidson, *Spencer Tracy*, 10.   **27**. Once when Kate and Spencer   Higham, op. cit.   **28**. "I don't understand"   *Harper's Bazaar*, September 1988.   **28**. "Yet he was enormously complicated"   *Newsweek*, January 1963.   **28**. Kate remained a disciplined artist   Higham, op. cit., 124.   **29**. LISTEN TO THE SONG OF LIFE   Anderson, op. cit., 92.   **30**. Georgia especially liked stories   Laurie Lisle, *Portrait of an Artist*.   **30**. "It's as if my mind" Georgia O'Keeffe, *A Studio Book*.   **30**. Anita takes the credit Anita Pollizer, *A Woman on Paper*.   **30**. "Steiglitz's gallery"   Lisle, op. cit., 79.   **31**. attracted to younger women Roxanna Robinson, *Georgia O'-Keeffe*.   **33**. "Love is an invention" *New York Times*, August 26, 1970.   **35**. Her mother   Margaret Mead, *Blackberry Winter*, 111. **38**. baby of her own   Mead, op. cit., 206.   **38**. Mary Catherine also Mary Catherine Bateson, *With A Daughter's Eye*. 11–30.   **40**. Psychiatrist Rollo May   Jane Howard, *Margaret Mead*, 367.   **40**. not the power of both ibid., 419.   **40**. "*My candle burns*"   Edna St. Vincent Millay, *Collected Poems*.

CHAPTER 2: WOMEN WITH MANY LOVERS

47.   Catherine's achievements   John Alexander, *Catherine the Great*.   **48**. "Everything that she desired"   Henri Troyat, *Catherine the Great*.   **49**. "I might have been fond"   Joan Haslip, *Catherine the Great*.   **49**. To keep herself intellectually occupied   *Voltaire & Catherine the Great: Selected Correspondence*.   **50**. Her love of reading   *Memoirs of Catherine the Great*, 108, 120.   **50**. When the empress died and Peter was crowned   ibid., 25–27.   **50**. But Catherine would not marry Orlov Alexander, op. cit, 73–75.   **51**. "Messieurs Senators are to be"   *Memoirs*, 68–69.   **52**. "I am burning"   Haslip, op. cit., 248.   **53**. "Catherine le Grand"   Troyat, op. cit., 398.   **54**. "the curse of boredom" Beryl Markham, *West with the Night*, 10.   **56**. One of her romances Noble Frankland, *Prince Henry: Duke of Gloucester*.   **57**. "Someone will say"   Errol Trzibinski, *Silence Will Speak*, 308.   **57**. "a keystone in an arch"   Markham, op. cit., 196.   **58**. "you are getting somewhere at last"   Mary Lovell, *Straight on Till Morning*, 131.   **58**. "Daredevil Society Woman"   ibid., 72–73.   **59**. "I believe in the future"   ibid., 170.   **60**. "acid and tender"   David Bertram Wolfe, *Diego Rivera*, 393.   **60**. Frida's paintings   Maurice Nadeau, *The History of Surrealism*.   **60**. "I suffered two grave accidents"   Hayden Herrera, *Frida*, 107.   **61**. Frida's . . . body was . . . seriously injured   James Randa, *Frida Kahlo*, 95–97.   **62**. "a daughter of the revolution"   taped interview, *Frida Kahlo*.   **63**. "Look, I have not come to flirt"   Herrera, op. cit., 87.   **63**. marriage between two monsters   Randa, op. cit., 153.   **64**. "I simply wanted to be free"   Herrera, op. cit., 277.   **65**. "*I have achieved a lot*"   Herrera, op. cit., 420.   **65**. legacy to Diego Wolfe, op. cit., 391.   **66**. " . . . a five-year-old is a complete individual"   Simone de Beauvoir, *Memoirs of a Dutiful Daughter*.   **67**.

"We were two of a kind" Claude Francis and Fernande Gontier, *Simone de Beauvoir*, 98. **68**. "If you were sleeping" ibid., 196. **68**. she met Nelson Algren D. E. F. Donohue, *Conversations with Nelson Algren*. **68**. *The Second Sex* was published Simone de Beauvoir, *The Second Sex*. **69**. "We had the same attitudes" Quoted in Axel Madsen, *Hearts and Minds*, 286. **69**. "The only public good" de Beauvoir, op. cit., xxviii. **70**. "contingent" affairs de Beauvoir, *The Prime of Life*, 22. **70**. "There was something innately shameful" Annie Cohen-Solal, *Sartre: A Life*, 105. **71**. "extremely self-controlled" Francis and Gontier, op. cit., xviii. **71**. "I have never met anyone" Ann Whitmarsh, *Simone de Beauvoir*, 18. **72**. In her memoirs Sarah Bernhardt, *Memories of My Life*. **72**. Sarah's earliest memories Sandy Lesprin, *The Memories of Sarah Bernhardt*, 13. **75**. Noted for her rich voice Clifford Fadiman, *The Little Brown Book of Anecdotes*, 59. **75**. She kept the coffin Sarah Bernhardt, *Memories of My Life*, 269. **76**. "reptilian mood" Cornelia Otis Skinner, *Madame Sarah*, 135. **76**. Sarah arranged for a successor ibid., 190. **76**. leg amputated Louis Verneuil, *The Fabulous Life of Sarah Bernhardt*, 6. **77**. "Madame, why do you" Fadimar, op. cit., 60.

CHAPTER 3: LOVE AND SOCIAL ACTION

80. The declaration affirms Paul Williams, ed. *International Bill of Human Rights*. **85**. Educated in a village school Eleanor Flexnor, *Mary Wollstonecraft*. **86**. "I cannot help viewing" Claire Tomlin, *Life and Death of Mary Wollstonecraft*, 185. **87**. "[Then] they would find us" Mary Wollstonecraft, *Vindication of the Rights of Women*, 263. **88**. "I would encounter" Tomlin, op. cit., 185. **89**. "You set my imagination on fire" Jean Detre, *A Most Extraordinary Pair*, 39. **90**. In the North Judith Papachistou, *Women Together*. **91**. to hide the injury Lerone Bennett, Jr. *Pioneers in Protest*, 134. **92**. "I had reasoned" Sarah Bradford, *Harriet Tubman*, 29. **93**. "I know of no one" Bradford, op. cit., 137. **95**. Alexandra's . . . utter commitment Linda Edmondson, *Feminism in Russia*. **97**. "If she must choose" Barbara Clements, *Bolshevik Feminist*. **97**. Because of her dissatisfaction Beatrice Farnsworth, *Aleksandra Kollontai*. **98**. Alexandra persuaded Lenin Donald Meyer, *Sex and Power*. **98**. Lenin, however, claimed Alena Heitlinger, *Women and State Socialism*, 22. **99**. "I am not the wife you need" Kollontai, *Selected Writings*, op. cit., 19. **100**. "The Soviet woman" Meyer, op. cit., 226. **100**. "woman will be judged" Kollontai, *Autobiography*, 4. **101**. "600,000 Berliners" poster described in Martha Kearns, *Käthe Kollwitz*, 130. **103**. "I have never been without your love" Käthe Kollwitz, *Diary and Letters*, 70. **104**. "I looked at her" Kollwitz. op. cit., 201. **105**. "If there is any logical explanation" Ralph Martin, *Golda*, 7. **107**. "The other day" Peggy Mann, *Golda*, 51. **107**. "I forced myself" Golda Meir, *The Land of Our Own*, 41. **109**. "I am not a nun" Martin, op. cit., 163. **109**. "It was the most reassuring" Golda Meir, *My Life*, 110. **109–110**. After David Ben–Gurion came into power Shabti Teveth, *Ben-Gurion*, 108. **110**. "Golda Meir is behaving like a grandmother" Meir, *My Life*, 370. **110**. "The inner struggles" Mann, op. cit., 89. **113**. "I never let anything physical" Eleanor Roosevelt, *This is My Story*, 140. **113**. "hides a primitive jealousy" Joseph Lash, *Eleanor and Franklin*, 371. **115**. "Eleanor Roosevelt is America's real ruler" Marianne Means, *The Woman in the White House*, 204. **115**. "On the whole" Eleanor Roosevelt, *This I Remember*, 350. **116**. "This I believe" Lash, *Eleanor: The Years Alone*, 327. **117**. "You have to have leisure" Cathy Porter, *Alexandra Kollontai*, 487.

CHAPTER 4: LOVE AND TRADITION

121. "simply a woman" E. B. White, *Essays*, 237. **125**. "Heedless and inaccurate" Phyllis Levin, *Abigail Adams*, 552. **125**. She sharply criticized Thomas Jefferson From Abigail to Thomas Jefferson, April 18, 1804, *Adams–Jefferson Letters*. **126**. The next time he called Catherine Bowen, *John Adams*, 232–234. **127**. "While she lived" Jack Shepherd, *The Adams Chronicles*, 272. **128**. John Adams attended the Continental Congress Letter from Abigail to John, July 31, 1777, *Familiar Letters*. **128**. "Remember the ladies" Letter, March 31, 1776, *Familiar Letters*. **129**. "There is a Lady" Levin, op. cit., xii. **129**. "Give me the man I love" *Familiar Letters*, 157. **129**. Abigail burned to establish equal rights Letter from Abigail to John, February 13, 1797, *Letters of Mrs. Adams*, 3rd edition. **130**. "the dear Partner" Letter from John Adams to Jefferson, *The Adams–Jefferson Letters*, October 20, 1818. **130**. "The mere departure" In speech to House of Representatives by Quincy Adams, quoted in Eleanor Flexnor, *Century of Struggle*, 95. **132**. last time she saw her father before the guillotine fell *Memoirs of Queen Hortense*, ed. Jean Hanoteau, 33. **133**. "I awaken full of you" Francis Mossiker, *Napoleon and Josephine*, 97. **134**. "Forgive me" ibid., 112. **134**. "a thousand kisses" ibid., 112. **135**. Josephine charmed the Pope Walter Geer, *Napoleon and Josephine*, 149–154. **136**. "She made everyone" Nina Epton, *Josephine: The Empress and Her Children*, 128. **137**. "Everything in this world" ibid., 128. **137**. "The laws of morality" Mossiker, op. cit., 225. **138**. As a loving stepfather V. M. Montagu, *Napoleon and His Adopted Son*. **138**. "Today she believes" Andre Castelot, *Josephine*, 459. **139**. "I truly loved her" ibid., 404. **140**. "had a firm belief in witches" Judy Taylor, *Beatrix Potter*, 19. **141**. "as quiet as the tame mouse" Margaret Lane, *The Magic Years*, 29. **141**. "My dear Noel" Beatrix Potter, *The Big Peter Rabbit Book*. **142**. "He did not live long" Taylor, op. cit., 104. **143**. Beatrix and William Jane Morse, *Beatrix Potter's Americans: Selected Letters*. **143**. "The portrait of two pigs" Taylor, op. cit., 134. **144**. "Life in the air" Anne Morrow Lindbergh, *War Within*, xv. **145**. Anne described herself Anne

Lindbergh, *Bring Me a Unicorn*, 2.   **145**. An adventuresome man Walter
Ross, *The Last Hero*, 47.   **146**. "[It is] where life meets death" ibid.,
38.   **146**. Lindbergh was twenty-five   Charles Lindbergh, *The Spirit
of St. Louis*.   **146**. "public hero stuff"   A. Lindbergh, *Bring Me a Unicorn*, 73.   **147**. "Charles is life itself"   A. Lindbergh, *A War Within*,
80.   **147**. nineteen-month-old son, Charles Jr.   George Waller, *Kidnap*.   **148**. "There is a place"   A. Lindbergh, *Locked Rooms*,
271.   **149**. Some forty years after the murder   A. Lindbergh, *Hour of
Gold*, 179.   **150**. "I have been overcome by the beauty"   A. Lindbergh,
War Within, 429.   **151**. *"Please do not die"*   Akiko Yosano, *Myojo*, September, 1904.   **152**. families arranged marriages   Alan Roland, *The
Search for Self.*   **153**. *"That secret"*   Akiko Yosano, *Tangled Hair*,
14.   **153**. It was a widespread custom   Chie Nakane, *Japanese Society*,
132–133.   **153**. like most Japanese children   Ruth Benedict, *The Chrysanthemum and the Sword.*   **154**. *"Only the sculptor's fame"*   Yosano, op.
cit., 162.   **154**. "The mountain-moving day"   Jane Condon, *A Half
Step Behind*, 299.   **154**. "If women get in the habit"   Yosano, *Collected
Essays*, 1985.

CHAPTER 5: VARIETY IN SEXUAL CHOICES

161 Yet the great historian   Emily Taft Douglas, *Margaret Sanger*, 1.
162. one could tell a person's age   Margaret Sanger, *Autobiography*, 474.   **162**. "Dammit, you killed my mother"   Madeline
Gray, *Margaret Sanger*, 25.   **163**. "That beast of a man"   ibid.,
30.   **165**. As she learned about how freedom   Havelock Ellis, *On Life
and Sex.*   **165**. "[Ellis] belongs"   Sanger, op. cit., 140.   **166**. "Margaret's love of Havelock"   Francoise Delisle, *Friendship's Odyssey.*   **166**.
"Look the world in the face"   Douglas, op. cit., 50.   **166**. "How do you
fit birth control"   Sanger, op. cit., 496.   **167**. "I found myself in the
position"   Sanger, op. cit., 188.   **167**. "She is the adventure of my
life"   Gray, op. cit., 224.   **168**. "I never asked myself"   Ruth Jordan,
George Sand, xiii.   **169**. To placate her husband   Felizia Seyd, *Romantic
Rebel*, 42.   **170**. "To live with a man,"   ibid., 43.   **170**. Her first job
as a journalist   George Sand, *My Life.*   **171**. "I feel that I love you"
Joseph Barry, *Infamous Woman*, 145.   **171**. "I will suffer"   Aurore Sand,
The Intimate Journal of George Sand, 21.   **172**. Chopin called her Aurore
Wm. Atwood, *The Lioness and the Little One.*   **173**. "a new Plato" ibid.,
36.   **174**. "She still fights triumphantly"   Joseph Barry, op. cit.,
338.   **174**. "A great woman"   Renee Winegarten, *The Double Life of
George Sand*, xi.   **175**. "loyalty to the idea"   Charles Higham, *Charles
Laughton*, viii.   **175**. "over-education"!   Elsa Lanchester, *Elsa Lanchester,
Herself*, 5.   **176**. "Keep each person separate"   ibid., 71.   **177**. "When
it came" ibid., 85.   **178**. "Charles needed" ibid., 141.   **178**. As
manager, Paul handled the publicity   Kurt Singer, *The Laughton
Story.*   **180**. "When Charles was alive"   Higham, op. cit., xiii.   **181**.
"The wives of geniuses"   Gertrude Stein, *The Autobiography of Alice B.*

Toklas, 14. **181.** in the style of Shakespeare   Howard Greenfield, *Gertrude Stein*, 7. **181.** relationship with her brother, Leo   John Brinnin, *The Third Rose*. **182.** "It is better if"   Elizabeth Sprigge, *Gertrude Stein, Her Life and Work*, 14. **182.** "Our life without a father"   Stein, op. cit., 19. **183.** writing in her own style   Greenfield, op. cit., 42–43. **183.** "She held my complete attention"   Alice B. Toklas, *What Is Remembered*, 23. **184.** "Baby Woojums"   Linda Simon, *Biography of Alice B. Toklas*, 99. **184.** Gertrude's one delight in dressing   Jean Gould, *American Women Poets*, 80. **184.** During World War I   Gertrude Stein, *Wars I Have Seen*. **185.** "What is the answer?"   Sprigge op. cit., 265. **185.** "Forget me as well as forget me not"   Alice B. Toklas, *Staying on Alone*, 364. **185.** "She has been"   Donald Gallop, *The Flowers of Friendship*, 203. **186.** erroneous, unscientific conclusions   Mary Leakey, *Disclosing the Past*, 148. **187.** "I never passed a single school exam"   ibid., 35. **187.** a conceited womanizer   Sonia Cole, *Leakey's Luck*, 120. **188.** At age thirteen   Nina Mulvey, *Digging Up Adam*. **189.** a kidney transplant   Rickard Leakey, *One Life*. **193.** As she observed her clients   Marcia Westcott, *The Feminist Legacy of Karen Horney*, 1–20. **193.** Like all theorists Ruth Monroe, *Schools of Psychoanalytic Thought*, 10. **193.** Karen disagreed with Freud's view   Peter Gray, *Freud: A Life for Our Times*. **194.** "In my own imagination"   Karen Horney, *The Adolescent Diaries of Karen Horney*, 64. **194.** two preeminent moral laws ibid., 81. **195.** As one of first women to study medicine   Susan Quinn, *A Mind of Her Own*, 101. **195.** "*Because* you understand" Horney, op. cit., 212. **195.** "reflection of the boy's narcissistic"   Jack Rubins, *Karen Horney: Gentle Rebel of Psychoanalysis*, 53. **196.** "There is nothing more unbearable"   Horney, *Diaries*, 245. **197.** She also perceived that infants needed care   Karen Horney, *The Neurotic Personality of Our Time*. **198.** New School for Social Research   L. Coser, *Refugee Scholars in America*. **198.** When . . . her second book was published   Karen Horney, *New Ways in Psychoanalysis*. **198.** Erich Fromm, as a member   Jack Rubin, op. cit., 232f. **198.** Another famous man Hannah Tillich, *From Time to Time*. **199.** "like a child"   Susan Quinn, op. cit., 385. **200.** in overly crowded Japan   Shidzue Ishimoto, *Facing Two Ways*.

CHAPTER 6: LOVE WITHOUT END

204. On their death certificates   Brian Wilkes, *The Illustrated Brontës*. **204.** During these times, when it was customary   Annette Hopkins, *The Father of the Brontës*, 63. **205.** "Unattractive—thin" Margot Peters, *Unquiet Soul*, 24. **206.** In Brussels   Winifred Gerin, *Charlotte Brontë*, 180–215. **206.** "To forbid me to write"   Thomas Wise and J. Alexander Symington, *The Brontës*, 69–70. **207.** Elizabeth Barrett Browning, who had been   Peters, op. cit., 265. **207.** "This indeed is a book"   ibid., 201. **207.** "They regard me as an old maid"   Janet Murray, *Strong Minded Women*, 116. **207.** "I am a *single* woman" Peters, op. cit., 384. **208.** "He entered—he stood before me"

Murray op. cit., 116.   **208.** So delighted was he   Wilkes, op. cit.,
195.   **208.** Tragically, the marriage was brief   Helene Moglen, *Charlotte Brontë*, 241.   **208.** "Oh I'm not going to die, am I?"   Edward
Benson, *Charlotte Brontë*, 305.   **209.** "I am inferior to no one"   Marilyn
Bailey, *Women in Science*, 76–78.   **209.** "She was a great man"   Samuel
Edwards, *The Divine Mistress*, 268.   **210.** she attempted suicide
Nancy Mitford, *Voltaire in Love*, 26–28.   **210.** "Emilie's tastes are impeccable" Edwards, op. cit., 11.   **211.** Since her husband was usually
away   Ira Wade, *Voltaire and Mme du Chatelet*.   **212.** "Do not look
upon me" Margaret Alic, *Hypatia's Heritage*, 147.   **212.** "I have become
a willing slave"   Edwards, op. cit., 129.   **212.** Emilie's professional
life   Louis Grinstein and Paul Cambell, ed., *Women of Mathematics*.   **212.** Her personal life   op. cit., 257.   **213.** Emilie gave birth
Edwards, op. cit., 266.   **213.** "I have not lost"   ibid., 268.   **213.**
descendants . . . married into royal families of Europe   Theo Aronson,
Grandmama of Europe.   **213.** "I proposed to Prince Albert"   Clifton
Fadiman, ed., *The Little Brown Book of Anecdotes*, 563.   **213.** total seclusion in Kensington Palace   Joanna Richardson, *Victoria and Albert*,
23.   **214.** 2,500 words each day   Christopher Hibbert, ed., *Queen Victoria*, 1.   **214.** "Albert's *beauty*"   Richardson, op. cit., 49.   **214.**
"what happiness is this!"   op. cit., 58–59.   **215.** "I gave Albert a last
kiss" Hector Bolitho, *Further Letters of Queen Victoria*, 3.   **215.** "I am
only the husband"   Fadiman, op. cit., 363.   **215.** "Albert stalked out"
Fadiman, op. cit., 563.   **216.** "We women are not made for
governing"   Richardson, op. cit., 152.   **216.** Victoria, in love with
love   David Duff, *Victoria and Albert*, 17–66.   **217.** excess of rings
Viscount Esher, ed., *Girlhood of Queen Victoria*.   **219.** "I wish they were
peanuts"   Helen Hayes with Lewis Funke, *A Gift of Joy*, 18–19.   **219.**
And Helen, in contrast   Jahn Robbins, *Front Page Marriage*, 113.   **220.**
"From your parents you learn"   Helen Hayes, *On Reflection*, 7.   **221.**
"I decided that Whistler's Mother"   ibid., 14.   **222.** "It might at first
have been anger"   Keith Barrow, *Helen Hayes*, 197–198.   **223.**
"Laughter is the sound of heaven"   Hayes, ibid., 49.   **223.** "I'm still
waiting"   Barrow, ibid., 202.   **224.** "the fatigue of growth and
study"   Marie Curie, *Pierre Curie*, 163.   **224.** Because Marie's father
was poor   Robert Reid, *Marie Curie*, 29–41.   **226.** "It would be a fine
thing"   Letter from Pierre to Marie in *Madame Curie* by Eve
Curie.   **226.** "I have no dress"   E. Curie, op. cit., 136.   **226.** "I
miss you very much"   ibid., 148.   **228.** "It is the picture"   ibid.,
283.   **228.** "husband snatcher"   Rosalynd Pflaum, *Grand Obsession*,
137–159.   **229.** "benefactress of the human race"   Francois Giroud,
Marie Curie.

BIBLIOGRAPHY

Adams, Abigail. *Letters of Mrs. Adams.* 3rd ed. Boston: Little, Brown, 1841. Letter to John Adams, Feb. 13, 1797.

Adams, Charles Francis, ed. *Familiar Letters of John Adams and His Wife Abigail Adams During the Revolution.* Boston: Houghton Mifflin, 1875. Letter dated July 31, 1777.

Alexander, John T. *Catherine the Great: Life and Legend.* New York: Oxford University Press, 1989.

Alic, Margaret. *Hypatia's Heritage,* Boston: Beacon Press, 1986.

Anderson, Christopher. *Young Kate.* New York: Henry Holt, 1988.

Aronson, Theo. *Grandmama of Europe.* Indianapolis/New York: Bobbs-Merrill, 1973.

Atwood, William. *The Lioness and the Little One: The Liaison of George Sand and Frederick Chopin.* New York: Columbia University Press, 1980.

Barrow, Keith. *Helen Hayes: First Lady of the American Theatre.* Garden City, N.Y.: Doubleday, 1985.

Barry, Joseph. *Infamous Woman: The Life of George Sand.* New York: Doubleday, 1977.

Bateson, Mary Catherine. *With a Daughter's Eye.* New York: Morrow, 1984.

Benedict, Ruth. *The Chrysanthemum and the Sword.* New York: New American Library, 1974.

Bennett, Lerone Jr. *Pioneers in Protest.* Chicago: Johnson Publishing Co., 1968.

Benson, Edward. *Charlotte Brontë.* Freeport, New York: Books for Libraries Press, 1932.

Bernhardt, Sarah. *Memories of My Life.* New York: Benjamin Bloom. First published 1908, reissued 1968.

Bernier, Oliver. *The Eighteenth Century Woman.* New York: Doubleday, in association with Metropolitan Museum of Art, 1981.
Blixen, Karen. *Out of Africa.* New York: Modern Library, 1986.
Bolitho, Hector, ed. *Further Letters of Queen Victoria.* Andover, England: Kraus, 1938.
Bowen, Catherine. *John Adams and the American Revolution.* Boston: Little, Brown, 1950.
Bradford, Sarah. *Harriet Tubman.* Originally published in 1868 but the details are not clear. Reissued in 1974 by Citadel Press, with introduction by Butler Jones.
Brinnin, John Malcolm. *The Third Rose: Gertrude Stein and Her World.* Reading, Mass.: Addison-Wesley, 1987. Remarkably detailed.
Browning, E. B. *Sonnets from the Portuguese.* Vol. XLIII. New York: Avon Publishing, 1950.
————. *Poetical Works of Elizabeth Barrett Browning.* Boston: Houghton Mifflin, 1974.
Butterfield, L. H., Marc Friedlander, and Mary-Jo Kline, eds. *The Book of Abigail and John: Selected Letters of the Adams Family, 1762–1784* Cambridge, Mass.: Harvard University Press, 1975. Original, uncorrected versions of their letters.
Cappon, Lester, ed. *Adams–Jefferson Letters.* 2 vols. Chapel Hill, N.C.: University of North Carolina Press, 1959. These letters are arranged in chronological order and are a vast resource for understanding the Revolutionary period.
Carey, Gary. *Katharine Hepburn: A Hollywood Yankee.* New York: St. Martin's Press, 1983.
Castelot, Andre. *Josephine.* Trans. Denis Folliot. New York: Harper & Row, 1967.
Clements, Barbara. *Bolshevik Feminist.* Bloomington, Ind.: Indiana University Press, 1979.
Cohn-Solal, Annie. *Sartre—A Life.* Trans. Anna Cancogni. New York: Pantheon Books, 1987.
Cole, Sonia. *Leaky's Luck.* New York: Harcourt, Brace, Javonovich, 1975.
Condon, Jane. *A Half Step Behind.* New York: Dodd, Mead & Co., 1985.
Coser, L. *Refugee Scholars in America.* New Haven, Conn.: Yale University Press, 1984.
Crompton, Margaret. *George Eliot: The Woman.* New York: Thomas Yoseloff, 1960.

Curie, Eva. *Madame Curie*. Trans. Vincent Sheean. Originally published in New York, Literary Guild of America, 1937. Reprinted by Doubleday, 1937. Letter from Pierre Curie to Marie Sklodovska, August 10, 1894.

Curie, Marie. *Pierre Curie and Autobiographical Notes*. New York: Macmillan, 1923.

Davidson, Bill. *Spencer Tracy: Tragic Idol*. New York: E. P. Dutton, 1987.

de Beauvoir, Simone. *Memoirs of a Dutiful Daughter*. Cleveland: World Publishing, 1959.

———. *The Second Sex*. Trans. H. M. Parshley. New York: Bantam, 1961.

———. *The Prime of Life*. Trans. Peter Green. New York: Penguin Books, 1984.

———. "A Very East Death," *Memories, Dreams and Reflections by Literary Daughters*. Ed. Susan Cahill. New York: New American Library, 1988.

Delisle, Francoise. *Friendship's Odyssey*. London: Delisle Limited, 1964.

Detre, Jean. *A Most Extraordinary Pair: Mary Wollstonecraft and William Godwin*. New York: Doubleday, 1975.

Donohue, H. E. F. *Conversations with Nelson Algren*. New York: Hill & Wang, 1963.

Douglas, Emily Taft. *Margaret Sanger: Pioneer of the Future*. New York: Holt, Rinehart & Winston, 1970.

Duff, David. *Victoria and Albert*. New York: Taplinter, 1972.

Edmondson, Linda Harriet. *Feminism in Russia, 1900–17*. Stanford, Calif.: Stanford University Press, 1984.

Edwards, Samuel. *The Divine Mistress*. New York: David McKay Co., Inc., 1970.

Edwards, Anne. *A Remarkable Woman*. New York: Morrow, 1985.

Ellis, Havelock. *On Life and Sex*. New York: New American Library, 1957.

Epton, Nina. *Josephine: The Empress and Her Children*. London: George Weidenfeld and Nicolson Ltd., n.d.

Esher, Viscount, ed. "The Girlhood of Queen Victoria." *Treasury of the World's Great Diaries*. New York: Doubleday, 1957.

Fadiman, Clifton, ed. *The Little, Brown Book of Anecdotes*. Boston: Little, Brown, 1985.

Farnsworth, Beatrice. *Aleksandra Kollontai*. Stanford, Calif.: Stanford University Press, 1980.

Flexnor, Eleanor. *Century of Struggle*. Cambridge, Mass.: Harvard University Press, 1968.

———. *Mary Wollstonecraft*. New York: Coward, McCann, & Geoghegan, 1972.

Francis, Claude, and Gontier, Fernande. *Simone de Beauvoir*. New York: St. Martin's Press, 1987.

Frankland, Noble. *Prince Henry: Duke of Gloucester*. New York: Weidenfeld and Nicolson Ltd., 1980.

"Frida Kahlo." Taped interview, *Arts in Video*, Greenwich, Conn.

Gallup, Donald. *The Flowers of Friendship: Letters Written to Gertrude Stein*. New York: Alfred Knopf, 1953.

Gardner, Howard. *Frames of Mind: The Theory of Multiple Intelligences*. New York: Basic Books, 1983.

Garson, Kanin. *Tracy and Hepburn: An Intimate Memoir*. New York: Viking, 1971.

Gay, Peter. *Freud: A Life for Our Times*. New York: Norton, 1988.

Geer, Walter. *Napoleon and Josephine: The Rise of the Empire*. New York: Brentano's, 1924

"Georgia O'Keeffe." Videotaped interview. Art Institute of Chicago.

Gerin, Winifred. *Charlotte Brontë: The Evolution of a Genius*. New York: Oxford University Press, 1967.

Giroud, Francoise. *Marie Curie: A Life*. Originally published in French as *Une Femme Honorable*. Trans. Francoise Giroud. New York: Holmes and Meier, 1986.

Gould, Jean. *American Women Poets*. New York: Dodd, Mead & Co., 1984.

Gray, Madeline, *Margaret Sanger: A Biography*. New York: Richard Marek Publishers, 1979.

Green, Jonathan, ed. *Famous Last Words*. New York: Quick Fox Publishers, 1979.

Greenfield, Howard. *Gertrude Stein: A Biography*. New York: Crow Publishers, 1973.

Grinstein, Louise, and Paul Campbell, eds. *Women of Mathematics*. New York: Greenwood Press, 1987.

Haight, Gordon S. *George Eliot: A Biography*. New York: Oxford University Press, 1968.

Hanoteau, Jean, ed. *The Memoirs of Queen Hortense, Published in Arrangement with Prince Napoleon*. Vol. 1. Trans. Arthur Griggs. New York: Cosmopolitan Book Corp., 1927.

Harper's Bazaar. September, 1988.

Haslip, Joan. *Catherine the Great*. New York: G. P. Putnam's Sons, 1977.

Hayes, Helen, with Lewis Funke. *A Gift of Joy*. New York: M. Evans & Co., 1965.

Hayes, Helen, with Sandford Dody. *On Reflection*. New York: M. Evans & Co., 1968.

Heitlinger, Alena. *Women and State Socialism: Sex Inequality in the Soviet Union and Czechoslovakia*. London: Macmillan Press, Ltd., 1979.

Herrera, Hayden. *Frida*. New York: Harper & Row, 1983.

Hibbert, Christopher, ed. *Queen Victoria in Her Letters and Journals*. London: John Murray Ltd., 1984.

Higham, Charles. *Kate: The Life of Katharine Hepburn*. New York: Norton, 1975.

Higham, Charles. *Charles Laughton*. New York: Doubleday, 1976.

Hobhouse, Janet. *Everybody Who Was Anybody*. New York: G. P. Putnam's Sons, 1975.

Hopkins, Annette. *The Father of the Brontës*. Baltimore: Johns Hopkins Press, 1958.

Horney, Karen. *The Neurotic Personality of Our Time*. New York: Norton, 1937.

————. *New Ways in Psychoanalysis*. New York: Norton, 1939.

————. *The Adolescent Diaries of Karen Horney*. New York: Basic Books, 1980.

Howard, Jane. *Margaret Mead: A Life*. New York: Simon & Schuster, 1984.

Ishimoto, Shidzue. *Facing Two Ways: The Story of My Life*. New York: Farrar and Rinehart, 1935.

Jones, Robert. *The Emancipation of the Russian Nobility, 1762–1785*. Princeton,N.J.: Princeton University Press, 1973.

Jordan, Ruth, *George Sand*. London: Constable & Co. 1972.

Kearns, Martha. *Käthe Kollwitz: Woman and Artist*. Old Westbury, N.Y.: Feminist Press, 1976.

Kollontai, Alexandra. *The Autobiography of a Sexually Emancipated Communist Woman*. Trans. Salvador Attanasio. New York: Herder and Herder, 1971.

Kollwitz, Käthe. *The Diary and Letters of Käthe Kollwitz*. Ed. Hans Kollwitz. Trans. Richard and Clara Winston. Chicago: Henry Regnery, 1955.

Lanchester, Elsa. *Elsa Lanchester, Herself*. New York: St. Martin's Press, 1983.

Lane, Margaret. *The Tale of Beatrix Potter*. Middlesex, England: Frederick Warne, 1946.

———. *The Magic Years of Beatrix Potter*. London: Frederick Warne, 1978.

Lash, Joseph. *Eleanor: The Years Alone*. New York: New American Library, 1972.

———. *Eleanor and Franklin*. New York: New American Library, 1973.

Leakey, Mary. *Disclosing the Past*. Garden City, N.Y.: Doubleday, 1984.

Leakey, Richard. *One Life*. Salem, N.H.: Salem House, 1984.

Lespren, Sandy, ed. *The Memoirs of Sarah Bernhardt*. New York: Peebles Press, 1977.

Levin, Phyllis Lee. *Abigail Adams*. New York: Ballantine, 1987.

Lindbergh, Anne Morrow. *Gift from the Sea*. New York: New American Library, 1955.

———. *Bring Me a Unicorn: Diaries and Letters of Anne Morrow Lindbergh*. New York: New American Library, 1973.

———. *Hour of Gold, Hour of Lead*. New York: New American Library, 1973.

———. *Locked Rooms and Open Doors: Diaries and Letters of Anne Morrow Lindbergh*. New York: Harcourt Brace Jovanovich, 1974.

———. *War Within and Without: Diaries and Letters*. New York: Harcourt Brace Jovanovich, 1980.

Lindbergh, Charles A. *The Spirit of St. Louis*. New York: Charles Scribner's Sons, 1953.

Lisle, Laurie. *Portrait of an Artist: A Biography of Georgia O'Keeffe*. New York: Pocket Books, 1986.

Litzmann, Berthold. *Clara Schumann: An Artist's Life*. 2 vols. Trans. Grace Hadlow. New York: De Capo Press, 1979. These two volumes are reprints from forty-seven books of diaries and journals.

Litzmann, Berthold, ed. *Letters of Clara Schumann and Johannes Brahms: 1853–1896*. Vol. 2. New York: Vienna House Edition, 1971.

Lovell, Mary S. *Straight on Till Morning*. New York: St. Martin's Press, 1987.

Madsen, Axel. *Hearts and Minds*. New York: Morrow, 1977.

Mann, Peggy. *Golda: The Life of Israel's Prime Minister*. New York: Coward, McCann, & Geoghegan, 1971.

Markham, Beryl. *West with the Night*. San Francisco: North Point Press, 1983. First published in 1942.

Martin, Ralph. *Golda*. New York: Charles Scribner's Sons, 1988.

Masters, Brian. *Sartre, A Study*. New York: Rowman & Littlefield, 1974.

Mead, Margaret. *Blackberry Winter: My Earlier Years*. New York: Simon & Schuster. 1972. First published in 1928.

———. *Letters from the Field*. New York: Harper & Row, 1977.

Means, Marianne. *The Woman in the White House*. New York: Random House, 1963.

Meir, Golda. *A Land of Our Own: An Oral Autobiography*. Ed. Marie Syrkin. New York: G. P. Putnam's Sons, 1973.

———. *My Life*. New York: Dell, 1975.

Memoirs of Catherine the Great. Trans. Katherine Anthony. New York: Knopf, 1927.

Meyer, Donald. *Sex & Power: The Rise of Women in America, Russia, Sweden and Italy*. Middleton, Conn.: Wesleyan University Press, 1987.

Miller, Betty, *Robert Browning: A Portrait*. New York: Charles Scribner's Sons, 1972.

Miller, Rosalind. *Gertude Stein: Form and Intelligibility*. New York: Exposition Press, 1949.

Mitford, Nancy. *Voltaire in Love*. New York: Harper & Bros., 1957.

Moffat, Mary Jane, and Charlotte Painter, eds. *Revelations: Diaries of Women*. New York: Random House, 1975.

Moglen, Helene. *Charlotte Brontë: The Self Conceived*. New York: Norton, 1976. An integration of her environment, personality, and writing.

Monroe, Ruth. *Schools of Psychoanalytic Thought*. New York: Henry Holt & Co., 1955.

Montagu, V. M. *Napoleon and His Adopted Son*. New York: McBride, Nast & Co., 1914.

Morse, Jane Crowell. *Beatrix Potter's Americans: Selected Letters*. Boston: The Horn Book, Inc., 1982.

Mossiker, Frances. *Napoleon and Josephine*. New York: Simon & Schuster, 1964. A documented study of their marriage.

Mulvey, Nina. *Digging Up Adam*. New York: David McKay, 1969.

Murray, Janet. *Strong-Minded Women and Other Lost Voices From 19th-Century England*. New York: Pantheon Books, 1982.

Nadeau, Maurice. *The History of Surrealism*. Trans. Roger Shattuck. New York: Macmillan, 1965.

Nakane, Chie. *Japanese Society*. Middlesex, England: Penguin, 1970.

Napoleon, I. *Napoleon Self-Revealed in Three Hundred Selected Letters*. Trans. and ed. by J. M. Thompson. Boston: Houghton Mifflin, 1934.

New York Times Magazine. August 26, 1970.

New York Times. June 18, 1967.

Newsweek. January, 1963.

O'Keeffe, Georgia. *A Studio Book*. New York: Viking Press, 1976. A large book of her paintings and memoirs which she had published to correct the misinformation and misinterpretation about her life and work.

Ogilvie, Marilyn Bailey. *Women in Science*. Cambridge, Mass: MIT Press, 1986.

Papachristou, Judith. *Women Together: A History in Documents of the Women's Movement in the United States*. New York: Knopf, 1976.

Peters, Margot. *Unquiet Soul. A Biography of Charlotte Brontë*. New York: Doubleday, 1975.

Pflaum, Rosalynd. *Grand Obsession: Marie Curie and Her World*. New York: Doubleday, 1989.

Pollizer, Anita. *A Woman on Paper: Georgia O'Keeffe*. New York: Simon & Schuster, 1988.

Polovtsoff, Alexander. *The Favorites of Catherine the Great*. London: Herman Jenkins Ltd., 1947.

Porter, Cathy. *Alexandra Kollontai: The Lonely Struggle of the Woman Who Defied Lenin*. New York: The Dial Press, 1980. The chronology of her political work is especially useful.

Potter, Beatrix. *The Big Peter Rabbit Book*. New York: Penguin Books, 1986.

Quinn, Susan. *A Mind Of Her Own: the Life of Karen Horney*. New York: Summit Books, 1987.

Randa, James. *Frida Kahlo*. Mexico Compana Editorial S.A., 1987.

Reich, Nancy. *Clara Schumann: The Artist and the Woman*. Ithaca, N.Y.: Cornell University Press, 1985.

Reid, Robert. *Marie Curie*. New York: Dutton, 1974.

Richardson, Joanna. *Sarah Bernhardt and Her Work*. New York: G. P. Putnam's Sons, 1977.

———. *Victoria and Albert*. New York: New York Times Book Co., 1977.

Robbins, Jahn. *Front Page Marriage*. New York: G. P. Putnam's Sons, 1982.

Robinson, Roxanna. *Georgia O'Keeffe: A Life*. New York: Harper

& Row, 1989. An authorized biography with many new pictures. Based on interviews and letters not previously available.

Roland, Alan. *The Search of Self in India and Japan: Toward a Cross-Cultural Psychology.* Princeton, N.J.: Princeton University Press, 1988.

Roosevelt, Eleanor. *This Is My Story.* New York: Harper & Bros., 1937.

———. *This I Remember.* New York: Harper & Row, 1949.

Rose, Phyllis. *Parallel Lives.* New York: Random House, 1983.

Ross, Walter S. *The Last Hero: Charles A. Lindbergh.* New York: Harper & Row, 1968.

Rubins, Jack. *Karen Horney: Gentle Rebel of Psychoanalysis.* New York: Dial Press, 1978.

Sand, Aurore. *The Intimate Journal of George Sand.* New York: Haskell House Publishers, Inc., 1976.

Sand, George. *My Life.* Trans. Dan Hofstodter. New York: Harper & Row, 1979.

Sanger, Margaret. *An Autobiography.* New York: Elmsford, 1970.

Sanson, G. B. *The Western World and Japan.* Tokyo: Charles Tuttle, 1977.

Selected Writings of Alexandra Kollontai. Trans. and commentaries by Alix Holt. Westport, Conn.: Lawrence Hill & Co., 1977. Includes extensive bibliography of Kollontai's writings in various languages.

Seyd, Felizia. *Romantic Rebel: The Life and Times of George Sand.* New York: Viking Press, 1940.

Shepherd, Jack. *The Adam Chronicles.* Boston: Little, Brown, 1976.

Showalter, Elaine. "Women Writers and the Double Standard." In *Women in Sexist Society,* ed. Vivian Gornick and Barbara K. Moran. New York: Basic Books, 1971.

Simon, Linda. *The Biography of Alice B. Toklas.* Garden City, N.Y.: Doubleday, 1977.

James Simpson, ed. *Simpson's Contemporary Quotations.* Boston: Houghton Mifflin, 1988.

Singer, Kurt. *The Laughton Story.* Philadelphia: John Winston Co., 1954.

Skinner, Cornelia Otis. *Madame Sarah.* Boston: Houghton Mifflin, 1967.

Spencer, Herbert. *Autobiography.* 2 vols. London: Williams & Norgate, 1904.

Sprigge, Elizabeth. *Gertrude Stein: Her Life and Work.* New York: Harper & Bros., 1957.

St. Vincent Millay, Edna. "Second Figs." In *Collected Poems*. New York: Harper & Row, 1956.

Stach, V. E. *How Do I Love Thee: The Love Letters of Robert Browning and Elizabeth Barrett*. New York: G. P. Putnam's Sons, 1969.

Stein, Gertrude. *The Autobiography of Alice B. Toklas*. New York: Random House, n.d.

———. *Wars I Have Seen*. Norris, Tenn.: Exposition Press, 1949.

Swindell, Larry. *Spencer Tracy*. New York: World Publishing Co., 1958.

Taplin, G. B. *Life of Elizabeth Barret Browning*. New Haven, Conn.: Yale University Press, 1957.

Taylor, Judy. *Beatrix Potter*. Middlesex, England: Frederick Warne, 1986.

Teveth, Shabti. *Ben-Gurion*. Boston: Houghton Mifflin, 1987.

Tillich, Hannah. *From Time to Time*. New York: Stern and Day, 1973.

Toklas, Alice B. *What Is Remembered*. New York: Holt, Rinehart & Winston, 1963. Reprinted by North Point Press, San Francisco, 1985.

———. *Staying On Alone*. New York: Liveright, 1973.

Tomalin, Claire. *The Life and Death of Mary Wollstonecraft*. London: Weidenfeld and Nicholson, 1974.

Troyat, Henri. *Catherine the Great*. Trans. Joan Pinkham. New York: Berkley, 1981.

Trzebinski, Errol. *Silence Will Speak: A Study of the Life of Denys Finch Hatton and His Relationship with Karen Blixen*. Chicago: University of Chicago Press, 1977.

Verneuil, Louis. *The Fabulous Life of Sarah Bernhardt*. Trans. Ernest Boyd. New York: Harper & Bros., 1942.

Wade, Ira. *Voltaire and Mme. du Chatelet*. New York: Octagon Books, 1967.

Waller, George. *Kidnap*. New York: Dial Press, 1961.

Westkott, Marcia. *The Feminist Legacy of Karen Horney*. New Haven, Conn.: Yale University Press, 1986. Reviews her work in a historical context.

White, E. B. *Essays of E. B. White*. New York: Harper & Row, 1977.

Whitmarsh, Ann. *Simone de Beauvoir and the Limits of Commitment*. New York: Cambridge University Press, 1981.

Wilkes, Brian. *The Illustrated Brontës of Haworth*. London: Willow Books, 1986.

Williams, Paul, ed. *The International Bill of Human Rights.* Glen Ellen, Calif.: Entwistle Books, 1981. A "must" for any library.

Winegarten, Renee. *The Double Life of George Sand.* New York: Basic Books, 1978.

Wise, Thomas, and J. Alexander Symington, eds. *The Brontës: Their Lives, Friendships, and Correspondence in Four Volumes.* New York: Oxford University Press, 1933.

Wolfe, Bertram David. *Diego Rivera: His Life and Times.* New York: Knopf, 1939.

Wollstonecraft, Mary. *Vindication of the Rights of Women.* Ed. Miriam Kramnick. Middlesex, England: Penguin Books. First published 1782. Reprinted 1978.

Wright, Constance. *Daughter to Napoleon.* New York: Holt, Rinehart & Winston, 1961.

Yosano, Akiko. *Myojo.* Tokyo, Japan, September 1904.

————. *Collected Essays.* Ed. Masanao Kano and Nobriko Kouchi. Tokyo: Iwanami-Shoten, 1985.

————. *Tangled Hair: Selected Tanka From Midaregami.* Trans. Sanford Goldstein and Seishi Shinoda. Rutland, Vt. and Tokyo, Japan: Charles Tuttle, 1987. Includes brief summaries and interpretations of her poetry by the translators.